THE HANDBOOK OF MINORITY STUDENT SERVICES

edited by
Charles A. Taylor

Published by Praxis Publications Inc.
P.O. Box 9869
Madison, Wisconsin 53715
Tel. (608) 244-5633

Library of Congress Cataloging-in-Publication Data
Taylor, Charles, 1950-
    The Handbook of Minority Student Services
    Bibliography:p.
    1. Minority college students--Services for--
United States. 2. Minority college students--United
States--Societies, etc. I. Title.
LC3731.T38 1985   378'.1982   85-72411

Praxis Publications, Inc. is an independent Multi-Cultural Business Enterprise which publishes educational and cultural literature; provides training programs, consultation and technical assistance to university and community groups. Praxis, headquartered in Madison, Wisconsin, is emerging as a leader in providing effective programs and services which seek to improve the quality of education for all people. We invite you to call or write us for additional information about our services and products.

Acknowledgments

Praxis Publications, Inc. gratefully acknowledges the following for their assistance in the completion of this book:

Julia Anderson, Clare Bir, Mary Girard, Sandra Hendrickson, and Elizabeth Johanna.

Dedication

This book is dedicated to college administrators and student support staff. May it assist you in your work with minority students.

About the Editor

Charles Taylor is currently the publisher and president of the Praxis Publications, Inc., a small publishing firm that publishes books and a wide range of literature pertaining to Minority Student Services. Mr. Taylor is presently working toward his Ph D. at the University of wisconsin-Madison, in Educational Technology. He earned his Masters in Education from the University of Oregon and his B.S. from Southeast Missouri State University. He's been involved in student services for over a decade.

Charles has served as a director of a Multicultural Education Center, as an academic advisor, financial aid officer and a dorm counselor during his illustrious career. He has served as an advisor to many student organizations and is founder of Wisconsin's Annual Minority Student Leadership conference. Mr. Taylor is also the founder and former publisher of the National Minority Campus Chronicle, one of the most contemporary newspapers in America covering the Minority Collegiate Scene. He continues to serve as a consultant to college campuses throughout America in the area of Minority Student Services.

TABLE OF CONTENTS

Foreword

This book was written with the practitioner in mind. Whether you're a newly appointed administrator entering minority student affairs for the first time or a seasoned manager, you will find a wealth of information in this publication.

We asked nearly a dozen administrators and faculty of successful programs to help us produce a book that would be of immediate use to the professional practitioner in better servicing minority students on campus. We're extremely proud of the final result. The **HANDBOOK** is filled with programming ideas that encourage student involvement on campus. The authors provide personal experience and advice in a manner that administrators and faculty can relate to.

If you need help in establishing a peer counseling program, or in looking for an effective counseling approach that works well with black women, or want to know what role minority student centers should play on predominantly white campuses, then this book is for you.

The authors cover a wide range of topics. Louis Sarabia, Director of Chicano Programs at New Mexico State University shares information on a Chicano student support program while Dr. Sandra Foster, Assistant Professor in the School of Social Work at Grambling offers tips on relating to black students. Dr. Alfonzo Thurman, Director Office of Special Projects at Northern Illinois University discusses factors worth considering when establishing special services on campus.

Other authors provide insight with regard to what professionals do, how they provide services and for what purposes. Supporting research is included in a manner that puts Minority Student Services on firmer footing.

If you're looking for entertainment sources, activities to improve cross-cultural interaction or want to know how to conduct a minority student leadership workshop, you'll be able to find it in this handbook. It's easy to see why this is an essential book for anyone involved in minority student programs. At last our helping profession has a book to assist campus planners provide the services that will enable minority students to grow and develop their full potential.

Charles Taylor, editor

Chapter 1

Establishing Special Services on Campus:
Factors to Consider

Dr. Alfonzo Thurman
Northern Illinois University

ABOUT THE AUTHOR

Dr. Alfonzo Thurman is a tenured Associate Professor in the Department of Leadership and Educational Policy Studies at Northern Illinois University in DeKalb, Illinois. He is also Director of Special Projects and Administrative Assistant to the Provost and Vice President for Academic Affairs. As Director of Special Projects, Dr. Thurman supervises the directors of the CHANCE Program, Upward Bound, Special Services, Talent Search and the University Tutorial Program.

Dr. Thurman received his M.A. and Ph.D. in Educational Policy Studies from the University of Wisconsin-Madison in 1973 and 1979 respectively. He received his Bachelor of Science degree in English from the University of Wisconsin-LaCrosse in 1971. He has served as a director and coordinator of Special Services, Minority Affairs, and Ethnic Studies at various institutions. Dr. Thurman has also taught educational leadership, policy, administration, and black history and literature at the University of Wisconsin-Whitewater, University of Wisconsin-Oshkosh and Northern Illinois University.

INTRODUCTION

Special programs for specific target populations have existed on some campuses for twenty years yet the need for them persists and for some populations, such as Blacks and Hispanics, the need increases. Establishing these programs calls for someone who is politically savvy, but who also understands the portent of effective program development.

In this article, discussion centers on the need for sound pre-assessment strategies, program design, program delivery (implementation) needs, and an awareness and knowledge of the institutional political environment in which the program designer must work.

The task is not an easy one, but it is exciting. Developing a sound proposal, whether seeking federal, state, foundation, or institutional funds is just the "tip of the iceberg." Laying the initial groundwork for campus implementation, seeking out alternative sources of funding, cultivating alliances, compromising and perservering through various pressures, assures an exciting adventure in academic politics.

ESTABLISHING SPECIAL SERVICES ON CAMPUS: FACTORS TO CONSIDER

by Alfonzo Thurman

History and Background

Programs which dispense "special services" have now been in existence for nearly two decades. They exist in various forms at many college and university campuses which serve minority or disadvantaged student populations. Indeed, they have expanded from recruitment and admissions programs to broad based academic, counseling, financial assistance, and cultural enrichment efforts (Astin, 1972; Thurman, 1979; and The College Entrance Examination Board, 1984).

The question arises, if special services have existed for two decades, why is there a need for a paper on factors to consider in establishing special services on campus? First, not all campuses who need such programmatic efforts have them. Second, established programs can be strengthened, perhaps through reviewing their current structure and political situation in light of the steps necessary for establishing new programs. Third, campuses with established programs may seek to restructure or put into place new educational opportunity programs. In restrictive academic disciplines such as engineering or computer science, campuses may choose to implement special services programs by college (rather than a general undergraduate program). I've previously stated that special services have existed on college and university campuses and they've existed to serve minority and disadvantaged students. The question, "what are they and what do they do" remains.

In short, special services is a mix of people, resources, and activities which are systematically blended together to meet an identified need for action for a specific population on the college or university campus. This need for action suggests that this mix of people, resources, and activities will be ongoing for a long enough period of time to satisfy or remedy the need.

Special services has come to denote a specific effort to provide assistance to underrepresented minorities (primarily Black, Hispanic, and Native American though programs are not exclusively comprised of these groups). Indeed, the federal government, through the Higher Education Act of 1965, established a set of programs, (Special Programs for Students from Disadvantaged Backgrounds), which have come to be known as TRIO Programs which provide funding to higher education institutions to provide "special services" to students underrepresented in higher education. One of these programs is aptly called Special Services. Special services, minority programs, and educational opportunity programs can be used interchangeably.

Special services programs have a variety of funding bases and provide a variety of services. Aside from the aforementioned federal funds, private foundations, special state grants, and institutional base budgets fund special services programs. Some of these programs simply recruit and admit students, as did the early programs.

Most, though, have expanded or given way to programs which provide a set of comprehensive services. They provide either financial aid directly or assistance in seeking such aid as budget management information, orientation activities, academic and personal counseling, career exploration and development services, cultural enrichment activities, remedial and/or developmental courses, study halls, skill development laboratories, and tutorial support. Some even provide credit bearing general education courses.

One of the most important services these programs provide—one which is often overlooked—is the psychological support; treating all of its students with dignity and respect, regardless of their prior experiences, financial status, or need for special attention. This positive reinforcement of ego and self-concept goes a long way in facilitating success.

Services have been offered via pre-college summer programs, pre-college academic year programs, transitional year programs, freshman year programs, freshman-sophomore programs, and four year programs, (Thurman, 1979). All have generally incorporated monitoring and follow-up efforts.

These programs grew out of the economic, political, and social forces of the 1960s when there was a (1) growing need for an educated work force, (2) an increasingly dynamic and demanding civil rights movement, (3) a renewed egalitarian education concept, and (4) a growing philanthropic support for higher education, (Gordon and Wilkerson, 1966). These factors have been minimized or eliminated, yet the need for the types of programs begun during the 1960s continues.

Minority and disadvantaged students continue to be underrepresented in higher education, especially in the professions, while their numbers in the population increase. Viable programmatic efforts are required to bring about the aims and goals of the early programs: equal educational opportunity for all. The following sections identify a practical process in establishing effective special services programs and the political factors which must be attended to in order to establish and maintain them.

Program Development Factors

Institutions of higher education have become increasingly bureaucratic and have attempted to have a heterogeneous population—one which represents a population mix of the greater society. These two factors have the capacity to introduce conflict between the goals of the institution and the heterogeneous population, (Borland, 1976). This is particularly true when race, gender, or physical appearance/dexterity are introduced into a system unprepared or underprepared to deal directly with these differences. These factors are compounded further if the students being introduced into the system are less academically prepared than the traditional population—regardless of why they are less prepared. Several key components become immediately apparent for the effective implementation of a durable, institution-

ally integrated special services program. Pre-assessment, goal clarification, and potential barriers must be identified as well as establishing implementation and alternative strategies.

Pre-assessment

It should be remembered that introducing special services onto
a campus significantly changes that entity; the program's students,
personnel, and services will be different from the norm generally
experienced. The political parameters which cross each of these
components must be given careful and studious attention. No program
exists of and by itself, therefore, the campus attitude, resources,
and environmental constraints must be attended to in all stages of
development. In other words, know or get to know the campus, what the
issues are and who the players are. Becoming familiar with the faculty, administrative and student leaders can help identify the above.
These concerns are addressed more specifically in the political process section.

The pre-assessment stage is crucial and raises several issues.
The professional seeking to establish a special services program
should ask several questions.

First, what is the need for the effort? If a discrepancy exists
between what is and what should be (the actual versus the desired or
required) then a need exists. This pre-assessment must take into
account which needs and for what group of students this special effort
is to address.

Second, who should be consulted regarding the need for the special program? Clearly, one would want to discuss the need for the
project with colleagues who have some understanding of the need for
such a project as well as those who might be against introducing a
special effort into the campus community. It is critical that this is
discussed with your immediate supervisor and with any higher authori-
ties as deemed appropriate.

Discussion with people who have some knowledge of the physical
and fiscal constraints of the institution would help identify
potential pitfalls and "sore points" to avoid when initiating the
proposal for the program. The fiscal aspect could be potentially
damaging to the successful implementation of a special services
program, particularly in these days of shrinking budgets; however,
this can be allayed if federal or other external sources of funding
are available. If an institutional fund source is being sought, then
timing is crucial as is the identification of re-allocated sources
and support during the budgetary process. It is important to have
your proposal designed and ready for scrutiny at the initial point of
the process unless some other provision has been made. A late entry
can doom even the best of efforts. During the pre-assessment phase it
is critical that the environment is scanned to establish the need and
determine the sources of support, the potential barriers, budgetary
constraints, institutional goals, and how the special program fits
with these goals and objectives.

Program Design

If program approval is to be obtained, those designing it should develop a vision of the program in its ideal state. This vision or master plan, though, should not be permanently fixed; rather it should give shape to what you wish to accomplish. Changes may occur in scope and size dependent upon the personnel, fiscal, and spatial resources available.

The design stage requires that the purpose be clearly identified and objectives specified in measurable terms. Whether using a management by objectives, PERT, or other planning mechanism, a clear statement of purpose, measurable objectives, and action plans are necessary. Accountability or evaluation mechanisms are extremely important. Because of the new clientele brought to the campus, the budget, personnel, and quantifiable data are scrutinized carefully to assure "quality control"--that students "who shouldn't be here" are not wasting valuable resources.

Other areas to be given careful attention in the design phase are the program delivery mechanisms: personnel patterns, budget determinations, space allocations and locations, working relationships with other administrative units, external commitments, time lines, and follow-up procedures.

Alternative means of delivery should be investigated and planned for in the program design. Plan A does not always work, but plan B just might, depending upon the contingencies that exist.

The space issue is important. New programs especially need to be in centrally located buildings. This gives the program a visible identity and certifies its centralness to the mission and purpose of the institution. It also demonstrates to students, particularly to underrepresented students, that they are a viable part of the institution. It also demonstrates to the faculty that the program has administrative support.

The program design is generally exhibited in a proposal. Federally funded programs have specific sets of guidelines and criteria. These should be followed closely, as rating points are distributed according to how well a proposal follows the designated determinants. Programs intended to be state or institutionally funded usually have guidelines to follow, and this should be done rigorously. Any deviation should be approved by the appropriate official prior to submission.

Careful attention should be given to the program's personnel. To the extent possible, program personnel should possess the same credentials as required of others in similar positions throughout the campus. For example, at four year comprehensive or doctoral degree granting institutions, special services directors should have a terminal degree, (i.e., Ph.D. or Ed.D.), if it is required of the Admissions Director or Financial Aids Director. The degree attainment, however, should not outweigh having someone with the experience, the commitment and desire, and the ability to "get the job done." (The director and staff should also, as much as possible, be representative of the target group.) Program designers should keep in mind that the university campus personnel recognizes and respects those who have attained their degree levels. It is also important to have staff who will foster the feeling, internally and externally, that the program's students can succeed. A committed staff is important.

Program Delivery

After the above components are in place, program delivery is affected. Several key elements must take place in this phase. One key is to promote the program to those who will use it, to those who will work with it, and those who work in it. A clear sense of purpose, well stated goals, and expected outcomes aid in the formulation of brochures, press releases, and special meetings to publicize and further the effort. A tone of excitement and enthusiasm should be pervasive. A second key element is to check all phases to assure that everything promised concerning the special program is in place—this includes people, materials, space, and time. The people who promised to help, the promotional materials, the location and the starting time must all be prepared and begun as planned.

A third element is to deliver what is promised; anything less can cause serious problems for continuation. This is extremely true if the special program is geared to minority and underprepared students.

One of the realities of university life on a predominantly white campus is that anything connected with minority related enterprises will be checked and rechecked and criticized if it does not flow as planned, as are most issues not fully understood or fully supported by the campus.

The Political Process

At the beginning of this article, I noted that program designers should pay careful attention to their environment; this is particularly important since the potential exists for conflict. I also noted that special services efforts are relatively new having been in existence for only twenty years. In those twenty years special services programs have introduced a different clientele, different personnel, and different services to the campus. While change is a constant on a university campus, it comes slowly. The introduction of special programs has been rapid and pervasive; the potential for conflict, then, is evident. The environment must be given adequate attention. As noted by (Baldridge and Deal, 1983):

> The relationship between the organization and its environment is like an everchanging kaleidoscope. The environment is a complex mixture of political support and control, competing organizations trying to steal clients or funds, supporters trying to build the organization up, and detractors working to tear it down. Government policies are

7

generous one minute and stingy the next. Every organization faces a bewildering whirlwind of environmental controls.

The above statement complements the concept of the university environment as an "organized anarchy," (Cohen and March, 1974). In an organized anarchy each individual is viewed as an autonomous decisionmaker. "The 'decisions' of the system are a consequence produced by the system but intended by no one and decisively controlled by no one." Decisionmaking in this type of setting is clearly political, and designers of programs should be cognizant of the politics which must be undertaken to gain approval, implementation, and survival of their programs.

The political milieu of the campus is similar to that of partisan politics where coalitions are built, pressure tactics are used, influence offered and sustained, and compromises arranged and terminated. Power is gained, and it dissipates over time. The environment is often hostile, but special programs must learn to negotiate the journey and compete for resources, as do all other programs. Moving politically within the college or university framework requires one to spend the necessary time to get to know the system--to identify those not only with the formal titles/positions but also those in the informal structure who can provide the needed entree, guidance, and support. This can assist the program designer in identifying those important or powerful individuals who can help or hinder establishment of the program. Obtaining the support of those with the authority to influence or make decisions can ease the tension or conflict which exists when a new program emerges. Identifying and nullifying or neutralizing potential enemies of the program is also necessary.

A key element in the success of special programs has been the support, the vocal and visible support, of the chief executive officer --the president and/or chancellor. As new programs emerge, tension usually surfaces around their legitimacy and domain or territory in which the program is to operate. Support from the top can help subdue known opposition to the new effort. The commitment of the chief executive will help ease the conflicts which generally arise from the establishment of a new program. Along with those who have authority, those with the power to influence the decision should also be identified, as they can be effective in allaying the fears of others on matters such as territorial infringement. As noted earlier an environmental assessment can assist in determining the campus climate as it relates to the receptivity of your program.

Because of the diverse nature of special services programs, fear of territorial infringement may appear in a number of places. Special services programs may have recruitment, admission, counseling, financial aid, career development, tutorial, cultural enrichment, and instructional components; all of which exist in other parts of the educational system. The potential for conflict, then, are numerous.

True conflict can be avoided if the issues are focused on the major concerns. The territory is generally broad enough to include everyone. Special programs have specific missions for a specific population which are usually not attended to by the rest of the community. Program specifics must be identified and publicized carefully and fully as noted in the process section of this paper.

Timing and the means of approaching the issues are paramount. If you are seeking institutional funding from a state supported institution, you should know the political process within the decision making structure of the campus; so that your proposal is read and evaluated in the appropriate climate and at a propitious time. If your proposal is read and reviewed by a group to which you have access, it may be helpful to offer your assistance or presence to answer any questions they may have. This may allow you the opportunity to make adjustments to the proposal.

It is difficult to get things done alone. A good campus politician will devise a way to work cooperatively with others of a similar interest. It is wise to include them in on the program design whether or not they are from the same department, division, or college. It is likewise helpful to include, if possible and feasible, your opposition in the decision making process. This can be effective in allaying fears and acts as a depressant to their opposition.

One key point which should be uppermost in the minds of those who design special programs is that the environment is fluid, and change is the constant. If you do not get the program implemented on the first try, persist! The time will come to resubmit the idea.

Good communication is a must in involving others. This involvement may range from simply informing to participation. The political communication system can also be used for testing ideas. Support for and against an idea will take place if it is put in the system. This can, in turn, lead to the identification of those with whom you wish to coalition build and/or involve as opposition leaders.

An important communication link which cannot be overlooked is your immediate supervisor. He or she can ease the pathway to the successful acceptance and implementation of the program. This can be of prime importance, for example, in determining the location of the program. New programs need not only promotion as addressed earlier, but also need the visibility of being in a central location. Space is generally at a premium. Setting the appropriate groundwork, recognizing the institutional priorities, and fitting the special services program within the institutional framework with your supervisor can ease his or her effort to get high visibility space for the program.

Conclusion and Summary

If the program development and political processes are followed, program designers should be able to establish special services programs on a college or university campus. Readers should remember that campus environments differ radically; thus, they must make as accurate an assessment as possible to determine the preparedness of the campus for a venture such as a special services program. This requires a knowledge and understanding of the formal and informal political systems of an institution, taking the time to cultivate alliances, compromise, and persistence. The necessary groundwork, however, must be laid to assure receptivity of the proposal to create a special services effort.

Special programs for minority and disadvantaged students have been successful on many campuses across the nation. Effective programs have several distinct characteristics: (1) a committed, dedicated, and capable administrator; (2) a staff fully committed to and believing in the program's students; (3) a well defined, comprehensive set of services to the clientele; (4) a clear set of expectations for staff and students as articulated via goals and objectives; (5) established promotional activities; (6) the support of the chief executive's office and the program's administrative unit; and (7) a firm and stable budgetary source.

REFERENCES

Astin, A.W. et. al **Higher Education and the Disadvantaged.** Washington, DC: Human Services Press, 1972.

Baldridge, J.V. and Deal, T. The Basics of Change in Educational Organizations. **In The Dynamics of Organizational Change in Education,** edited by J.V. Baldridge and T. Deal. Berkeley, California: McCutchan Publishing Company, 1983.

Boland, D.T. Student Development Implementation Through Expanded Professional Skills, **Journal of College Student Personnel,** 1976, 17, 145-149.

Cohen, M.D. and March J.G. **Leadership and Ambiguity: the American College President,** New York: McGraw Hill, 1974.

Gordon, E.W. and Wilkerson, D.A. **Compensatory Education for the Disadvantaged,** New York: College Entrance Examination Board, 1966.

The College Entrance Examination Board, **Equality Postponed.** New York: The College Board Publication, 1984.

Thurman, A. **Factors in the Institutionalization of Educational Opportunity Programs,** An unpublished dissertation. The University of Wisconsin-Madison: Madison, Wisconsin, 1979.

The Role Minority Student Centers Play on Predominately White Campuses

Lawrence W. Young
The Pennsylvania State University

ABOUT THE AUTHOR

Lawrence W. Young is currently the Director of the Paul Robeson Cultural Center at The Pennsylvania State University. Mr. Young is well known for his leadership in making minority student centers responsive to student needs. His numerous articles and essays have been published in leading newspapers around the country. He received his B.S. and M.S. from Miami University in Oxford, Ohio. His professional experience includes being the Director - Minority Student Affairs, and Director of the Educational Opportunity Program at Miami University; a reading and English teacher at several public school districts and holding a position in private industry. Larry is a linguist who speaks fluent French and understands several other languages. He is both a student and teacher of Afro-American culture and its impact on the behavior of Black and White Americans.

INTRODUCTION

Faced with the certain alienation and isolation of small Black student populations on campus, some predominantly white colleges created Black cultural centers on campus for a variety of reasons. To some these centers were to be pacifiers to quell the demands of Blacks for a more relevant total environment. To some they were to be a temporary bridge to help ease the transition of black students into the mainstream of college life. To others they were viewed as a misguided concession to Black demands by weak-kneed, pseudoliberal whites and a further polarization of the campus constituencies on the issue of race. Perhaps most importantly they were viewed by most Black students as "an island in a sea of whiteness" that offered them a sense of identity and protection in an environment which they viewed as hostile or indifferent.

This article examines the history of minority, (Black), cultural centers; and while the focus is on Afro-Americans, the material applies to women, Hispanics, Native Americans, and other ethnic groups to varying degrees. This article also examines the implications and impacts of minority cultural centers on students, the collegiate environment, and the intellectual community at large.

Do minority cultural centers have a permanent role to play on predominantly white campuses, or is this simply another fad of the academy soon to be forgotten and discarded? What role will these centers play if minority enrollment shrinks? Or if it increases drastically? These are issues that every one in higher education will and should face head-on with a rational, just, and humane plan for managing change.

The Role Minority Student Centers Play on Predominantly White Campuses

by Lawrence W. Young

The advent of minority student centers on predominantly white campuses is a relatively new phenomenon in higher education. These centers were created as a part of some universities' response to the civil rights movement, the increased enrollment of minority (particularly Black), students, and the assassination of Dr. Martin Luther King, Jr. They were part of packages that also featured Black Studies, minority affairs, and special admissions programs and financial aid. It should be clear that not all universities responded to the pressures of the late '60's, and only a relative few began and have maintained minority cultural centers as units outside of a Black or ethnic studies program.

Because the impetus for most of these centers was the activism of Black students on white college campuses, I shall devote my attention to those centers with a specifically Black cultural focus, although I believe there is relevance in these observations for Hispanic, Native American, or Asian cultural centers as well.

In his introduction to Carter G. Woodson's **The Mis-Education of the Negro** reprinted in 1977, Charles H. Nilon says that **"Woodson was interested in the content of Black education, the input and the results of it--the output."** He felt that the content of education in Black colleges was similar to that in white colleges, and that it prepared Black students to accept white Anglo-Saxon values and to function in a society where those values were coercive. This education, however, did not provide them a knowledge of and respect for themselves. It resulted, Woodson felt, in Black persons feeling inferior or hating themselves. When they avoided feelings of inferiority and self-hate, they were likely, Woodson felt, to feel superior to the mass of Black persons, (Woodson, 1977).

Woodson (1875-1950) is regarded as the "father of Negro history" and as such was quite concerned that even at "Black" colleges, students were "taught to admire the Hebrew, the Greek, the Latin, and the Teuton and to despise the African," (Ibid, p.1). It was this attitude of contempt toward their own people that most disturbed and moved Woodson, for he concluded that those who felt this way were **"all but worthless in the development of their people."**

The minority student entering a predominantly white college today walks in to what John Egerton has called **"the white sea of higher education."** (Altman and Snyder, 1971) Recent government statistics show the decline in the enrollment of Black and other minority students from a high of 9.4% in 1976-77 to the 8.5% of 1984-85. It is not unusual to find college campuses with under 5% Black enrollment. The environment on campus is influenced by an overwhelmingly white student body, faculty, administration, and curriculum, which is assumed by most to be the natural order of things. It is in this circumstance that the student must struggle for a relevant environment or submerge his or her cultural heritage and attempt total assimilation, which has as a basic assumption Woodson's concept of self-hatred and which is neither logical or mentally healthy. Because conformity is a very important social value among whites as well as unreconstructed Blacks, cultural centers are often looked upon as "separatist", "special interest," even as "subversive." We must clearly understand that the history of American education has as its foundation the concern for special interests.

Originally education was the "special interest" of the children of wealthy landowners, that is, the dominant American white male elite. Other institutions were created "to preserve indigenous culture and beliefs and to combat undue influence of the dominant culture," (DHEW, 1979). Religiously distinctive schools, Catholic and Jewish, fall into this category. Their role was to preserve the culture while preparing members of the group for professional and economic assimilation into the mainstream. However at the heart of the educational process was an intense reinforcement of values and beliefs that prepared the groups for acculturation. Likewise repressive notions about women, led to the creation of college dominated by and exclusively for women. Although lessened in urgency by the acceptance of women to nearly all formerly male universities, those women's colleges remain an important and vital option. Their relevance is underscored by the difficulty in gaining grudging acceptance for women's studies and women's centers on many campuses today.

The precursor of the Black cultural centers on white college campuses were the historically Black colleges (HBC) established after the Civil War. Like the colleges for religious groups and women, the historically Black colleges were a function of a society which excluded some. Unlike the former two groups, however, Blacks faced even more pervasive and debilitating discrimination rooted in code and in custom in America. Even though these colleges were controlled and dominated by whites who held the purse strings, they still had as part of their primary focus **"psycho-socially congenial settings in which Blacks can develop and ... bastions of Black culture and thought ...,"** (DHEW, p.13) The HBC's were then a part of the struggle for "a relevant environment" and as such represented one of the few and first formal institutions to stress and nurture pride, identity and respect for Black culture.

These historically Black colleges assumed an impressive role in not only building leadership, but in promoting and preserving Black culture and all of America owes them debt. Some of these schools realized that the purpose of education was more than just preparation for a job and more than just training for competency. Some there knew that the only sure advocates for the interests of Black people would be people who were Black in color, consciousness and culture. One need only reflect on the hundreds of leaders of the civil rights movement, like Martin Luther King, Jr., who received schooling and nurture at a historically Black college, to underscore the value of such institutions.

To appreciate the role of minority cultural centers on predominantly white campuses, we must return to Woodson who said, **"If you can control a man's thinking you do not have to worry about his action. When you determine what a man shall think you do not have to concern yourself about what he will do.** If you make a man feel he is inferior, you do not have to compel him to accept inferior status, for he will seek it himself. If you make a man think that he is justly an outcast, you do not have to order him to the back door. He will go without being told, and if there is no back door, his very nature will demand one," (Woodson, 1933 p.84-85).

Since we live in a society which believes that "real education" only takes place in organized classrooms, we must then closely examine that which passes for education in American colleges.

We must recognize that the emphasis is weighted heavily in favor of a western orientation that functions to **"help socialize succeeding generations to accept a system based upon class and inequality, to accept rules unquestioningly, to compete, to label one another and themselves, to accept as truth the values we teach as fact, and determine, by the process of selection based upon conformity, who will be allowed access to the great middle and professional classes with their concomitant wealth and leisure,"** (Kern and Needham, 1981). Thus learning takes a back seat to accreditation and socialization in American education. And while this represents a problem for white Americans, it is an unmitigated disaster for Black Americans.

The inculcation of Black students with a value system that only works well for whites is a commonplace occurrence in America. When Blacks accept that Columbus discovered America without wondering about the people Columbus "discovered" living here, when "American History" is accepted as the story of white people in the United States without questioning whether Canada, Mexico, Central and South America were ever part of the Americas, when "World History" is accepted as a study of Egypt, Greece, Rome, and Europe, then we recognize that Black people in this process are in need of help. In a society that values conformity, thinking is a dangerous and unde-sirable practice. After all, thinking sometimes leads to challenge, and challenge usually leads to struggle. Education for Black students on predominantly white campuses came to be a process of separating "us" from "them", and many Black students and teachers have accepted this class-based assumption. Few have chosen to **"define education as a process of learning to liberate ourselves from oppressive and alienating forces,"** (Kern and Needham, 1981, p 103).

The first Black cultural centers were viewed by students and staff as safe havens in an alien environment. These students, who arrived on white college campuses that were unprepared for their presence, suffered feelings of isolation, loneliness and alienation. Because they viewed the campus as a hostile environment, many reacted with either anger, or depression, and apathy. In their search for esteem, love, and belongingness on white campuses, they were able to find few refuges. Moreover, the very nature of white campuses served to deflate the self-esteem of Black students. They viewed the anglo-centric curriculum, extracurricular activities and social life as an indictment of their lifestyle. Minority centers were viewed as a necessary and just alternative to this environment. They were to serve as a means of facilitating the transition from the Black community to the University, while helping the student to discover and identify with Black culture and heritage; and in some instances, they would also serve as a social center for the Black population. As time passed and universities were forced to deal with the dual challenges of Black recruitment and Black retention, the value of Black centers became apparent; and the dimensions of their roles began to slightly change. In an extensive study of the problems of recruitment and retention at selected white universities in 1980, a panel recommended, **"Universities should encourage, not discourage Black student awareness of their heritage in all of its positive aspects. Black students need their own organizations and cultural activities as important means to deal with hostile environments and insure the development of healthy attitudes toward themselves and other Black people,"** (Doe, 1981). That report went on to say that the poor quality of Black campus life was the underlying cause of Black attrition.

In addition to the roles stated above, the centers took on additional roles as imparters of Black ideology and values, as cauldrons for Black political thought, as the crossroads where African, African-American, African-Caribbean, Asians, and Europeans met to exchange points of view on neutral to friendly turf. The centers began to move from a service orientation to an educational orientation. In some instances this shift aroused suspicion and anxiety in white administrators and resentment and hostility among "party-time" and assimilationist Blacks. The emphasis of the centers was fashioned by directors whose ideology was shaped by the events of the '60's and '70's and who were well versed in the literature of Black studies. These directors saw the center as a natural community extension of the intellectual thrust of Black Studies and as a compliment to the aims of Black Studies. While pride and identity and preparation for the "mainstream" are still important, the centers of the '80's and '90's are attempting to do more. They are attempting to fill vital gaps in knowledge and understanding and to provide young Black people with the weapons to combat rampant resurgent racism in our society.

This effort is precisely what Harold Cruse proposed as the **"special function of the Negro intellectual...he should tell Black America how and why Negroes are trapped in this cultural degeneracy, and how it has dehumanized their essential identity, squeezed the lifeblood of their inherited cultural ingredients out of them, then relegated them to the cultural slums. They should tell this brainwashed white America, this "nation of sheep," this overfed, overdeveloped, overprivileged, (but culturally pauperized), federation of unassimilated European remnants that their days of grace are numbered,"** (Cruse, 1967). The truly progressive leaders of centers today believe deeply that we must **"define education as a process of learning to liberate ourselves from oppressive and alienating forces,"** (Kern and Needham, 1981, p. 84).

17

The new breed of leaders in these minority student centers have come to the realization that they may hold the last hope for our young people who are being lured astray by the siren songs of material acquisition, hedonistic narcissism, self-indulgence, indifference for others, status as success, and an Anglo-centric view of the world. It is through the presentation of alternative views of the world that the centers can provide the opportunity for the psychological liberation which must precede political and economic liberation. The need for a relevant environment in the **"white sea of higher education"** is pointed out by Dr. Carolyn Dejoie when she says **"...the university is not geared to those of non-majority status. Fraternities, sororities, homecoming activities, and student govern-ment maintain the white status quo. As in academic areas, the social aspects of university life systematically follow the interest of the white students--the majority group.**

Standard student activities that are planned well in advance, as movies, concerts, theatre, lectures, seldom include presentations which demonstrate artistry talents and scholarship of Blacks. There is a dearth of positive Black imagery on white campuses. Entwined with the white-oriented social affairs is the cultural starvation of Black students," (Dejoie, 1985). The reduction of this "cultural starvation" is a basic tenet of minority cultural centers. Whether it is the Bolinga Black Cultural Resources Center at Wright State University in Ohio which states, **"it is not our responsibility only to promote an understanding of who we are and where we are going, but more importantly to equip Black children with the knowledge and wisdom necessary for them to continue on from that foundation to acquire critical skills which will help to assure the survival of Black people in America,"** or the Afro-American Cultural Center at the University of Connecticut whose director states, **"One goal of the Center is to transmit to the University of Connecticut community the wealth of information about the Black experience in order for there to be a creation of mutual respect with the majority of cultures gathered,"** or the Black Cultural Center at Purdue University in Indiana whose director says, **"Our purpose here is to destroy myths for both Black and white people and to acquaint all people with the heritage of Black America. We are here for the socialization of minority students. They need to relate to their own ethnic background in a nurturing environment in order to get the most from their time at Purdue."**

Black cultural centers like the Nyumburu Center at the University of Maryland, the Afro-American Cultural Center at the University of Virginia, the Multi-Cultural Center at Marquette University, the Gwendolyn Brooks Cultural Center at Western Illinois University, and the Paul Robeson Cultural Centers at Rutgers and Penn State, share a common mission and duty with the historically Black colleges and universities like Central State University of Ohio. The Paul Robeson Center located at Central State is a beacon of dignity, pride, respect, integrity, intellect, and responsibility.

Historically Black colleges and Black cultural centers at predominantly white colleges share a common obligation to the students

18

who use them to assist them in meeting their personal educational goals, in promoting the pursuit of excellence, in cultivating an appreciation and respect for Black culture, in preserving our precious heritage, and in preparing young Black minds for the reality of the struggle that is and the struggle that will be. Black cultural centers at predominantly white campuses can help Black students, (and white students, too), to discover who they were, who they are, and where they should be going. These centers provide an alternative view to customs and conventions of American education and offer to Black students a relevant environment. They promote, rather that impede, the process of self-discovery. The poet E.E. Cummings perhaps said it best:

> "To be one's self in a world which is trying its hardest, night and day, to make you somebody else... is to fight the hardest battle any human being can fight."

Footnotes

Altman, Robert A. and Patricia Snyder (eds) **"The Minority Student On Campus"** Center For Research and Development in Higher Education, University of California, Berkeley, and Western Interstate Commission for Higher Education, PO Drawer P, Boulder, Colorado, 1971. p. 35.

Cruse, Harold. **The Crisis of the Negro Intellectual.** New York, Quill, 1967. p. 455-456.

Dejoie, Carolyn. **Readings From a Black Perspective: An Anthology.** Madison, Wisconsin. Health and Human Services. University of Wisconsin-Madison, 1985. p. 106.

Department of Health Education and Welfare. **Black Colleges and Universities: An Essential Component of a Diverse System of Higher Education.** Prepared by National Advisory Committee on Black Higher Education and Black Colleges and Universities. 1979. p. 8.

Kern, Iris and Needham, William. **Quid Nunc: The Contemplative Perspective of the American Dream Turned Nightmare.** Washington, DC. Bond Publishing Company, 1981. P. 101.

U.S. Department of Education. **Admission and Retention Problems of Black Students at Seven Predominantly White Universities.** National Advisory Committee on Black Higher Education and Black Colleges and Universities, 1981. p. 17.

Woodson, Carter G. **The Mis-Education of the Negro.** Washington: Associated Publishers, 1933. With new introduction by Charles H. Nilon, 1977.

What Minority Students Need to Know About Financial Aid

Elba Chavez
Waubonsee Community College

ABOUT THE AUTHOR

Elba Chavez is a Financial Aid/Minority Recruitment professional at Waubonsee Community College. She received her B.A. in Spanish Translation and Business and is currently pursuing an M.B.A. degree at Aurora University. Elba has begun her career at Waubonsee and serves as a source of financial aid information for students. Working in a community college setting, she is responsible for minority recruitment and marketing the college through travel publications, and local agencies. She has also performed translating and interpreting duties for the court system and private industry. She understands the financial need of many minority students and works diligently to ensure that students obtain the information they need to matriculate. Her financial aid workshops for students have proved an effective strategy in keeping minority students on her campus informed.

Chapter 2

What Minority Students Need to Know About Financial Aid

INTRODUCTION

In her new position as financial aid advisor and minority recruiter, Ms. Chavez has found that the economically disadvantaged and their families not only need to be encouraged but also need to be emotionally supported while attending college. She has found that many of her clients are disillusioned after taking the initiative to start school or to return to school. They find themselves trapped in an ongoing labyrinth of political red tape. One agency requests this verification while another wants a cross check. It is her hope that in reading this chapter one may be able to obtain a different insight and be able to view minorities in a different light. After all, she says,

> "red, black, brown, or white, we were all raised in different environments, cultures, and sometimes different countries. We all have our own sets of values and beliefs about how education fits into our lives."

This country is undergoing a dynamic face lift, and when it is through its population will mainly consist of relatively young generations—young minorities that require assistance now if we are to expect them to run the country.

What Minority Students Need to Know About Financial Aids

by Elba Chavez

Most of us are not unaware that the type of aid students receive has a great effect on their achievements. Receiving grants and scholarships have a positive effect, while loans conjure mixed emotions. Minority students rely heavily on a financial aid package to enable them to go to school, because they often begin college with heavy financial responsibilities. Before one attempts to discern the needs of minorities, it is important to realize how they differ from their Anglo counter parts. Unless one happens to be a minority, it is difficult to realize that the chances of a Mexican American ever completing a college education are much less than for an Anglo or a Black. Out of every 100 Chicanos entering their freshman year, only 17 make it to their senior years. Once they are seniors one can assume that they will graduate.

One of the reasons why Mexican Americans do not finish college is that they, as a group, tend to do poorly on traditional Anglo tests of academic achievement. They also do not perform as well in subject academic evaluations. Still another reason, and probably the most important, is the difference in culture. Schools attempt to teach ideals and the American way of life--both of which do not resemble their home environment. According to Thomas P. Carter and Roberto D. Segura,

> **"...Measures of the internationalization of American culture—in the form of standardized test aptitude, intelligence, and achievement—show that Mexican Americans, Blacks, and the poor in general are not learning the skills, knowledge, and values so diligently taught by the school,"** (Rudzitis, 1985).

The reason that minorities do not learn these skills is due to the difference in the culture and in the economic values. Minorities, like other disadvantaged groups, attempt to incorporate the values and patterns of the dominant society, but are still made to feel like second class citizens. This occurs in the child's early development, when he/she realizes the role assigned to him by many members of the Anglo-American society. This coupled with feelings of discrimination, has caused many minorities to experience self-hatred. Some low status students do succeed in school and in society. They usually share, or are assumed to share, middle class values, or have some personality characteristics akin to Anglo students.

With demographic studies showing that minorities will become an increasingly large part of this country's population, it becomes necessary to bring them into the mainstream of post-secondary education. Not only do they need to be encouraged to attend college, but they need to consider entering disciplines in which they are highly under-represented, such as math and science. Demographics show where minorities exist and will continue to exist, but there are many factors that determine whether or not a minority will attend college. These include: the family's socio-economic status, the student's scholastic ability and achievement, and the family's perception of a college education. Many minorities belong to low income families whose adjusted gross income does not exceed $10,000 annually. This would explain why minorities rank among the highest student aid recipients, but it does not explain why low income students still remain under-represented in the college community. Perhaps this is due to the high drop-out rate among minorities and as a result of current reductions in federal student aid.

Unlike many of their Anglo counterparts, minority families do not have the same options to send their children through college. They cannot borrow from private lenders, because they have no credit established; they also cannot borrow against assets which they do not hold. They often have no home to mortgage and no substantial income to contribute, and they also cannot tap into any savings.

If the student works, he is expected to contribute his earnings to the household, rather than to save it for college. In a financial aid need analysis the student's earnings are counted as part of the family's contribution towards educational expenses. Most low income families rank college attendance last with emergencies and basic necessities as top priorities. According to the **Professional Journal of College Guidance Research,** **"...there is a great deal of aid available to these students, and yes, these programs provide access to college for many who otherwise would have no hope of attending. But the facts are that low income students and their families are paying a substantial portion of the costs of college attendance and, despite the availability of student aid, a college education remains financially out of reach for many of these families,"** (Journal of College Guidance and Research, 1986). Even when students receive aid, there still remains a major portion of college costs that are not covered by grant or scholarship assistance—aid that is usually termed "gift aid" since it does not have to be repaid or earned. The real cost to any family is the total cost of education after grants received by the students has been subtracted.

While low income students are generally eligible for federal aid, not all of them qualify, nor do they all apply. It is not that he has no desire to apply, but rather that he is often unaware of what is available. Even when he knows what is available, the family may not be giving the support he needs to attend college. Some students are not eligible for federal grants because they receive significant untaxed income from various sources—i.e., Social Security, Aid to Families of Dependent Children (AFDC), or veteran's benefits. However, the Pell Grant program and others similar to it are especially important for low income students.

Since federally funded programs are important to minority students, they should be made aware of what is available to them in order to finance their education. Students should review and consider information about a school program before they enroll. They should also be aware of financial aid. This requires planning ahead by obtaining the necessary forms as soon as they are available and to promptly return them completely filled out. One should also make arrangements to take required examinations--PSAT/NMSQT, Scholastic Aptitude Test, ACT exams, and College Entrance Examination Board Exams. Failure to take these tests in advance may hinder the opportunity for college admission and/or financial aid approval. A student must also make sure that the examination scores, high school transcripts, and personal letters of recommendation are forwarded to any institution or source of aid that requests them. One should be made aware that it is important to keep careful and detailed family financial records. Filing early cannot be over emphasized; this is the student's responsibility and the key to obtaining limited sources of aid.

Once the financial aid application has been processed, the student may be required to provide additional documentation of any dollar amounts reported. Also corrections and/or new information requested by the financial aid office or the agency to which the application was submitted needs to be submitted. To be eligible for federal aid, a student must be a U.S. citizen or an eligible non-citizen. Non-citizens may be required to show proof of status. In addition, male students reaching their 18th birthday must be registered with selective service. Similarly, the student must show evidence of financial need as indicated by an approved needs analysis service.

The two most commonly used forms to determine need are the "Financial Aid Form", (FAF), put out by the College Scholarship Service, (CSS), and the "Family Financial Statement" distributed by the American College Testing, (ACT), Program. Other need analysis forms are the United States Department of Education's Application for Federal Student Aid," (AFSA), the "Pennsylvania Higher Education Assistance Application," (PHEAA), and the "Student Aid Application for California," (SAAC).

To be eligible for any federal or state assistance, students must be enrolled in at least 6 semester hours and must be making satisfactory progress as determined by the college of attendance. Students cannot be in default of federally guaranteed student loan programs while receiving aid for attendance at their college.

There are five federally funded programs available that all students should be aware of: The first is the Pell Grant. When a student qualifies, he/she does not have to repay it. It is considered "gift aid" and is meant to be used for undergraduate studies only. The eligibility is determined by a standard formula designed by the Department of Education. In this formula all available resources and assets are taken into consideration. The formula produces a student aid index number that is used to award a certain amount of funds to the student. The amount of the award is based on the cost of attendance at the particular school the student wishes to attend, enrollment status, and length of attendance. A student receiving a Pell grant may be eligible for up to $2,100.00 per academic year, but the actual amount a student receives will depend largely on his student aid index number and the cost of education at his school.

The second type of aid available is the Supplemental Educational Opportunity Grant, (SEOG). Like the Pell Grant, this too does not have to be repaid, and is for undergraduate study only; this type of grant is a campus-based program, because it is administered by the financial administrator at the college. The amount the student actually receives depends upon availability of funds. A student may be eligible to receive up to $2,000 a year depending on need, the availability of funds for SEOG at the school, and the amount of other aid the student receives.

A third type of aid is college Work-Study. This program provides the student with an on-campus job to earn money for school. This aid is available to both undergraduate and graduate students. Similar to the SEOG, it is a campus-based program. The amount of the award is based on the student's need and availability of funds. A student is paid at least the current federal minimum wage, and the student cannot exceed twenty work hours per week while attending school. Some work study jobs are available off-campus, but most are on campus.

A fourth type of aid is the National Direct Student Loan, (NDSL). Loans, unlike grants, must be repaid. Payment begins six months after the student has graduated or has stopped attending college. This type of aid is available to undergraduate and graduate students. It is also a campus-based program, and the amount of the loan is based on need and availability of funds. An NDSL is a low interest loan, (usually 5%), designed to help the student pay for his/her education in college. With an NDSL a student may be able to borrow up to $6,000 as an undergraduate student having completed 2 years of study toward a Bachelor's degree. (This total includes any amount borrowed under NDSL for the first two years of study.)

Finally, the fifth source of financial aid is Guaranteed Student Loans. Like the NDSL, this too must be repaid after graduation. This type of loan can be used for undergraduate as well as graduate studies. The student must have filled out a financial aid form and have been found ineligible in order to apply and qualify for a GSL. A Guaranteed Student Loan (GSL) is a low interest loan made available to the student by a lending institution. It is intended to be used for a student's college education. The interest rate for students is 8%, and one is allowed to borrow up to $2,500 per academic year.

A student will usually receive one or a combination of the above mentioned aid as part of his/her financial aid package. A financial aid package consists of Federal and non-Federal aid such as loans, grants, or work-study combined in a package to help one meet college costs. Similarly, a student can combine his school's financial aid package with privately funded scholarships from groups or corporations. Some of these companies establish funds for scholarships in specific fields of study, while civic groups award scholarships based on merit and recognition to outstanding students.

Because the financial needs of minority students differ from most other students, it is important for them to receive guidance in order to have a better opportunity to attend college. One must also realize that as a group, minority students have a tendency to do poorly due to the emphasis placed on Anglo culture in school. All one can do to help a student is to guide him/her through the overwhelming bureaucracy by making sure that the student is aware of all the possible resources available to him/her. Once one has done this, it is essentially up to the student to follow through to meet all of the requirements.

BIBLIOGRAPHY

Carter, Thomas P., and Segura, Roberto D., **Mexican Americans in School: A Decade of Change.** New York: College Entrance Examination Board, 1979.

How Low Income Families Pay for College, **The Professional Journal of College Guidance and Research.** Kansas City, Missouri: The National Research for College and University Admissions, 1986.

Making It: A Guide to Student Finances. Harvard Student Agencies, Inc., New York: E.P. Dutton & Co., Inc., 1973.

Rudzitis, Unose, **How to Put Your Children Through College Without Going Broke.** New York: The Research Institute of America, Inc., 1985.

Scholarships

AMERICAN GEOLOGICAL INSTITUTE
Requirements: Under Graduate, Graduate, geoscience, Black, Native American, Hispanic; based on need

Type of Aid: Scholarships

Application Deadline: February 1
For Application and Further Information:
American Geological Institute
Director of Education
4220 King Street
Alexandria, VA 22302

MUSIC ASSISTANCE FUND
Requirements: Minority student, orchestral playing; based on need

Type of Aid: Grants

Application Deadline: September 1; May 1
For Application and Further Information:
Music Assistance Fund
New York Philharmonic
Broadway at 65th Street
New York, NY 10023

HERBERT LEHMAN EDUCATION FUND
Requirements: Under Graduate, Black, enter formerly segregated school in deep South

Type of Aid: Scholarships

Application Deadline: April 15
For Application and Further Information:
Herbert Lehman Education Fund
99 Hudson Street, Suite 1600
New York, NY 10013

AMERICAN INSTITUTE OF CERTIFIED PUBLIC ACCOUNTANTS
Requirements: Under Graduate, graduate, minority, accounting major, need, transcript, U.S. citizen

Type of Aid:Scholarship
For Application and Further Information:
Sharon L. Donahue
American Institute of Certified Public Accountants
1211 Avenue of the Americas
New York, NY 10036

NSPE MINORITY SCHOLARSHIPS
Requirements: High school senior, minority, engineering, top 25% of class, United States citizen

Type of Aid: Scholarships

Application Deadline: December 15 (confirm data with local Chapter)
For Application and Further Information:
National Society of Professional Engineers
Educational Foundation
142 King Street
Alexandria, VA 22314

NATIONAL ACTION COUNCIL FOR MINORITIES IN ENGINEERING, INC.
Requirements: Under Graduate, Black, Hispanic, Indian, engineering, need, United States citizen

Type of Aid: Grants

Application Deadline: None
For Application and Further Information:
Contact the participating Guidance Counselor at the college or Write:
National Action Council for Minorities in Engineering, Inc.
3 West 35th Street
New York, NY 10001

NATIONAL ASSOCIATION OF BLACK JOURNALISTS SCHOLARSHIP PROGRAM
Requirements: Under Graduate, graduate, Black, journalism, nomination, competition

Type of Aid: Scholarship

Application Deadline: May 31
For Application and Further Information:
Ruth Allen
KRLD-TV-33
8001 Carpentry Freeway
Dallas, TX 75247

BLACK SCHOLARSHIP FUND
Requirements: Black ministerial student, Christian church member

Type of Aid: Scholarships and Loans

Application Deadline: March 1
For Application and Further Information:
Black Scholarship (Star Supporter) Fund
Department of Ministry
P.O. Box 1986
Indianapolis, IN 46206

STUDENT OPPORTUNITY SCHOLARSHIP (UPCUSA)
Requirements: Church member, racial or ethnic group, United States citizen, need

Type of Aid: Scholarships

Application Deadline: April 1
For Application and Further Information:
Student Opportunity Scholarships
Presbyterian Church, (U.S.A.)
475 Riverside Drive, Room 430
New York, NY 10115

NATIONAL ACHIEVEMENT SCHOLARSHIP FOR OUTSTANDING NEGRO STUDENTS
Requirements: High school student, black, test scores

Type of Aid: Scholarships

Application Deadline: PSAT/NMSQT Test, usually taken in October of junior year
For Application and Further Information:
For PSAT/NMSQT Student Bulletin describing the award.
Write:National Achievement Scholarships—Outstanding Negro Students
One American Plaza
Evanston, IL 60201

AIA MINORITY/DISADVANTAGED SCHOLARSHIP PROGRAM
Requirements: Under Graduate, graduate, minority or disadvantaged, architecture, nomination, scores, need

Type of Aid: Scholarships

Application Deadline: Nominations April 1; Final Applications June 1
For Application and Further Information:
Scholarship Programs
American Institute of Architects
1735 New York Avenue, NW
Washington, DC 20006

ARMCO MINORITIES IN ENGINEERING SCHOLARSHIPS
Requirements: High school senior, Black, Hispanic, Indian engineering. recommendation, scores

Type of Aid: Scholarships

Application Deadline: November 15 of senior year in high school
For Application and Further Information:
Armco, Inc.
730 Curtis Street
Middletown, OH 45043

LULAC NATIONAL SCHOLARSHIP FUND

Requirements: College entry, Hispanic, proximity to local LULAC, need, United States citizen

Type of Aid: Scholarships

Application Deadline: June 1
For Application and Further Information:
LULAC National Scholarship Fund
400 First Street NW, Suite 716
Washington, DC 20001

LEO S. ROWE PAN AMERICAN FUND

Requirements: Under graduate, graduate, Latin American, student visa, transcript, need

Type of Aid: Loans

Application Deadline: None specified
For Application and Further Information:
Organization of American States
Leo S. Rowe Pan American Fund
17th Street & Constitution Avenue, NW
Washington, DC 20006-4499

COLLEGE BOARD-ENGINEERING SCHOLARSHIPS

Requirements: Under graduate, minority, transfer to four-year college, engineering

Type of Aid: Scholarships

Application Deadline: Fall nomination cycle
For Application and Further Information:
Contact the academic dean or write:
College Board-Engineering Scholarships-CEEB
888 Seventh Avenue
New York, NY 10019

MISSISSIPPI STATE FUNDED PROGRAMS

Requirements: Mississippi resident

Type of Aid: State Aid

Application Deadline: None
For Application and Further Information:
Institutions of Higher Learning
Student Financial Aid Office
P.O. Box 2336
Jackson, MS 39225-2336

UNITED METHODIST HANA SCHOLARSHIPS
Requirements: College junior, senior, or graduate, Methodist, specific minorities

Type of Aid: Scholarships

Application Deadline: April 1
For Application and Further Information:
United Methodist Church
Scholarship Program
P.O. Box 871
Nashville, TN 37202

ROY WILKINS SCHOLARSHIP PROGRAM
Requirements: College accepted, minority, full-time, need, letters, academic

Type of Aid: Scholarships

Application Deadline: June 6
For Application and Further Information:
NAACP
186 Remsen Street
Brooklyn, NY 11201

JIMMY A. YOUNG MEMORIAL SCHOLARSHIP (ARTF)
Requirements: Under Graduate, minority, respiratory therapy, "C+" average, need, recommendation, United States citizen

Type of Aid: Scholarships

Application Deadline: June 15
For Application and Further Information:
American Respiratory Therapy Foundation
1720 Regal Row
Dallas, TX 75235

MICHELLE CLARK FELLOWSHIP
Requirements: Minority, journalist, experience, electronic journalism

Type of Aid: Scholarship

Application Deadline: March 31
For Application and Further Information:
Ernie Schultz, Secretary
Radio Television News Directors' Foundation
1753 De Sales Street, NW
Washington, DC 20036

Financial Aid Resources

Directory of Special Programs and Financial Assistance for Black and Other Minority Group Students
Urban League of Westchester, 2 Grand Street,
White Plains, New York 10601.

EDUCATION FELLOWSHIPS FOR INDIAN STUDENTS

Office of Indian Education has grants for Indian students interested in courses in business administration, natural resources, medicine, engineering, law, education and related fields. Grants range from $2,300-$14,000. The average grant received is $5,000. For application or information, contact: Office of Indian Education, Department of Education, 400 Maryland Ave. S.W., Washington, DC 20202.

A Selected list of Post-Secondary Education Opportunities for Minorities and Women

U.S. Dept. of Health, Education, Welfare, Office of Bureau of Higher Education, Room 4913, ROB-3, 400 Maryland Avenue, S.W., Washington, D.C. 20202.

FINANCIAL AID DIRECTORIES

SCHOLARSHIPS, FELLOWSHIPS AND LOANS VOLUME VII

Available for $75 from Bellman Publishing, P.O. Box 164, Arlington, MA 02174.

STUDENT WORK, STUDY, TRAVEL CATALOG

Available from the Council on International Educational Exchange, 205 E. 42nd St., Ny, NY 10017.

INFORMATION ON SCHOLARSHIPS

Area Community Services, Inc., 500 South Pasadena Avenue, Pasadena, CA 91105. Information on scholarships for Blacks, American Indian and Spanish-speaking students.

FINANCIAL AID

The Department of Education has released a report on methods of securing financial aid. For information contact: Student Liaison, Department of Education, FOB MS 6350, Rm 3073, 400 Maryland Avenue SW, Washington, DC 20202.

SOURCES OF FELLOWSHIP INFORMATION

Selected List of Major Fellowship Opportunities and Aids to Advanced Education for United States Citizens, Fellowship Office, National Academy of Sciences, Washington, D.C. 20418.

ASSORTED AID

Business Administration or Career Advancement. Mary Reynolds Babcock Foundation, 102 Reynolda Village, Winston-Salem,NC 27106.

Dentistry. Robert Wood Johnson Foundation Forrestal Center, P.O. Box 2316, Princeton, NJ 08540.

Engineering. Cabot Foundation, 125 High Street, Boston, MA 02138.

Environment or Health Sciences. Jessie Smith Nayes Foundation, 16 E. 34th Street, New York, NY 10016.

Law, Medical or Music. Helena Rubinstein Foundation, 261 Madison Avenue, New York, NY 10016.

Vocational. Altrusa International Foundation, 332 South Michigan Avenue, Chicago, IL 60604.

MISCELLANEOUS RESOURCES

You may also refer to the following resources available from the addresses below.

*College Blue Book, 18th Edition: Scholarships, Fellowships, Grants and Loans** is a comprehensive list of financial aid resources at every level of study. MacMillan Publishing Co., Inc., 866 Third Avenue, New York,NY 10022. Available at libraries.

*Educational Financial Aids: A Guide to Selected Fellowships, Scholarships and Internships in Higher Education,** American Association of University Women, Sales Office, 2401 Virginia Avenue, NW, Washington, DC 20037. $4/copy.

*Financial Aid: A Partial List of Resources for Women, 1982** Project on the Status and Education of Women, Association of American Colleges, 1818 R Street, NW, Washington, DC 20009. For $2.50 a copy.

*Financial Aid: Where to Get It, How to Use It.** Business and Professional Women's Foundation, Scholarship Department, 2012 Massachusetts Avenue, NW, Washington, DC 20036. $1/copy.

*Grants, Scholarships, & Fellowships Bibliography The American Anthropological Association, 1703 New Hampshire Avenue, NW, Washington, DC 20009. Free.

THE DIRECTORY OF FINANCIAL AIDS FOR MINORITIES, 1984–1985 By GAIL ANN SCHLACHTER

While numerous sources offer information on financial aids programs open to all segments of society, rarely do these cover more than a few of the programs designed primarily or exclusively for minority groups. As a result, many advisors, counselors, librarians, scholars, researchers, and students remain uninformed about the impressive array of financial aids programs established for minorities. In today's political and economic climates, the minority student and researcher, more than ever, need access to resources to finance continuing education or training. **The Directory of Financial Aids for Minorities, 1984–1985** now provides comprehensive, up-to-date information about the special resources set aside for Asians, Blacks, Hispanics, Native Americans (American Indians, Hawaiians, Eskimos, Samoans), and minority groups in general. The programs described are sponsored by government agencies, professional organizations, corporations, sororities, fraternities, foundations, religious groups, educational associations and military/veterans organizations. For price information please contact: ABC-CLIO Information Services, Promotion Dept, P.O. Box 4397, Santa Barbara, CA 93103.

THE AMBITIOUS STUDENT'S GUIDE TO SCHOLARSHIP AND LOANS

Is available for $2.50 (prepaid) from the Project on the Status of Women, Association of American Colleges, 1818 R Street, NW, Washington, D.C. 20009. Checks should be made payable to AAC/PSEW, Bulk rates are available.

Financial Aid Booklets

Garrett Park Press, Garrett Park, MD 20896 has a series of booklets specializing in financial aid programs for Minority students (graduate and undergraduate) in the fields of Allied Health, Business, Education, Engineering, Law, Mass Communications, Medicine, and Science. In addition, each booklet contains an employment outlook summary and a tabulation of Minority group members currently employed in the field. Each booklet costs $3.00.

ADDITIONAL FINANCIAL AID RESOURCES

*Five Federal Aid Programs–A Student Consumer's Guide, U.S. Department of Education, Consumer Information Center, Pueblo, CO 81009.

*Education Handbook for Black Families, Anchor Press and Doubleday, New York, NY 10167.

*Education Scholarship Program, Division of Howard G. Norback Assoc., 227 E. Sunshine St., Springfield, MA 65807.

*Financing Medical Education 1982-1983, National Association of Medical Minority Educators, 1720 Massachusetts Avenue NW, Washington, DC 20036.

*Scholarship Search, 1775 Broadway, New York, NY 10019.

*Directory of Special Group Programs for Minority Group Members-Financial Aid Sources, 3rd Edition, Edited by Willis L. Johnson, Garrett Park Press, Garrett Park, MD 20766.

*Student Aid and the Urban Poor, Ford Foundation, P.O. Box 559, Naugatuck, CT 06770.

*Scholarships, Fellowships, and Loans News Service and Counselor Information Services, Bellman Publishing Co., P.O. Box 34937, Bethesda, Maryland 20817

*The Directory of Special Programs for Minority Group Members, Garrett Park Press, P.O. Box 190F, Garrett Park, MD 20896. Available in its fourth edition and costs $22.50. The directory includes career information services, employment skills banks and financial aid sources.

*Mortgaged Futures: How to Graduate from School Without Going Broke, Hope Press, P.O. Box 40611, Washington, DC 20016. Explains how students can apply for financial aid, set up financial plans and seek counseling, provides lists of available programs and resources. $10.95, postage paid. Contact: 202/337-4507.

*The College Board, College Scholarship Service, 888 Seventh Ave., NY, NY 10102. Has publications that describe financial aids to parents.

*American College Testing Program, Iowa City, Iowa 52240.
Has a withdrawal form that asks the types of questions that will assist administrators in helping students stay in school or at least find out the reasons why students leave.

Chapter 3

Developing an Effective Peer Counseling Program for Entering College Students Who Are Low Income and/or Minority Students

Mary Frances Howard
Associate Dean of Students
The University of North Carolina at Charlotte

About the Author

Mary Frances Howard is the Associate Dean of Students at The University of North Carolina at Charlotte. She received her B.A. degree in 1976 in Speech and Dramatic Arts and M.A. in 1977 in College Student Personnel Administration at The University of Iowa. Her major areas of interest are minority retention programs, orientation, commuter life and grantsmanship. She has worked with low-income and minority students from 1978-1984 through the TRIO Programs - Special Services for Disadvantaged Students. At UNCC, She designed, implemented, and coordinated the first peer Mentoring Program for incoming Black freshmen. She also coordinates the Black Freshmen/Parent Orientation Program and developed a UNCC Black Student Handbook.

INTRODUCTION

The purpose of a Peer Counseling or Peer Mentoring Program is to provide minority students with a "Big Brother" or "Big Sister" relationship to lessen the stress of their transitional period to the campus community. These students encounter not only the pressure of being a freshman but also being a minority student on a predominantly white campus. The mentors are trained to guide them throughout their freshman year providing academic and personal support so they may be able to persevere and matriculate successfully through their first year.

A Peer Counseling Program is designed as a short run and high impact strategy to provide students with positive role models they can identify with quickly, strengthen and foster unity among the Black students, and ultimately to reduce the dropout rate of those students who may be placed on probationary status.

The reader should be able to glean from this paper how to implement a peer counseling program, the selection and training of peer counselors, and the need to involve the campus and community with the Peer Counseling Program.

Developing an Effective Peer Counseling Program

by Mary Frances Howard

"The students were asked `Has any professor really taken you in hand and helped you become a professional in your field'? While one out of four white students answered `Yes,' just one out of twenty minority students did so," (Katz and Hartnett, 1976).

Peer Counseling Defined

There is a growing need in counseling centers and student advising offices to reach students of culturally disadvantaged backgrounds, and those students who have had inadequate preparation for college work, and to prepare them for the culture shock of college campuses. To fill these needs the concept of peer counseling is being used and expanded on college campuses, (Brown, 1972).

Peer counseling involves the training of students to help other students toward a successful adjustment to college. The scope of students' influence on one another is enormous, ranging from their academic lives to their personal lives, (Upcraft, 1984). Feldman and Newcomb, (1969), describe eight functions peer groups serve for students.

1. Help students achieve independence from home and family.
2. Support, and facilitate, or impede the institution's academic and intellectual totals.
3. Offer students general emotional support and fulfill needs not met by the curriculum, classroom, or faculty.
4. Give students practice in getting along with people whose backgrounds, interests, and orientations differ from their own.
5. Provide students support for not changing.
6. Provide students support for changing. Peer groups can challenge old values, provide intellectual stimulation, and act as sounding boards for new viewpoints, present new information and new experiences to students, help clarify new self directions, suggest new career possibilities, and provide emotional support for change.
7. Offer an alternative source of gratification and self image, and reward a variety of non-academic interests for students not satisfied academically. Peer groups can also discourage voluntary withdrawal from college for non-academic reasons.
8. Help students' post-college careers by providing general social training and developmental ties.

Studies done by Brown, (1972) and Smith, (1974) show that the majority of students said they prefer peer counselors to professionals as a source of help for their personal, social problems. Peer counselors from the same ethnic and socio-economic background as the counselee could contribute uniquely in behavioral growth, (Ware, Gold, Mensel, Perry, 1971). Programs of this type can be done at a relatively moderate cost, and peer programs stimulate experimentation and replication for other college programs (Ware, et. al, 1971). There are still a number of precautions involved in using the semi-trained paraprofessional group, (Brown, 1972). As well intentioned and empathetic as these counselors may be, the fact still remains that peer counselors have only a limited amount of training and may not recognize the point at which a problem exceeds their capabilities, (Brown, 1972). Without proper training and supervision, peer counselors may compound student problems (Brown, 1972).

The peer counseling program to be effective has to be an integral part of the institution with matriculation between it and the departmental program in which it is a part. The program should be thoroughly integrated with counseling curricula and student activities for a great degree of success. These issues and a deeper assessment of peer counseling programs will be discussed further in my paper.

"What determines whether or not entering students adapt to their new environment? There are several factors, but undoubtedly the most important is the influence of students on one another. The scope of this influence is enormous. Peer groups help achieve independence from home and family, support or impede academic goals, support, develop interpersonal skills, change or reinforce values, and influence career decisions," (Feldman and Newcomb, 1969; Upcraft, 1984).

Peer Counselors as Role Models

Delworth, Sherwood, and Casaburri (1974) gives the reader a good definitive conception of a paraprofessional and his/her role:

...A person without extended professional training who is specifically selected, trained, and given ongoing supervision to perform some designated portion of the tasks usually performed by the professional, (Ibid, p.12).

Delworth et. al, (1974), warns that the paraprofessional is not a "cheap professional." He is not a full-time staff member and can't do all tasks assumed by the professional. The use of peer counselors, (paraprofessionals), offers advantages not available if professionals alone are employed, (Warnath and Associates, 1983). McCann, (1975), sees peer counselors as students who have been taught helping skills and who in turn help to create a proper climate for the development of positive mental health in the school setting.

Dawson, (1973), and Gumaer, (1973), have similar opinions about the role of the peer counselor. They state that this student is one who is able to lead small group discussions and encourage other group members to explore their ideas and feelings; he or she is able to use such techniques as reflection, interpretation, confrontation, active

41

listening, clarifying, and empathy. The responsibilities of the peer counselors should be restricted to those tasks which can be performed without disrupting the personal relationships between the counselors and their fellow students such as disseminating information, giving assistance with immediate situational problems, academic advising, and helping with orientation (Warnath, 1973).

The idea of "service to indigenous people by indigenous people" has been incorporated by a number of Educational Opportunities Programs. It has helped college students develop social skills and overcome loneliness, (McCarthy and Michaud, 1971).

Peer counselors can be a valuable asset to a program for ethnic minorities within the program they are facing, (Warnath, 1973). Many entering minority students may be moving from an environment where there were significant numbers of minority peers to a setting where they have to cope with being only one, (Upcraft, 1984). Without significant minority peer group support, students may feel lonely and alienated and lose self confidence, (Upcraft, 1984).

The peer counselors will thereby alleviate minor problems placed upon the shoulders of the incoming minority student by mentoring them and playing a significant role in their intellectual, social, and cultural development on a predominantly white campus. Quoting a paragraph from Lewis, (1976), he states the following about Black peer counselors:

> **...Peer counselors are simply another group of paraprofessionals, who, by virtue of their training, skills, and status among their peers, are to offer support and help to other students in addition to that which comes through a traditional counseling program. In programs in which the student population is predominantly Black, this means that Black students would be trained to help other Black students.**

Role of the Professional

Warnath, (1973), states that the counselor of the professional literature is someone who is accepting, who is able to establish an empathetic relationship with another individual, and who can give insights and clarifications to another person based on understanding of the person's experiences and thought processes. Vontress, (1971), states that a well-trained counselor should be able to function in any environment.

I have cause to disagree with such a statement. It has been this writer's experience in high school that counselors, especially white counselors, tell Black students not to attend college, and to prepare for vocational trades, or attend a nearby community college and work. Therefore, a stigma has been placed upon white counselors as being uninformative, biased, and too busy to listen to the problems of Black students. The Black student recognizes that his counselor has based his advice primarily on his assumptions about appropriate goals for Blacks rather than individual considerations, (Warnath, 1973).

The typical college counseling center staffed primarily by whites is generally perceived as a potentially hostile agency whose structure and office atmosphere projects to the Black student a sense of **"going to see the Man,"** (Warnath, 1973). According to Burrell and Nayder, (1971), white counselors are perceived as being insensitive to the needs of Black students, white counselors lack the training and experience necessary to work with Black students, and they allow bias and preconceived stereotypes to influence their judgment. Many minority students go to professional counselors only when they are in deep academic trouble.

Since peer counselors are involved with the student's day to day activities, they could intercept the student who is having academic difficulty and refer him/her to the appropriate professional staff member. Having peer counselors for minority students adds a broad dimension to any staff or counseling center. Lewis, (1976), believes that:

> **Black counselor educators have the responsibility to incorporate this technique into their own counselor education programs. In-service workshops might be conducted, demonstration projects undertaken, and courses in peer counseling added to the curriculum, (p.7).**

Arbuckle, (1972), gives the reader several issues which are related to the counselor and his professional involvement with indi-viduals who are members of minority groups:

1. It is clear, of course, that the counselor, as a member of the human species, carries with him into the counseling relationship his own values; and a major factor affecting one's own values over the years is whether one has been a member of a majority or a minority group. It should be stressed, however, that it is only one of many factors; and one cannot say that all black clients will react in one way and all white clients in another way.

2. Any person who is a member of a minority group in a one-man-one-vote culture has had and will be likely to continue to have for the foreseeable future special kinds of problems which are not those of the members of the majority group.

3. It is crucial, of course, that the counselor, whether he be a member of a minority or a majority group, has achieved a level of self identity and self-actualization such that he is totally understanding and acceptant of differences in human beings.

4. A multiplicity of cultures make up America, and it is naive to assume that every American is going to have a deep understanding and appreciation of all of these cultures.

One of the problems has been that counselors with extensive formal training find it difficult and sometimes impossible to establish meaningful relationships and contacts with Black students particularly those from backgrounds of poverty and apparent alienation, (Lewis, 1976).

To most Black students a white counselor already has one strike against him because of the students previous experiences with whites, (Mitchell, 1970). They have not been able to communicate a sense of safety and a "you can trust me" understanding to these Black youths who are inclined to be suspicious of counselors with the middle class value system, (Lewis, 1976).

Banks, Berenson, and Carkhuff, (1967), did a study on Blacks and counselors, (of white and Black races), at the University of Maryland, Their outcome and summary is as follows:

> **In a counter-balanced design, an inexperienced Negro and three white counselors of varying degrees of experiences saw eight Negro counselees and were assessed on the dimensions of counselor empathy, positive regard, genuineness, concreteness, and client depth of exploration...The Negro counselor and the two inexperienced counselors (white) ... functioned significantly higher than the white counselor with his Ph.D. All of the Negro counselees indicated that they would return to see the Negro counselor, and none indicated that they would return to see the white Ph.D. On all of the rank orderings by the counselees, the experienced white Ph.D. was ranked last, (p,72).**

Black counselors as a group are not immune to the aforementioned weaknesses, because most Black counselors are of middle-class training, if not background, (Lewis, 1976). The problem of the Black counselor who has not examined himself, is that he has a tendency to project his attitudes and feelings on other Blacks, according to (Mitchell, 1970). Mitchell, (1970), also states that he, (the Black counselor) can be just as ineffective as the white counselor and just as ineffective if the Black student sees him for what he really is.

Another study done by Peter Cimbolic in 1972 shows the opposite data than that of Banks, et al., in 1967. Cimbolic's study was implemented at the University of Missouri in Columbia. His subjects were 83 Black freshmen. The counselors were one Black and 3 whites at differentiating experience levels. To much surprise the experienced counselors were rated highly, and most students were willing to return for future counseling to at least one of the white counselors.

Professional counselors usually work toward achieving the level of personal growth at which they can naturally accept people with broadly different values and lifestyles. Societal influences work against this kind of personal growth, however, consequently not all counselors are able to overcome such pervasive societal influences, (Lewis, 1976). The busy and confusing role of the professional counselor gives one more reason for implementing a peer counseling program for minority students. Peer counselors are able to relate to their fellow classmates as peers, and because of their special training experiences they are in a position to offer help, (Lewis, 1976).

The following are seven requirements suggested as essential elements in a successful program of student-to-student counseling (Brown, 1972).

44

1. Formulation of meaningful peer counseling goals. The objectives for all student-counseling-student-activities should be carefully spelled out in a manner that clearly recognizes student and institution needs, problems, and resources.
2. Development of informed peer counseling support. The student-counseling-student approach should be effectively sold in a manner that assumes the appropriate support and involvement of administration, faculty, and students.
3. Delineation of realistic peer counseling activities. The counseling activities to be performed by student counselors should be carefully defined.
4. Provision of adequate office and classroom space properly spaced and centrally located.
5. Selection and training of peer counseling personnel. Should be carefully selected and given appropriate training.
6. Supervision of peer counseloring activities. The ongoing program of student-counseling-student-activities should be adequately supervised by professional personnel workers in order to assure efficient, realistic, and coordinated program operation.
7. Evaluation and revision of peer counseling effort. All aspects of the student-counseling-student program should be evaluated systematically, and the individual counselor activities should be eliminated, revised, or expanded, as appropriate, on the basis of their proven effectiveness. **"Upperclassmen need to share the responsibility of the success and persistence of new students,"** (Noel, et al.,1985).

Selection of Peer Counselors

Selection of peer counselors is the key to any paraprofessional program as a success variable. Delworth, Sherwood, and Casaburri, (1974), suggest five ways in which students should be selected and how the paraprofessional programs merit implementation:
1. A systematic procedure for selection of positions should be established.
2. The positions should be described to include the paraprofessional as an integral part of the major system or central agency.
3. A specific, clear job description should be written.
4. Qualities and skills for the position should be specified.
5. Arrangements regarding training, supervision, and evaluation must be specified.
Qualifications of a minority peer counselor should follow the general guidelines set forth by (Warnath, 1973). The peer counselor is a student with emotional needs and anxieties similar to those students he's counseling. The peer counselor must remain on good terms with his fellow students.
These are the qualifications set forth by (Delworth et al., 1974). The student should have sufficient experience with the institution so that he can help others find their place or make changes.

45

The student should possess an amount of interpersonal competence and communication skills that allows him to deal effectively with a variety of individuals and groups. The student should be minimally able to organize his daily life. The student must be able to work with an understanding of the philosophy of the department in which he is apart of. In choosing Black peer counselors, Lewis, (1976) suggests four considerations:

1. **Interest.** Students should be students who show an interest in wanting to help other students.

2. **Commitment.** It is important that students who show an interest in the program also show with a fair amount of commitment to the idea of the program, because their participation will entail the sacrifice of a large part of their time and energy.

3. **Peer Respect.** Even though a student possesses interest and shows commitment to the peer counseling program, he or she must also have the respect of the student population if he or she is to be effective.

4. **Assertiveness.** Black peer counselors should exhibit a certain amount of assertive behavior inasmuch as they will have to be able to translate concerns of Black youths to the counselor or teacher.

Training

There are many designs for training programs for peer counselors: they vary with the purpose, philosophy, and personalities of those who design them, (Lewis, 1976).

Delworth and Aulepp, (1976), state that the overall goal of training is to enhance each person's ability to function well in his or her position. In programs such as a minority peer counseling program, it is very important that the training program is complete with professional staff and well prepared and knowledgeable about counseling skills and interpersonal skills. Also, a variety of training techniques should be used for the training sessions.

Some positive side effects of training are: **"Peer counselors developed strong feelings of group purpose and cohesiveness,"** (Dawson 1973; Lewis, 1976); many other students want to become peer counselors themselves, (McCann, 1975; Lewis, 1976); and peer counselors experience positive psychological growth, (Dawson, 1973; Gutsch, Spinks, and Aitken, 1969; Varenhorst, 1974; Lewis 1976).

Lewis, (1976), feels the following skills should be implemented in the Black peer counseling programs:

1. **Listening Skills.** If you are not able to listen to another person, you will be little help or no help. Nonverbal cues will escape you, and there's no way that you can read the other person's mood.

2. **Facilitating Responses.** The background environment influences of most youth have taught them that "telling" and "advice giving" is the way that the world operates; this is

especially true of Black youths. These youths will have a particular need to learn such facilitating techniques and clarifying, reflection, and the giving of positive, meaningful feedback.

3. **Group Process.** Although peer counselors will probably spend a lot of their time working with one student at a time, they can be effectively used in small group settings. Training should include a heavy dose of group processing in which theory and practice are combined.

4. **Assertiveness Training.** Black youth are usually not very verbal or outspoken. A good dose of assertiveness training would overcome this tendency and give such youth the confidence to deal with situations as they arise and not become aggressive.

The most successful approach to training has been an intensive, 3-5 days of workshops prior to the beginning of the academic school year with a combination of Lewis' training skills and academic/university information. Ongoing staff meetings and special workshops should be continued 1-2 times per month with arranged individual sessions between the Peer Counselor/Mentor and the Coordinator of the Program.

Funding

Sources of funding for a peer counseling project should be included in the departmental budget for each fiscal year. Paraprofessionals are usually paid out of the college work-study funds. Time sheets or other record keeping systems should be used to determine work output, as well as compute the salary for each pay period, (Delworth et al., 1974).

"If institutions are really committed to providing equal opportunity for college success, they must not only grant access, they must develop orientation programs and activities that help minority students make a successful transition from their previous environments to the collegiate environment," (Upcraft, 1984).

Role of Peer Counselors in Orientation Programs

Helping minority students' transition to college is the responsibility of the institution's orientation staff, (Upcraft, 1984). Traditional orientation programs devote little time to the new student as an individual, (Snider, 1970). Entering minority students, particularly those who may be first generation college students, may have received little of the mentoring or role modeling that has been shown to facilitate personal and intellectual development, (Upcraft, 1984). Orientation programs should introduce entering minorities to the campus and should provide an assurance of belonging or understanding of academic and social expectations, and a knowledge of campus resources, (Smith and Bauch, 1981; Upcraft, 1984). Minority peer counselors can be used effectively as small group facilitators during a Black student/parent orientation program. This type of program can be implemented by providing an additional session at the beginning or end of the institution's orientation program. A Black student and parent/guardian program should be implemented so that the entire family and student can assess the supportive environment they are leaving the student in, as well as meet the Black faculty, staff, and peer counselors. Entering minority students do not come to college alone; the entire family enrolls vicariously, (Upcraft, 1984).

"Less than thirty years ago, over 90% of Black students, (approximately 100,000 in 1950), were educated in traditionally Black schools. About two-thirds to three-fourths of the Black students in college are now in predominantly white educational settings, (Boyd, 1974; Gurin and Epps, 1975; Fleming, 1984).

Conclusion

It is important to note that many of the Black students who are attending predominantly white institutions do not remember the Bakke decision and have no knowledge of the Brown vs. The Board of Education case in 1954. It is important for Black students to have Black peers and professional role models on these campuses to help them adjust to their new environment and remember the civil rights struggle in the 1950's and 1960's that opened the doors of higher education to them.

The need for a special orientation program and peer counselors during the freshman year for Black students should be the focal point at any predominantly white institution. The problem of being away from one's family and friends coupled with the added task of making new friends among many whites and few Blacks adds to the Black's dilemma of adjusting on the white campus, (Harper, 1975).

The Black freshman needs a role model and mentor to help him/her cope with the academic rigors, adjust to a new environment, and develop socially and emotionally at their respective institutions. A peer counseling and special orientation program will insure the successful matriculation of the Black student who is exploring his/her extraneous and new university home.

Bibliography

Arbuckle, Dugle S. Counseling With Members of Minority Groups. **Counseling and Values,** 1972, 16, 239-251.

Banks, G., B. G. Berenson, and R. R. Carkhuff. The Effects of Counselor Race and Training Upon Counseling Process With Negro Clients in Initial Interviews. **Journal of Clinical Psychology.** 1967, 23 70-72.

Boyd, W. M. **Desegregating America's Colleges,** New York: Praeger, 1974.

Brown, W. F., **Student to Student Counseling.** University of Texas Press, Austin, 1972.

Brown, W. F., Student to Student Counseling:For Academic Adjustments. **Personnel and Guidance Journal,** 1965, 43, 811-816.

Cimbolic, P., Counselor Race and Experience Effects on Black Clients. **Journal of Consulting and Clinical Psychology,** 1972, 39 328-332.

Dawson, R. K., Personality and Peer Counselors:An Australian Study. **Personnel and Guidance Journal,** 1973, 52, 46-49.

Delworth, U., G. Sherwood and N. Casaburri. Student Paraprofessionals: A Working Model for Higher Education. **Student Development Series No. 17.** American College Personnel Association, 1974.

Delworth, U., and L Aulepp. Paraprofessional and Allied Professional Programs. **Western Interstate Commission for Higher Education,** 1976.

Feldman, K. A. and T. M. Newcomb (Eds). **The Impact of College on Students.** San Francisco. CA.:Jossey-Bass, 1969.

Fields, A. L. **Unpublished Interview.** 1976.

Fleming, J. **Blacks in College.** Jossey-Bass, 1984.

Franklin, A. J. To be Young, Gifted and Black with Inappropriate Professional Training and a Critique of Counseling Programs. **Counseling Psychologist,** 1974, 2. 107-112.

Gurin, P. and Epps. E. G. Black. **Consciousness, Identity and Achievement.** New York: Wiley, 1975.

Gumaer, J. Peer Facilitated Groups. **Elementary School Guidance and Counseling,** 1973, 8, 4-11.

Gutsch, K. U., S. L. Spinks and J. R. Aitken. Counselor Aids in Action: Hattiesburg Public Schools, Mississippi. **Counselor Education and Supervision,** 1969, 9, 61-63.

Harper, F. D. **Black Students, White campus.** APGA Press, 1975.

Jones, C. M. **Unpublished Interviews,** 1977.

Katz, J. and R Hartnett. **Scholars in the Making: The Development of Graduate and Professional Students,** 1976.

Lewis, S.O. Black Peer Counselor Educators use Peer Counseling. **Journal of Non-White Concerns,** 1976, 5, 6-20.

McCann, B. G. Peer Counseling: An approach to Psychological Education, **Elementary School Guidance and Counseling,** 1975, 9, 180-187.

McCarthy, B. W. New Approaches to Mental Health Services in Colleges and Universities. **Psychological Reports,** 1970, 27, 420--422.

Mitchell, E. The Black Experience in Higher Education. **Counseling Psychologist,** 1970,30--36.

Noel, L., R. Levitz, D. Saluri and Associates. **Increasing Student Retention: Effective Programs and Practices of Reducing the Dropout Rate.** San Francisco, CA., Jossey-Bass, 1985.

Smith, D.H. and B. M. Baruch. "Social and Academic Environments of Black Students on White Campuses." **Journal of Negro Education,** 1981, 50 (Summer), 299-306.

Smith, Joel and Franklin Westbrook. Assisting Black Resident Students at a Predominantly White Institution: A Paraprofessional Approach. **Journal of College Student Personnel,** 1976, 17, 205.

Snider, P.A. A Student comes to us. **Journal of the National Association of Women Deans and Counselors,** 1970, 33-141.

Tolson, H. Counseling the "Disadvantaged." **Personnel and Guidance Journal,** 1972, 50, 735-738.

Upcraft, Lee (Ed.). Orienting Students to College. San Francisco, CA., Jossey-Bass, 1984. **New Directions for Students Services,** No. 25.

Varenhorst, B. B. Training Adolescents as Peer Counselors, **Personnel and Guidance Journal,** 1974, 53, 271-275.

Vontress, C.E. Counseling Blacks. **Personnel and Guidance Journal,** 1970, 48, 713-719.

Ware, Gold, Mensal, Perry. The Los Angeles City College Peer Counseling Program. Washington, D.C.:American Junior College Association, 1971, **The Urban College Project Series No. 2.**

Warnath, C. F. and Associates. **New Directions for College Counselors,** Jossey-Bass, San Francisco, Chapter 9, 1973.

Wrenn, R. L. and R. Menke. Students Who Counsel Students. **Personnel and Guidance Journal,** 1972, 50, 687-689.

Student Affirmative Action-Implementing the Program and Developing Positive Role Models

Sylvia Lopez-Romano
California State University, Chico

ABOUT THE AUTHOR

Sylvia Lopez-Romano is director of Educational Equity Services, comprised of Disabled Student Services, the Educational Opportunity Program and Student Affirmative Action at California State University-Chico, California. She received her B.A. and M.A. at California State University-Chico and is currently working toward a Doctorate in Organization and Leadership and Multicultural Education at the University of San Francisco. She has had extensive experience working in the area of student services and established a model student affirmative action program at California State University, Chico. She has done extensive work in cross-cultural communication. Other accomplishments include directing a successful Upward Bound project for four years, serving as an elementary school vice principal and teacher, as well as an instructor on the college level. Ms. Lopez Romano has earned a host of honors including Who's Who of American Women for two years in a row and was awarded a California State University Administrative Fellowship, (1982-83).

INTRODUCTION

During the sixties many programs were created to address and attempt to correct some of the concerns that spawned the civil rights movement. Some of these programs focused on educating low income and educationally disadvantaged students and parents as a means of breaking the poverty cycle. One such program was Headstart. Headstart utilized teachers and teacher aides to work with low income youngsters and often parents were employed as classroom assistants. Parental involvement was critical to the programs' success. For many parents, this was the first positive experience they had with educational systems (i.e. principals, teachers, and teacher aides). Ms. Romano was heavily involved with Headstart during its infancy and later in life she had a chance to work with her former students again when she was director of one of President Johnson's Great Society Programs, **Upward Bound,** for high school students. In Upward Bound, students are selected from the same economically and educationally disadvantaged populations as the Headstart program.

The charge was to identify students who were potential dropouts, and provide tutoring and counseling, during the academic year, and summer programs. The Upward Bound Program provides basic skills in English, Math, Science, study skills, career exploration, and cultural enrichment much like the goals of Headstart. Again the goal was to prepare students for completing high school successfully and to encourage college as a means of providing more options and to break the poverty cycle in which low employment levels or unemployment was a daily reality. Ms. Lopez-Romano says, **"Most students will live up to your expectations. If you expect their success, they will follow your lead."** The author's former position as Director of Upward Bound led her to the administration of Educational Equity Services at California State University, Chico where this paper begins.

The information included should prove helpful in working with minority students.

Student Affirmative Action

by Sylvia Lopez-Romano

Concerned legislators in Sacramento drafted the Assembly Concurrent Resolution (ACR 151) which was a mandate to the California State University System to address the underrepresentation of ethnic students on all nineteen state college campuses in 1979. The Chancellor's Office was charged with initiating and implementing a program to work toward meeting this mandate; thus the Core Student Affirmative Action Program (CSAA), was created. Six colleges out of nineteen were chosen to conduct pilot programs in the 1979-80 academic year. The following year, 1980-81, the remaining thirteen campuses were busy initiating and implementing Core SAA programs. This was the year I became Director of the Core SAA Program at California State University, Chico.

The thrust of each campus' response to the mandate was to conduct a needs analysis to determine which ethnic group was the least represented on the particular campus, and to determine which population in the service area of the college needed to be more represented. Ideally the college population was to reflect the population of the service area it served. California State University, Chico has always been 98% Anglo-American which reflects the demographics of the service area only too well. The needs analysis however indicated that the least represented group on the campus was the Hispanic; second, American Indian; third, Black Americans; and finally the re-entry ethnic women over 25 years of age.

The task of initiating and implementing a program tailored to attract, retain, and graduate ethnic students on a campus which as stated earlier, is 98% Anglo-American, was a challenge which I soon found to be an overwhelming task. As the only Hispanic administrator in Student Affairs at Chico State, implementing the CSAA Program took all the knowledge, skill, and experience I could muster. It has been my experience that attaching the name "Affirmative Action" can produce a resistance from the very people you need to work with; so it's like fighting an uphill battle at times. Yet the goals of the program were so near and dear to my heart that the work was well worth the effort it took. The program is now in it's fourth year and is successful in meeting the objectives and goals year after year.

Why is the program important? Why should the CSU system be concerned with ethnic students, reentry women, and be especially interested in attracting Hispanics to higher education? Primarily, because the State of California along with the entire Southwest, is becoming increasingly an ethnic area and the largest single ethnic population is Hispanic. This creates a need to provide an educated populace in order to maintain the level of society some of us are enjoying now.

I will outline some of the basic components to implement the Core SAA program below:

1. **Outreach Component:** Developing programs, activities, policies, and perspectives that ensure equitable access in junior high

school and senior high school by all students to those prog rams and services that develop the skills, outlook, and motivation needed to become eligible for college.

2. **Retention Component:** Developing programs, activities, policies, and perspectives that ensure the equitable dissemination of academic and multi-cultural information about opportunities in higher education and career alternatives.

3. **Educational Enhancement Component:** Developing programs, activities, policies, and perspectives that ensure that the educational process and environment of the university is a relevant experience that is sensitive to the cultural background of all students, and that college is a successful endeavor for those who earnestly try.

A vital ingredient for the success of a program begins with the identification of competent staff to direct and provide service to students. Once staff is selected, the program goals and objectives are delineated and put in a framework which includes timeliness and identification of the personnel responsible for accomplishing the goals and providing the activities described in the objectives. The next task was to select the target high schools and the community colleges for the outreach component. This entailed contacting the key school personnel, starting with the superintendents, principals, and head counselors in the high schools and community- colleges slated to receive full service. Full service meant that a student outreach paraprofessional would visit the school and meet with students on a weekly basis.

I would caution anyone starting a new program of this type to carefully assess what a staff can realistically accomplish. The first year my outreach advisor and I thought we could save the world with her working part-time and with a staff of five untrained student paraprofessionals working approximately 20 hours per week. We started with the grand plan which included providing weekly visits to 19 high schools and 5 community colleges. Needless to say, when a service area is as large as the State of Ohio, it is a "next-to-impossible" task to accomplish.

Meetings were scheduled with the target school personnel, and the Core Student Affirmative Action program was explained. At these meetings we explored ways to more effectively serve the school, the students, their parents and still meet the program's goals and objectives. Schedules for visitation of school sites and the contact persons were identified. At the same time that the program staff was orienting the service area school personnel, the director was orienting the University Student Affairs' units, Academic Affairs, Administration, and staff regarding the program's mission in the Retention and Educational Enhancement component. At these meetings special attention was placed on the importance of creating a campus environment which would be supportive of ethnic students and assist in the retention of targeted program participants.

Faculty workshops, faculty and staff informational meetings, visits with deans, department chairs, and top administrators were

54

scheduled on an ongoing basis. TV media and local radio stations and newspapers along with periodic information flyers were utilized to spread the word about the program. Church presentations were also made to area churches which served the local ethnic communities.

Students were utilized in workshops to sensitize faculty and to provide first hand experiences with the educational process on this and other campuses and at their local elementary and high schools. Ethnic students, for the most part, have experienced some very unique and unpleasant instances of insensitivity in the schooling process whether from teachers, counselors and other students. It never feels good to be at the brunt of this kind of action.

An article written by Harold L. Hodgkinson in **THE EDUCATION DIGEST** cites the following,

> **"The conclusion for higher education is inescapable: American public schools are now very heavily enrolled with minority students, large numbers of whom will be college eligible. Private elementary and secondary schools do not enroll enough students, (mostly white), to alter this trend.** Previous policies like **"benign neglect" seem reasonable to some when the percentage of minorities was 10-12 percent, but what state can neglect 40-45 percent of its youth? Such a policy would be suicidal for states like California and Texas if not the nation.**
>
> **Out of sheer self-interest, it behooves the higher education community to do everything to make sure that the largest possible number of minority students do well in public schools and thus become college eligible. If this is not done, and significant numbers of minority students leave the public schools before graduation or graduate without the aspiration for college, the potential decline in the college cohort could amount to nearly half of the present college population,"** (Hodgkinson, 1983).

The challenge for those of us who are ethnic and who are striving to succeed in a system which has been traditionally "elitist and exclusionary", is to provide the support and assistance available to those who are following in our footsteps. The few ethnic administrators and faculty on the various campuses across the state wear many hats. We are teachers, counselors, friends, Socratic gadflies, and role models for the students we represent. On this campus the ethnic student population numbers 1,423 or 10%. Therefore the few ethnic faculty and professional staff members spend a significant portion of their time advising and counseling ethnic students; and, as a result, we are sometimes penalized in the retention and tenure process because we have not published or been actively involved in "scholarly" activities.

A recent example given to me by a graduate ethnic student confirmed the need for a support base for ethnic faculty also. As the students feel isolation, so do the faculty and staff from ethnic backgrounds. In the student's words,

> **"I have had the opportunity of taking classes from the only Black professor in my department, and finally now that I have someone to communicate with, I have a fear that he**

will not remain at this institution because he confided in me that he cannot fit in. He is not given the respect that his position warrants as a professor in the field. Students who comprise the classes he teaches are 99% Anglo-American and do not relate to his teaching style; and they will not interact with him, but instead go directly to the department chair if they have a question about the course content."

This causes a feeling of isolation which ultimately causes most ethnic faculty to leave this institution for one that is more ethnically balanced. This feeling of isolation is also one of the major reasons why it is difficult to retain faculty from ethnic backgrounds which then becomes a vicious cycle.

"We lose our role models as fast as we get them."

Working as a change agent in a bureaucracy which has no desire to change is hard work and never ending. A Chicano colleague once told me,

"working in a university setting as one of the few affirmative action persons was like walking down a hallway made of foam rubber; as long as you keep your fist in the foam you make a dent—take your fist out of the foam and it returns to it's undented state. Life goes on, and it's business as usual."

I have to agree with this description. Despite these bureaucratic obstacles and the resistance to change which is obvious at almost all levels, the critical need for successful ethnic professionals who are willing to serve as role models encourages me to continue working in this position. The American College Dictionary gives several definitions of the word, model:

1) model as a standard for imitation or comparison; 2) to form or plan according to a model; 3) to give shape or form. In addition role has the following definitions: 1) proper or customary function, 2) the teacher's role in society.

The importance of a role model and faculty mentor is noted in the literature on that subject as one of the essential keys in the retention of students. Over the past four years, CSAA has also found that the use of ethnic faculty, staff, and students as role models for our target CSAA students has proven to be one of the keys to the outreach and retention efforts of the program.

The lack of ethnic role models on college campuses has even reached the attention of the Ford Foundation. Frank Press, President of the National Academy of Sciences announced that the Ford Foundation will establish a nine million dollar fellowship program to increase the number of minority group professors. The program began in September, 1985. He also states that,

"the competition for the fellowships will make a substantial contribution to increasing the pool of minority students who will be candidates for positions on faculties across the country."

The Reverend Timothy S. Healy, President of Georgetown University said,

> " Minority students often feel alienated because they do not find role models either in the student body or on the faculty. This program will help address that problem."

The national attention that the lack of ethnic role models on a campus is receiving is long overdue. Those of us who were ethnic students at the campus experienced this lack of role models as we pursued our educations, and, therefore, we can relate very well to an ethnic student who is currently experiencing this same sense of anomie.

The Ford Foundation on the national level might have been influenced by the report submitted to the CSU Chancellor, Anne Reynolds (by the Commission on Hispanic Underrepresentation) in September, 1984 which presented a total of thirty-five recommendations for the CSU to consider in addressing the needs of underrepresented groups. On page 21 of this report under the heading, **Faculty and Staff as Role Models and Change Agents,** the following is taken directly from the text and follows with the thirtieth recommendation also taken directly from the text.

Faculty and Staff as Role Models and Change Agents

There is virtual consensus around the proposition that CSU would be more successful in its efforts to overcome underrepresentation if there were greater numbers of faculty and professional staff from these same groups. Deliberate efforts are required to recruit and retain minority faculty.

For Hispanics in particular, the shortage is so serious as to constitute an emergency requiring extraordinary action. In 1983 only 3.2 percent of CSU faculty were Hispanic. Although the 7.5 percent of professional staff identified as Hispanic suggests a healthier situation, it is unlikely that this category would be comparable were it not for the large numbers of Hispanics occupying positions in special programs such as the Educational Opportunity Program. Today we compare 3.2 percent of faculty with the 11.3 percent of entering freshmen who are Hispanic, a proportion almost three times as great. Unless extraordinary measures are taken, this discrepancy will grow, due to the predictable low rate of output of Hispanics with terminal degrees at least in the near future.

Competition will be keen for these few, as other universities and especially business and industry seek to meet their needs as well. Resolution of this problem will be achieved only when underrepresentation of both undergraduates and graduate students has been overcome. Meanwhile, the Commission believes that the following actions would lead to significant improvement.

30. **"To increase enrollment in and completion of advanced degree programs, the CSU should establish a program whereby outstanding CSU Masters degree candidates are identified through a competitive process and awarded fellowships for up to two-three years of advanced graduate study in return for a commitment to serve in either a temporary or tenure track position upon completion. Criteria for participation in this program should be membership in a group underrepresented among faculty, projected need for faculty in the candidate's field, as well as academic and other characteristics germane to the prospective faculty position."**

Core Student Affirmative Action has often found the ethnic students that are recruited are usually the first persons in their families to attempt higher education. This then calls for a supportive cadre of professional people whom they can comfortably interact with, and who will inspire them to stay in school. We have also discovered that it is very useful to utilize ethnic seniors and ethnic graduate students to fulfill the recruiting role and have found that it is easier for these college students to establish trust and rapport with target students in high schools and junior colleges.

The ethnic recruiters usually come from the same population and can relate well to the young person's fears and expectations about college life. This is not to say that only ethnic students can recruit ethnic students, because that is not always the case. It is to say however that the ethnic student often talks the same "lingo" as the prospective student and, therefore, has an easier time establishing rapport quicker.

These trends are very encouraging to the SAA program staff and will prove beneficial in the long run and make our jobs easier. It follows that once the ethnic student is on campus the SAA retention effort goes into operation and utilizes the expertise and interest of ethnic faculty and staff to provide a link with the students.

As ethnic students on a campus which is 98% Anglo, the reality of being the "one and only" in a class is almost assured, which is a very unsettling experience; and one simply has to have a support system to share feelings and fears with when the need arises. Knowing that a person has and is experiencing the same feeling of isolation, but maybe at a different level now, is very encouraging and could make the difference between a student "toughing it out" or going back home. Having someone who can say "Quetal? Mira Nomas, que bien vas en tus estudios!" is uplifting to the student. Seeing the pride on the student's face is reward enough for me for the work that is embodied and goes with the territory of serving as a role model. Also, if I serve only to say "if I can make it, you can too!" And if this inspires a student to keep striving, then I've been successful in my efforts. Seeing is believing, as the saying goes, For instance, as a

Chicana role model I spend time mentoring Chicanas who are entering school as re-entry women, single parents, and with little or no support systems. Two young women come to mind—one a single parent with two children, and the other a single person who was unmarried, but in a heavy relationship with a man from another ethnic culture. I was able, because of my background and experience of entering college as a mother with five children who existed as a single mother, to relate to the single parent who is struggling to stay in school with little or no support from her parents or friends. I have spent many hours just listening, sharing ideas, and being a friend, someone she could talk openly with. She has told me and others on many occasions that she would not have been graduating this Spring if I had not been there to counsel, direct, and inspire her as a role model.

Then there is a young Chicana student who was involved with a young man from another culture. She was very confused and having a difficult time with her family who disapproved of her choice of boyfriend, and because of the pressures, she was not doing well in her classes. She and I were able to go through the values clarification that she needed, and I was for awhile her only support base on campus. She has since left town and has, in fact, married a man who is a teacher; and she is pursuing a teaching credential. She still keeps in touch, and when I met her husband she introduced me as the one who served as her friend, counselor, and role model. The success of these and many other students serves to remind me of the critical need that exists for role models who can be supportive and relate to students at a campus level.

I'll always be thankful for the Student Affirmative Action program which has allowed me the opportunity to serve as a role model for ethnic students. The psychic pay is something one cannot measure.

Hopefully, CSAA will provide the State of California with a significant number of ethnic professionals who can experience the challenge, excitement, and reward that I have gained from serving as a positive role model.

BIBLIOGRAPHY

Archiniega, Thomas A., Chair. "Faculty and Staff as Role Models and Change Agents." **Hispanics and Higher Education a CSU Imperative, Part I of the Report of the Commission on Hispanic Underrepresentation,** September 1984, Page 21.

Desruisseaux, Paul. "Ford to Establish $9-Million Fellowship Program to Increase Number of Minority-Group Professors." **The Chronicle of Higher Education,** May 8, 1985, page 16.

Hodgkinson, Harold L. "College Students of the Future-Regional, Ethnic and Class Differences are Increasing; College Students in the 1990's: A Demographic Portrait." **The Education Digest,** November 1983, pages 28-29.

AN EXPLANATION OF CORE STUDENT AFFIRMATIVE ACTION 1980-81
THE CALIFORNIA STATE UNIVERSITY AND COLLEGES

BACKGROUND

The student affirmative action plans submitted by each of The California State University and Colleges campuses were the result of sensitive inventories of local needs and resources by many relevant constituencies. Participating in the formulation of campus plans were students, CSUC faculty and staff, community representatives, high school faculty and staff, and the faculty and staff of other post-secondary educational institutions.

While each plan presented many approaches and avenues for action, there were several activities and areas relating to student affirmative action that were identified in common by all campuses. Nearly identical to the components comprising the current regional outreach effort and the components comprising the student affirmative action pilot programs, three components, (comprised of seven elements), were systematically mentioned by each campus as being essential to any student affirmative action, (SAA), plan. These elements have been combined to form what is referred to as the "campus core student affirmative action program" approach.

PURPOSE OF CORE SAA

The purpose of the core approach is to expand the Student Affirmative Action Coordinated Regional Outreach Program begun in 1979-80, and to augment the overall CSUC student affirmative action effort on each campus through increased activity in the major areas of:

* Intensive outreach at the undergraduate and graduate levels.
* Expansion of basic retention efforts for minority/low income students.
* Educational enhancement/improvement in counselor and teacher preparation.

COMPONENTS OF THE CORE APPROACH

The three major components of the proposed core approach are:
1) **Intensive Outreach at the Undergraduate and Graduate Levels**
    Elements of this component include:
    * Student/parent/family outreach.
    * Community/university relations.
    * Counselor/staff intersegmental cooperation between high schools, community colleges, and the University of California.
    * Better information dissemination methods and more focused media and information units.

2) Retention
Elements of this component include:
* Reconfiguration of existing retention resources to make them more applicable to underrepresented students.
* CSUC faculty/staff in-service programs.

3) Educational Enhancement/Improved Counselor and Teacher Preparation
This component is concerned with providing such preparation on CSUC campuses during a prospective teacher's original education and with providing in-service training to those in the field.

IMPLEMENTING THE ELEMENTS OF THE CORE APPROACH

The following discussion details the seven elements that comprise the three major components of the core approach:

1) Student/Parent/Family Outreach
Any successful outreach effort requires the development of innovative and effective information and service dissemination systems that will positively impact the prospective applicant. Since parents and family play an important role in the lives of ethnic minorities, and since ethnic minorities are a major SAA target, an effective outreach effort must also reach directly to the family unit. Individual CSUC campuses should initiate student/parent/family outreach that will feature community events, cultural events, direct community outreach and servicing, home visits, and other approaches.

2) Community-University Relations
A primary action item for each campus should be the implementation of new programs designed to foster more direct relations between the university and the minority community. Through such programs as campus tours, campus cultural events campus-administered outings, more effective dissemination of university news throughout target communities, community function speaking engagements, and other activities, each campus hopes to better explain higher education and foster dialogue between the campus and the community.

3) Information Dissemination
Sharing information with target students requires non-traditional, culturally sensitive media and dissemination practices. Central to the core student affirmative action approach should be a campus-by-campus examination of currently utilized outreach media.

A high priority should be the restructuring of existing media into more culturally consistent information packages. Campuses should utilize special bilingual media, regional media, and cultural media. The CSUC and each campus in the system recognize that educational opportunities are based on the availability of useful information about those opportunities. We, therefore, want to insure that underrepresented target groups are provided information about such opportunities in formats and structures with which they are most comfortable.

4) Retention
Campuses should concentrate on the relevance of current supportive services (both academic and para-academic) for underrepresented stu-

dents and on the identification of additional services required by these target students. Programs designed to develop a more supportive college environment should be implemented. Such programs should include (where appropriate) peer advising, cultural programs, continuous information to parents and family units, diagnostic testing, bilingual information sharing, economic counseling, and special academic/career/personal counseling and advising.

5) **CSUC Faculty/Staff In-Servicing Activities**

CSUC campus faculty and staff shape the environment in which the target student will exist. Campuses should seek to modify curricula and practices where appropriate and to reconfigure supportive services into a more supportive environment that will facilitate the advancement and retention of target students. Activities under this heading include: (1) faculty and staff orientations regarding cultural sensitivity, tenets of student affirmative action, and methods of fostering interpersonal relationships with target students, (2) re-evaluation of literature and available information on a department-by-department basis, (3) faculty review of opportunity to enhance some of their curricula, and (4) staff review of opportunity to enhance approaches used for interacting with students.

Such activities will provide faculty and staff with an understanding of cultural differences, current campus approaches to student affirmative action, and models for interacting in more efficient ways with underrepresented students.

6) **Intersegmental Cooperation**

At the heart of the CSUC's Student Affirmative Action Program is the enhancement of intersegmental cooperation between high schools, community colleges, the University of California System, and other post-secondary institutions. Such intersegmental cooperation permits more effective use of resources, more effective servicing of students, and adds continuity to the process of higher education.

The core SAA approach stresses the intensive cooperation of all key education segments through such avenues as joint college information days, joint career days, coordinated counseling/ tutoring/advising, joint membership on local and regional advisory committees, joint information dissemination campaigns, intersegmental staff in-service opportunities collection techniques, comparable student tracking methods, and other approaches.

Such joint efforts should be planned and implemented under the direction of an advisory group including representatives of the professional staff of area secondary and post-secondary educational segments, as well as representatives of the community, business, and industry.

7) **Counselor/Teacher Preparation**

The CSUC prepares nearly 70 percent of the certificated public school teachers and counselors who graduate from California institutions of higher education. The CSUC and each campus recognizes the need for improvement and augmentation of counselor education programs and intersegmental leadership by CSUC schools of education.

Each campus should evaluate course offerings and approaches rela-

ting to bilingual-cross-cultural programs, counselor credential programs, and other education programs that produce individuals that will
interact effectively with target students.

Campuses should develop more internships and placements at
schools with predominantly high concentrations of ethnic minorities.
They should develop more culturally sensitive curricula and train
prospective teachers and counselors how to identify and assist
prospective college students.

Other activities include campaigns designed to recruit more
underrepresented students into these educational disciplines and
campaigns designed to make prospective teachers and counselors fully
aware of college admissions procedures and requirements (including
financial aid, national tests, housing, and supportive services).

Summary of Core Student Affirmative Action

Student Affirmative Action (SAA) is a continuing process that
encompasses three components:
1) Outreach   2) Retention   and 3) Educational Enhancement
1) **SAA Outreach** encompasses:
* Student/parent/family contact and interaction
* Intersegmental coordination of activities between the university
  and appropriate community colleges, University of California,
  private universities, high schools, junior high schools, community
  agencies, community influentials, business, and others).
* More sensitive, thorough, effective university-community relations
* Utilization of multi-cultural, multi-lingual communication, media,
  correspondence, forms.
2) **SAA Retention** encompasses:
* Where necessary, revamping existing supportive services
* Coordinating existing supportive services
* Development of supportive campus environment through services,
  special activities, cultural acknowledgment, perspectives.
3) **SAA Educational Enhancement** encompasses:
* CSUC faculty and staff in-service training opportunities in such
  areas as cultural sensitivity, inter-racial communication, female
  and ethnic minority perspectives, differences in the socialization
  processes of various underrepresented groups.
* Field in-service training sessions for junior high schools, high
  schools, community colleges, faculty, staff, counselors in those
  areas described above, as well as sessions on understanding admission requirements, financial aid opportunities, motivational
  techniques, available educational support programs, etc.
* Enhancement of teacher education programs through the identification and provision of the additional skills and courses students
  need in order to become well-rounded counselors and teachers in
  public education.

A general working definition of student affirmative action can be viewed as containing three charges:

Working Definition of SAA:

* Developing programs, activities, policies, and perspectives that ensure equitable access in junior high school and senior high school by all students to those programs and services that develop the skills, outlook, and motivation needed to become eligible for college.

* Developing programs, activities, policies and perspectives that ensure the equitable dissemination of multi-cultural information about opportunities in higher education and career alternatives.

* Developing programs, activities, policies, and perspectives that ensure that the educational process and environment of the university is a relevant experience that is sensitive to the cultural background of all students, and that college is a successful endeavor for those who earnestly try.

At the outreach stage, SAA can be viewed as the delivery of a package of coordinated, special services to students and other individuals who may ultimately be admitted to higher education on a regular or special admit basis. A primary objective of SAA Outreach will be to ensure that regularly eligible individuals from under-represented groups are not bypassed by services and information regarding college.

In order for SAA to become institutionalized existing programs involved in outreach, retention, educational enhancement should be coordinated. Examples of programs and/or offices that could be coordinated within each of these SAA components are as follows:

Outreach

Admissions Records Evaluations, (ARE)
Relations With Schools, (RWS)
Educational Opportunity Program, (EOP)
Minority Engineering Program, (MEP)
MESA
TRIO
Public Affairs
Special SAA targeted outreach programs

Retention

Educational Opportunity Program (EOP) Support Services
Office Advising Services
Counseling
Tutoring Center
Learning Resource Centers, (LRCs)
Financial Aid
Housing
Testing
Career Planning Placement, (CPP)
Student Affairs
Ethnic Studies
Women's Centers

65

Educational Enhancement
Dept. of Education
Ethnic Studies
Bilingual-Bicultural Programs
Teacher Certificate Programs
Personnel Office
Graduate Studies
Extended Education
Academic Planning
Women's Centers
Affirmative Action Officer

Coordination may be defined as a five-step process:
Coordination: Coming together in order to:
1) Share basic programmatic information.
2) Identify tasks, respective priorities, program components, and constituents.
3) Establish operating agreements, resolve differences and programmatic overlap, identify gaps in service.
4) Develop commonly understood work plans, master calendar of activities/targets, and master goals and objectives statement.
5) Periodic sharing of review of service efforts, activities, and outcomes.

Campuses may want to consider designating an appropriate individual within each of the three program spheres (outreach, retention, educational enhancement) to chair coordination sessions.

Campuses should develop procedures that resolve differences and programmatic considerations that cannot be satisfactorily addressed in coordinating sessions.

Campuses may want to consider designating a specific individual to oversee all aspects of SAA (e.g., outreach, retention, educational enhancement, general campus strategies, etc.).

By way of information, some campuses have proposed creating new positions such as Assistant Vice President for Academic Affairs, SAA Coordinator, etc., and recruiting for that new position. Other campuses have proposed to upgrade an existing position to an appropriate level. Examples here include designating the EOP Director, AA Officer, etc., to Assistant Vice President for Academic Affairs, or Director of University SAA Affairs.

Campuses should support systemwide emphasis on Outreach SAA efforts as the primary concern for campus SAA-funded activities for the next several years. Thus, campuses should develop programs and budget requests that reflect financial and human resource expenditures that approximate the following breakdown:
60% Outreach
30% Retention
10% Educational Enhancement

Subject to legislative approval, FY 1980-81 CSUC Systemwide Student Affirmative Action funds available for disbursement to campuses may approach $1.7 million (combining Program Change Proposal and

Program Maintenance Proposal request). No specific level of System-wide SAA funding is guaranteed for any campus: rather, campuses will have access to SAA funds through a competitive proposal process.

Summary Statement

Underrepresentation of ethnic minorities and women in college and university student populations is a severe societal issue. Like other post-secondary educational segments, the CSUC does not today have a student body that reflects the ethnic composition of high school graduates statewide. Underrepresented students have created a challenge for postsecondary institutions to implement viable, sensitive programs now. The CSUC is confident that the core approach to student affirmative action will provide the University-wide focus and commitment to adequately and successfully meet that challenge.

Getting Minority Students to Participate by Understanding their Needs: A Case For Bradley University

Dr. K. Paul Kasambira
Bradley University

ABOUT THE AUTHOR

DR. K. Paul Kasambira is the director of Minority student activities and associate professor of Teacher education at Bradley University in Peoria, Illinois. A graduate of the University of Zimbabwe, Africa; Taylor University; Upland, and Ball State University, he holds a BA, MA, and Doctorate. He is also licensed by the National Board of Certified Counselors. Dr. Kasambira has co-authored a textbook and has had numerous articles published in the United States, Canada, and Africa.

Dr. Kasambira conducts presentations to student affairs, teacher education, religious, minority, college, and university audiences at the state, national, and international levels. He does consulting work on a variety of topics relating to minority student services.

INTRODUCTION

Today a lot of institutions of higher education are spending a lot of money, human power and time recruiting minority students into their programs. What most of these institutions forget is the fact that enrolling these students does not necessarily guarantee their retention. How to retain minorities, especially on predominantly white college campuses, has become a big controversial issue in university administrative circles.

The issue of apathy among college students, especially minorities, is one that has university personnel, particularly those in student affairs, rethinking and reevaluating their mission. Some people have written, in publications such as **THE CHRONICLE OF HIGHER EDUCATION**, about the prevalence of this phenomenon. Translated simply, apathy might very well be a sign or symptom of lack of motivation. The desire to learn or to participate in campus activities is where true education begins.

Some minority students do not participate because their needs are not recognized by university communities at large. However, these needs can be easily understood by university personnel if the minority students are given an opportunity to express themselves. This article describes a research study whose major aim was to get minority students at Bradley University in Peoria, Illinois, to participate by understanding their needs.

Getting Minority Students to Participate by Understanding Their Needs: A Case for Bradley University

by Dr. K. Paul Kasambira

Historically, the attrition rate of Black College students on the predominantly White campus has been substantially higher than that of White students. The variables attributed to this phenomenon would appear to lend themselves to all minority students. Academic factors play a big part in student attrition rates and to a large degree are strongly influenced by the other factor, i.e., a feeling of alienation within the environment. The subcategories of alienation that seem to stand out, are feelings of meaninglessness, powerlessness, and social estrangement.

Minority students comprise a category of individuals whose racial, educational, social, cultural, and economic experiences vary significantly from that of the majority student population because of their past historical experiences which in some cases included some form of oppression. For these people there are four modes of reaction towards oppression of any sort. Minority students on university campuses have a tendency, as a representative sample of society in general, to fall into one or more of these four modes. These modes may be manifested in the following reactions:

1. Movement towards the perceived oppressor in a desire for integration into the mainstream of society.
2. Movement away from the dominant society.
3. Movement against the oppressors and to express hostility through aggressive action directed at white individuals or institutions.
4. Movement in no particular direction and the manifestation of signs and symptoms of apathy.

The above cited modes of reaction or movements ironically seem to coincide with the civil rights movements in this country. The movement towards the oppressor, in an effort to integrate into the mainstream, occurred in the early 1960's and is typified by minorities such as James Meredith. Meredith was the young man who had personally integrated the University of Mississippi in 1962 (Scott King, 1969).

The short period of movement towards the oppressor was followed by the movement of minorities away from the dominant society, and anyone visiting university campus cafeterias during meals would obviously observe cliques mainly determined by ethnic or racial lines. The anger bottled by minorities after the passage of the Civil Rights Act of 1964 was unleashed during the university campus unrest which prevailed during the late 1960's and the early 1970's. These events marked the third movement in which oppressed minorities expressed hostility toward white or majority institutions, (Gollnick and Chinn, 1983).

The fourth stage, which is virtually not a movement towards anything and is typified by apathy among students on university campuses, in my opinion is where we are now. Students, and particularly those from minority groups are in some cases so apathetic about

70

university life or activities that they just want to be left alone and not be involved in campus activities.

Research literature compiled within the last ten or so years seems to point to the fact that the number of minority students on American university campuses is going to steadily increase. In his article, entitled "Guess Who is Coming to College," Harold Hodgkinson, who is probably one of the leading researchers on demographics and higher education, pointed out the following statistics:

1. Blacks and women are now proportionately represented among college populations, while Hispanics are not.
2. Higher education institutions would have to prepare themselves for increasing minority enrollments. For example...a new 97% population in the District of Columbia, 75% in Hawaii, 57% in New Mexico, 51% in Mississippi, 46% in Texas, 43% in California, 34% in Maryland, 32% in New York State, and 29% in Illinois to mention only a few examples.
3. Higher Education will have to provide new programs in order to attract minorities, older adults, and programs offered in conjunction with industry, the military, and other educational services users.
4. By 1990 minorities of all ages will constitute 20 to 25 percent of the American total population, while their youth population will be 30%. In some states such as Texas and California minorities will be over 45% of the state birth cohort.
5. Today the number of Native Americans, Hispanics, Asians, Mormons, and Seventh Day Adventists are increasing rapidly due to either ethnic or religious values regarding family size, family planning or divorce.

In reviewing literature on university campus needs for minority students, the author came across some interesting studies, but they were rather specific in scope. For instance, Burrell and others conducted a study to determine how minority students viewed academic advising. These researchers concluded that the majority of the University students they had surveyed perceived academic advising as their most important resource (Burrel et al, 1983).

Particular needs of Chinese students on American university campuses were revealed in a study conducted by Esther Lee Yao. After her study Yao concluded that one of the needs Chinese students had was to acquire skills in adjusting to the American life style, new language, value system, and new teaching/learning methods (Yao, 1983).

A 1981 study by Perry and Tucker recommended that institutions of higher education should adjust their organization based upon the determination that students will succeed regardless of how long it takes or how much effort is expended by the institution (Perry and Tucker, 1981).

A study to determine university students' perceptions of a university environment was conducted by Madrazo-Peterson and Rodriquez using the College Student Questionnaire and the Environmental Satisfaction Questionnaire. The researchers found significant differences between ethnic groups, between sexes within ethnic groups,

71

and differences by class, college, and sex (Madrazo-Peterson and Rodriquez. 1978).

Scherini and others did a study in which they were trying to determine the needs of immigrant and refugee students to the University of California, Berkeley. Their study revealed that the major areas of difficulty for these students were the large amount of course work reading, relations with instructors and peers, and adjustment to the USA society and institutions. While seriously taking into account what researchers such as Harold Hodgkinson and other researchers have found, the director of Minority Student Services (MSS) at Bradley University, Peoria, Illinois, conducted a research study to assess the needs of minority students enrolled at Bradley, in the Spring semester of the 1985 academic year.

Purpose of the Study

The purpose of this study was to obtain information concerning some of the basic needs of minority students enrolled by Bradley University during the Spring semester of 1985. At that time, 13.2% of the Bradley University enrollment of 4,950 was made up of minorities. The results obtained from the study would then be used in programming activities or improving the services delivered to minority students by the Office of Minority Student Services. In this Needs Assessment Survey, the term "programming" is defined as the **"creating, planning, and implementation of activities for students, staff, and faculty, which builds a sense of community responsibility, and enthusiasm on campus."** This would involve the inclusion of activities or extra-curricular activities such as entertainment, parties, speakers, cultural programs, and academic support services.

Significance of the Study

In this day and age when institutions of higher education are faced with the harsh reality of declining enrollments and consequent financial exigency, these institutions are expected to deliver services in a more efficient and cost-effective manner than ever before. This set of circumstances then compels those people directly in charge of the services area, student affairs, or activities area, to systematically determine what the recipients of the services they deliver feel or perceive as their needs. In this respect Bradley University is no exception.

One of the ways to find out the needs of service recipients, in this case the students, is by surveying them. A variety of surveying approaches can be used and in the case of this study a survey questionnaire was used. This method was chosen over the other methods since it seemed to be the most economical method. This study is significant, since it seems to involve the first comprehensive study of its kind conducted by the Office of Minority Student Services at Bradley University. The data collected in the study would be used to strengthen, improve, or initiate programmatic strategies used in the delivery of services to minority students.

Method

The Subjects:

The subjects who were surveyed are those people who are considered "minorities" at Bradley University . For all intents and purposes Bradley University, as do most federal agencies, defines minorities as people who belong to one or more of the following racial/ethnic group: American Indian, Alaskan, Asian or Pacific Islanders, Black/Afro-American, Hispanic, and People from Brazil, Guyana, Surinam, or Trinidad.

Procedure

The survey instrument was the result of several activities. These activities included the author's reviewing of research literature related to minority student needs, informal survey of other Bradley University student activity offices, examination of the existing minority student program, and informal discussions with minority student leaders on campus. The instrument or questionnaire had three major parts and thirteen different items. The first part of the instrument was of a demographic nature, dealing with information on the respondent's sex, college classification (Freshman, Sophomore, Junior, or Senior), his/her hometown, and current residential address.
The second and third parts of this instrument dealt with decision factors. These decisions and activity/interest factors were arranged randomly on the survey instrument and included the following variables:
Best day and time for attendance at campus activities
Best means of informing students of campus activities
Preferred programs
Type of music preferred
Type of movies preferred
Type of speaker/lecture preferred
Campus membership activity/interest profile
Campus location most conducive to participation in campus activities
Academic courses in which review or tutorial services were needed
Suggestions or recommendations on additional programs,activities, or services
Additional comments

Data Collection and Analysis

Three hundred questionnaires were distributed to minority students who lived in dorms on Bradley's campus, and the respondents either mailed their completed questionnaire to the Office of Minority Student Services or gave them to their residence advisors who then in turn sent them to the Minority Student Services Office. Some of the questionnaires were mailed to off-campus students whose mailing addresses were still filed with the Office of Minority Students. Of the 300 questionnaires sent out, 114 (38%) were returned. The instrument which was specifically designed and developed for this particular study is included as an Appendix in this report.

The data collected from this study were sent to the Bradley Computer Center for analysis. Due to infrequency of responses, it was deemed fit to collapse and to tabulate the respondents' top three and bottom three choices.

Results and Discussion

Items 1 and 2

Since items 1 and 2 in Part I of the instrument dealt solely with demographic data, the information obtained in these sections will not be discussed in this report. Instead, information obtained in Parts I and II which dealt with decision factors and activity interest profiles are what this report will focus on. Information from item numbers 11 and 12 dealing with respondents' suggestions or comments was separately extracted and is included in this report.

Item 3 - What is/are the best day (s) and time (s) for your attendance at campus activities?

Respondents to this question indicated that the three days which would be most favorable for them to attend activities on Bradley's campus are Friday, Saturday, and Sunday. Friday (7:00 p.m. to 11:00 p.m.) got the highest (59) voters from the respondents, followed by Saturday (7:00 p.m. to 11:00 p.m.). The least favored day and time of the three top favorite days was Sunday (3:00 p.m. to 5:00 p.m.). The least favored day and time was Monday before noon followed by Tuesday and Wednesday before noon. The last two days and times got 3 and 4 responses respectively.

Item #4 - What is the best way to inform you of campus activities?

A total of 321 responses were indicated on this item.

According to the respondents, the three top best ways for them to get information were through: mailbox flyers (72 votes), posters (62 votes), and the **Bradley Scout** (52 votes), the University's weekly newspaper. The least favorite mode of communication as indicated by the 34 people who responded to this item was organization representatives (20 votes) followed by radio/television. Word of mouth was the best of the three bottom or least favorite choices.

Item 5 - I would prefer to attend the following types of programs.

The most favored programs were popular music concerts, with 44 of the total 183 votes cast, followed by movies with 38 of the third place with 19 votes each. The three bottom or least favored programs were art exhibits, sports events, and dances or lectures/speakers.

Item 6 – What types of music do you prefer ?

Respondents to this question cast a total of 357 votes*. The top three favorite types of music were soul (65 votes), swing (49 votes), and classical music (45 votes). The three least liked types of music were hard rock, rhythm/blues, folk, and punk.

Item 7 – What types of movies do you prefer?

In this item, the top three movie choices were comedy, films with Black stars, and mystery films. The comedy movies received 90 of the 367 votes while movies with black stars got 48 votes followed by mystery films which got 41 votes. The respondents' three bottom choices were foreign, western, and horror movies.

Item 8 – What type of speaker/lecture presentations do you prefer?

In response to the above question, respondents indicated that their top three speaker/lecture choices, in descending order were current events, minority issues, and comedians. Science lectures, political lectures, and religious presentations were their three bottom or least favorite programs.

Item 9 – In what campus organizations are you involved?

Respondents to this question indicated that the top three organizations in which they were involved were, in descending order: special interest groups, (e.g., Dorm Council, Little Sister, Sweetheart, Psychology Club), intramural sports, and Black Student Alliance. The bottom three organizations in which respondents were least involved were varsity athletics, student senate, and the Scout publication.

Item 10 results were ommitted.

---

* In this report, the words, votes and choices will be used interchangeably to indicate the frequency with which respondents made that particular choices.

Item 11 - What locations are conducive to your participation in campus activities?

A total of 144 choices was indicated by the 85 people who responded to this item. Their top three choices of conducive locations were the Field House (32), the Civic Center (21), and the Romeo B. Garrett Cultural Center (12 choices). The three least favorite places were "other places," outdoors, and residence halls.

Item 12 - In which academic areas would you like to have review or tutoring sessions? (Check as many as appropriate).

Table
Summary of Data Concerning
Tutoring needs by Course

Course	Responses
Mathematics	22
Statistics	15
Computer Science	15
Calculus	13
History	12
Economics	11
Physics	11
Accounting	10
Chemistry	8
Engineering	6
Biology	4
Sociology	4
Business Management	3
English	3
Journalism	2
French	1
Finance	1
Geology	1
International Studies	1
Psychology	1
Nursing	1

Item 13 - Suggestions for additional programs to be provided and additional comments.

*   Indicates number of respondents who made that suggestion.
**   Minority information center with minority alumni in different fields
**   More Black students should be encouraged to integrate more into campus-organizations as well as just Black Greeks and BSA.
*   More in-depth information on events happening on campus such as

information telling who Romeo B. Garrett was and why such a commotion over him...There should be more informative and persuasive information provided.

*** More inter-racial programs

* More religious activities, e.g., Bible studies in dorms

*** Black radio station - one that gets more air time

* Specific class and teacher description available before registration

* More West Indian programming

* Fewer parties and dances - more cultural and academic events

* More effort in individual counseling

* BSA candidates for president should be selected from a wide range of capable candidates.

*** Emphasize conscious raising of academic support and assistance services - steps for planning academic coursework around future careers.

* More minority scholarships should be made available

* Counseling services on the morale of Blacks/minorities on this campus

*** Would like to see the Minority Services get involved with other organizations on campus. For example, maybe co-sponsor with ACBU on one of their film Festivals (e.g., A Sidney Portier and Bill Cosby Night).

* Would like to see the Minority Services hold an Open House to dispel doubts that the Garrett Center is "the Black people hang-out." Instead of holding all of our functions there, we should consider using the Hartmann Center and/or Dingledine

* If there is anything coming to Peoria that you feel that we as students should see, buy a block of tickets. For example, many students did not realize that "Ain't misbehavin'" would get sold out so early.

* Time management workshops

** I Would like to see the Black minorities start a drama production. I am seriously willing to start a Black production workshop concentrating on Black plays using a majority of black actors and actresses. If this is possible, let it be known; and I will get in touch with you.

* Before we help minority students on campus, there has to be student communication between those who are not minorities. This school is too conservative, and the students are stagnant. The Reggae band showed at least some of the so-called "melting pot" theory in this school. We need more interchanging activities to educate the majority.

** More community oriented activities, i.e., Big Brother-Big Sister City Clean-up (cleaning streets), donating food baskets to poor families, planting flowers for senior citizen homes, etc.

* In the case of ACBU, it is the activities council for all of Bradley University. Confront the council as to why it isn't sponsoring any events for minority students, since it is allocated a budget from SABRC in the neighborhood of $75,000.

Conclusions

Based upon the data collected and analyzed in this needs assessment study, the following conclusions can be made:

*   Respondents seemed to be interested in attending campus activities on weekends from 7:00 to 11:00 p.m. but were least interested in doing so before noon on Monday, Tuesday, and Wednesday.
*   Respondents were interested in getting their information through reading material such as flyers or the University newspaper as opposed to getting it through radio or television.
*   Popular music concerts would be more acceptable than sport event activities. Soul music programs would be most acceptable to the minority students, while punk rock would be least acceptable to them.
*   Comedy movies would be most popular among minority students, while horror movies would be least acceptable.
*   Speakers/lecturers dealing with current event issues would be most popular, while those dealing with religious topics would be least popular.
*   The bulk of the respondents seemed to belong to special interest groups such as Dorm Councils, Little Sisters, Sweetheart groups, the Psychology Club, or the Black Student Alliance, while virtually none of them worked on the **Scout** publication.

Recommendations

Based upon the data analysis and the suggestions or comments made in item 12, the following recommendations are made for serious consideration as well as implementation:

-   As much as possible most minority student services activities should be scheduled during the weekend and preferably between the hours of 7:00 p.m. and 12:00 p.m. to allow most students to participate. Unless absolutely necessary, weekday mornings should be left free for students to work on their studies.
-   To effectively disseminate information to minority students, some kind of newsletter or flyer mailed to minority students should be started by the Office of Minority Student Services.
-   Funds for comedy movies should be provided.
-   More speakers/lectures dealing with current political issues should be invited to give presentations on Bradley's campus.
-   Minority students should be encouraged to run for offices or to actively participate in organizations such as the Bradley University Student Senate so as to minimize "isolation."
-   There should be more interaction between minority and white students through social activities.
-   The possibility of a Black student Christian organization should be explored.
-   The BSA with the help of the Office of Minority Student Services should seriously look into the possibility of starting a minority drama organization.

- More activities such as the Reggae band which are specifically designed to bring students of diversified cultural backgrounds together should be brought to campus.
- Minority students should be encouraged to be involved in community projects such as food drives, city clean up, and helping senior citizens in the community.
- The Office of Admissions should be encouraged to organize weekend programs here on campus for prospective minority students.

Implementation

Based upon the results of this research study, particularly the students' recommendations or suggestions to the Office of Minority Student Services, the director along with the student advisory council implemented the following recommendations:

1. In response to the tutorial needs indicated in Table 1, a systematic tutorial network has been established by the Office of Minority Student Services.
2. A concerted effort is being made to schedule student activities during the weekend between the hours of 7:00 and 12:00 p.m.
3. A newsletter called The Minority Network published twice a month by the MSS office was launched. This document, which is mailed directly to all minority students, faculty, staff, all university student activities and co-curricular activities offices has received a very high evaluation from its recipients. The Network informs students of upcoming events and important deadlines for financial aids and other application forms.
4. Funds for comedy movies have been provided for different kinds of movies with minorities in them by the all minority student council.
5. The MSS office has provided films and lectures through minority student organizations dealing with current issues such as Apartheid in South Africa.
6. Minority students have been encouraged to run for all university student senate seats, and they have won!
7. Social activities involving white, black, and other minority students have been organized. For instance, a Reggae band, **Safari**, from Chicago, has been invited to perform on campus. This event was probably the best attended multi-ethnic activity on campus.
8. Plans are under way to develop a minority theater group on campus.
9. In conjunction with the Bradley Admissions Office, the MSS office along with minority students have given a number of recruitment seminars to prospective high school students from the Peoria high schools and a number of minority students from Chicago area schools.
10. Minority students have been involved in community projects such as food drives for the needy.
11. A minority student leaders' Advisory Council to the Director of Minority Student Services was launched. This group works as the liaison between minority students and the MSS office.

Summary

My experience as the Director of Minority Student Services at Bradley University has taught me that if minority students are allowed to express their needs and to actively participate in the decision-making process, they become very motivated to participate in campus activities. They are also likely to break down racial, cultural or ethnic barriers and to feel that they are part and parcel of the Bradley University community.

Selected Bibliography

Burrel, et al. "Advising with Students on Predominantly White Campuses." **Journal of College Student Personnel,** V24/N2, (March, 1983), pp. 121-126.

Gollnick, D. & Chinn, P. **Multicultural Education in a Pluralistic Society.** C.V. Mosby Company, 1983.

Hodgkinson, Harold, "Guess Who Is Coming to College" Your Students in 1990." **Minoratric Abstracts.** V5/N13, (April,1983).

Hodgkinson, Harold. "What's Still Right with Education," **Phi Delta Kappan,** (December, 1982), pp. 231-235.

Madrazo, P. & Rodriquez. "Minority Students' Perceptions of a University Environment." **Journal of College Student Personnel,**19, (3), (May 1982). pp. 259-263.

Perry and Tucker. "Organizing the Institution to Meet the Needs of Minority and Disadvantaged Students," **College Student Personnel,** V15/N2, (Summer, 1981), p. 1985.

Ross, Douglas N., ed. **Population Trends and Implications.** Report no. 735. New York: The Conferences Board, 1977.

Steward, Ian. "Higher Education Faces Hard Times Ahead." **American Demographics,** (June, 1979), pp. 12-13.

Scherini, R. et al. **Survey of Immigrant and Refugee Students at the University of California, Berkeley.** California University, (October, 1980).

Scott-King, C. **My Life with Martin Luther King,** Jr. Holt, Rinehart, and Winston, Inc., 1969.

U.S. Department of Commerce, Bureau of the Census. "Projections of the Population of the United States: 1977 to 2050." **Current Population Reports.** May, 1979, P-25, N. 805.

Westoff, Charles F. "The Decline of Fertility. "American Demographics, (February, 1979), pp. 16-19.

Yao, E.L. "Chinese students in American Universities." **Texas Tech. Journal of Education,** V10, (Winter, 1983), pp. 35-42.

Increasing Minority Student Participation on Campus

by Charles A. Taylor

Program Ideas

The following list is provided to assist program coordinators in planning activities that will help to involve minorities in student services. Serving as mental stimulation for possible future "brainstorming," this list includes activities that have been successful in achieving minority involvement.

    Sponsoring a bus tour during spring break to Black colleges
    Sponsoring a picnic for all minority students and then passing out information
    Sponsoring a dance with campus "reps" conducting a sales pitch at intermission
    Sponsor ethnic dinners and/or tournaments.
    Interacting with minority groups at colleges around the area.
    Cross-cultural workshops
    International Day; Multi-cultural Arts Festival
    Speakers, conferences, panels
    Campus radio program, T.V., or other media program on minority culture
    Black History Week, American Indian, or Latino Week
    Minority Health Symposium
    Movies; fund raising activities
    Anything by Richard Pryor/Comedy Night
    Student Talent Shows, fashion shows, hair styling clinics
    Person-to-Person Committee to increase interaction between whites and minorities
    Saturday Children's Program for minority children
    Outreach programs in minority communities
    Documentary, scrapbook, slide show
    Minority parents weekend; Minority alumni day
    Greek Day
    Peer Counselors
    Cosmetic demonstration
    Minority Author of the Month Discussions
    Personal growth, assertiveness training, Minority awareness workshops
    Vocational and Career Seminars and Exhibits
    Special study nights; Library tours
    Play some cultural games - make race relations fun!
    Form a friendship league, or host a Mix & Match night
    Set up a cultural SWAP shop; get- acquainted day
    Recognition nights, Brotherhood/Sisterhood Week
    Sponsor an annual multi-cultural festival
    Brown bag programs, breakfast seminars
    Establish a cultural training center
    Sponsor minority community tours

Language classes, Bilingual tutors
Learning Resource Centers
How-to-workshops on term papers, study habits, research, modern technology, etc.
Sponsor demonstrations on "How to Cook Soul Food, Mexican, Indian, or Chinese Food"
Contests on Black history themes, Women issues, Indian themes, etc.
Bailes theater groups; Help students form touring gospel choir.
Reserve several tables in the Student Union for national and international cultural exchanges
Ethnic buffet, international correspondence; Third World tours
Community outreach programs, children's program and elderly programs
Peer or Buddy System for social, cultural or educational purposes
Short Course Classes, Bulletin Boards, Orientation programs
Support student exchange programs (national and international).
Place cultural cards, calendars and miscellaneous information on student union tables
Add your own...

The goal of sponsoring any of these activities is to bring people together for an educational and learning experience. Campuses that have minority-related activities as part of the university program have provided a means of minimizing the alienation that minorities often feel.

Problems Related to Minority Programming

There are certain difficulties associated with Minority Programming that must be identified, understood and dealt with if Minority Programming is to be effective. Several of the obstacles to effective programming are listed below.

Minorities uninvolved in the planning of programs
Lack of general campus support
Nationalism and separatism movements on the part of minority students
Low expectations
One-shot funding approach
Lack of objective evaluations in assessing minority student programming
Ignoring cultural needs of minority students
Attitudes on the part of some minority students
Lack of understanding of minority student needs
Tokenism programming
Inadequate funding
Lack of minority student organization, therefore no perceived need

Low priority and/or stereotyping
Benign neglect; institutional racism
Inexperience on the part of minority students
Pie dividing - pitting minorities against minorities
Viewing funding for minority programming as supporting
segregation
No commitment; as a result can't determine what constitutes an
adequate amount of programming
Attitudes - faculty and administrators don't believe in
minority programming
Lack of overall plan or calendar on part of minority
students

Here, as in other situations, identifying the problem is
only the first step. Be careful not to let this list deter
taking positive action. The hope is to view these not as
problems but as challenges that can be over come.

Factors That Prohibit Minority Involvement

Cultural Conflict - Many Campuses operate as white cultural institutions with an emphasis on middle class values. Often minority
cultural values are ignored or rejected. This can result in an identity crisis on the part of the minority student. Universities should
promote cultural pluralism and the inclusion of the minority
experience as an integral part of the curriculum.

**Self-determination Positions Taken by Minority Groups Which The
University Interprets as Segregation** - Minority Student Organizations
(MSO's) serve a very important function for minority students. The
challenge is to allow minority students autonomy while at the same
time encouraging them not to limit their involvement solely to MSO's.

**Minority Students absent from top positions in Student Services
Hierarchy** - Students need role models they can identify with and peer
groups in which they feel comfortable.

**Inflexible Guidelines That Ignore Cultural Needs of Minority
Students** - Early closing of Student Unions is an example we frequently
encounter. To the Urban student this presents a problem. All university policies should be evaluated in terms of bias and their perceived
or real impact on minority students.

Tokenism - Many minority students feel their viewpoints won't be
accommodated or that they will be put in a figurehead position without
any real power. Universities should make sure that committees, Advisory Councils and Task Forces truly reflect a fair representation of
minorities.

Struggling to Survive Academically - If you can't make the
grades, involvement tends to be a low priority. The establishment of
supportive services by many campuses has proven to be an asset in
helping minority students achieve academically. The payoff will hopefully result in students taking a more active interest in campus
affairs.

Campus Administrators and White Students Leaders Not Attending or

Showing Little Interest in Minority Initiated Activities – It is important that students know there is a sincere commitment and interest in activities they initiate. Although it is unrealistic for administrators to attend all minority oriented programs, it is devastating to student morale if administrators don't attend any.

Lack of Familiarity with Parliamentary Procedure – Many student government meetings are run using parliamentary procedures. Students unfamiliar with this procedure often feel inadequate or intimidated. Universities that are sensitive to this plight have either encouraged other forms of operating procedures or provided students with parliamentary procedure training.

Peer Group Pressure – Some minority students are into "racial nationalism," and they feel their energy and time should be spent with their particular racial group. What we've encouraged college officials to do is help students move beyond racial polarization by helping them understand that we're all here together. Students can learn to be secure in their own culture while at the same time joining hands with others to address problems that affect everyone.

Alienation – Over the years many minority students have expressed their belief that most campus activities on predominantly white campuses are geared towards white students. An administrator who was successful in getting minority students involved revealed his secret. He said, "Make them feel comfortable." Once a student feels a part of the institution, chances are good that he/she will participate.

also...

Having to assume the role of "minority student" representative rather than "student representative."
Hassles of obtaining and justifying "separate" funding
Racial bias as perceived by the minority student
No one on campus ever encouraged them to become involved
Involved in the sub-culture of alternative activities organizations on campus

Minority Celebration

Recognition of culturally significant days that are either sponsored or recognized by the university helps to foster environmental conditions that demonstrate sensitivity to significant cultural distinctions. The following provides a synopsis of Minority Celebrations that are intrinsically important to minority cultures. It is recommended that dates relevant to the multi-cultural composition of your institution be recognized and incorporated into your calendar planning. A complete description of these holidays can be found in the **FACT SHEETS** located in chapter 8.

It is important that universities are aware of minority holidays and events that are traditionally celebrated by a substantial percentage of the minority population. We have listed only the major celebrations that are national in scope.

85

<u>American Indian:</u> The most popular and celebrated events are:

American Indian Day - celebrated by many tribes the day after Thanksgiving
Feasts of Thanksgiving - celebrated by different tribes dates are determined by tribes
American Indian Week - celebrated by different tribes on different dates

<u>Black:</u> The most popular and celebrated events are:

January 15 - **Martin Luther King, Jr.'s Birthday**
February - **Black History Month**
June 19 - **Juneteenth Day** (Black Person's Fourth of July).
Texas is the only state that has made Juneteenth Day a state holiday.
December - January 1 - **Kwanzaa Celebration** - Kwanzaa is based on the traditional African holiday and seven principles of the "new" Black value system. Kwanzaa means "first".

<u>Asian:</u> The most popular celebrated events are:

Chinese New Year - Usually falls between January and March (based on lunar calendar), and normally lasts about two weeks with a Lantern Festival culminating the holiday.
Hmong New Year - Usually starts somewhere in mid-November to December depending on the rhythm of nature itself.
Laotian celebration - Boon Hok Nam - This is the Laotian New Year, May 1-5 every year. This holiday is used to wash away evil and to bring good luck (Known as the throwing of water).
Vietnamese Tet - Celebrated at the beginning of the Lunar Year. Includes three important days: The First Day or Head-day is to celebrate Tet with one's parents. The second day is to celebrate with one's wife's parents, and the third day is to celebrate with one's teacher.

<u>Chicano/Hispanic:</u> The most popular and celebrated events are:

September 16 - Commemorates **Mexican Independence Day**
December 12 - **Patroness of the Americas**
May 5 - **Cinco de Mayo;** Commemorates the Battle of Puebla

We encourage universities to sponsor or recognize these minority celebrations!

Using Strategies That Work

Sponsor A Minority Leadership Conference for Students

Annually many universities sponsor a one-to-three day intensive
leadership conference for students providing them with developmental
skills. New freshmen students should be especially encouraged to
participate so there will be a continuous pool of trained students.
The leadership Conference covers topics on leadership styles, parliamentary procedures, establishing campus contacts, creative programming, time management, decision making, cross-cultural communication,
assertiveness training and ways to increase minority student participation on campus. Students are then provided with leadership roles on
campus. For an overview of what an actual leadership workshop is like
see chapter 9.

Sponsor a Cultural Retreat

Are you having a problem with white and minority students
interacting? We know of no better method to break down racial barriers, to dispute myths and stereotypes, than to get students in an
isolated setting and literally submerge them in minority culture for a
weekend. The retreat should have a representative mixture of Minorities and Whites. Praxis has developed a structured social and educational program that combines cultural awareness with fun sessions that
lead to a total cultural experience. Praxis', **How to Sponsor a Cultural Retreat Handbook** sells for $19.95 plus postage. See Chapter 12,
"Related Books of Interest", for ordering information.

Establish a Tradition of Minority Events on Campus

Develop a tradition so that students have something to look
forward to and can plan their activities around. This really spurs
students into becoming involved. The ethnic celebrations are a good
starting point in establishing a sense of tradition.

Develop an Effective Public Relations Plan Geared Specifically Towards Minority Students.

This Public Relations plan should include a monthly newsletter
with items of interest for minority students, flyers of upcoming
activities mailed regularly to their mail box, special announcements
in the campus media (radio, newspapers, etc.), personal telephone
calls, and invitations. It is also important to announce minority
activities in all "official" inter-campus newsletters.

Create an Advisory Council

Form a Multi-cultural advisory council of students and faculty to
advise on activities and program planning.

<u>Sponsor Rap Sessions and Orientation Sessions in the Residence Halls.</u>

These sessions should be led by other students and should be a general discussion of minority concerns on campus. Minority student leaders should meet with residence hall staff and student government leaders to work out strategies of mutual concern.

<u>Use Minority Faculty as Resource Persons</u>

Talk with minority faculty and administrators on your campus, and use their suggestions on how to reach out to minority students. Encourage minority faculty to get involved in minority student activities.

<u>Provide leadership from the top</u>

Have the president of the university sponsor an informal "mingle and tingle" night for minority students as a way of introduction.

Conclusion

It will take consistent and long range efforts to reach the desired level of minority involvement. In order for the full benefits of these ideas presented to be realized, minority students need to be provided with information and have access to educational facilities and resources that foster self-identity and self-determination. This in turn will give them the power to influence their educational environment and affect positive social change.

Chapter 5

Perspectives on Counseling Black Women in Academia

Dr. Herbert A. Exum
North Carolina State University

ABOUT THE AUTHOR

Dr. Herbert Exum is Associate Professor of Counselor Education in the school of Education at North Carolina State University. He received his B.A. from Federal City College, his M.A. and his Ph.D in Counseling and Student Personnel Psychology from the University of Minnesota. He has held a number of significant positions in his illustrious career, including: Associate professor, Department of Counseling and Guidance, UW-Madison, and Assistant Professor, Division of Counselor Education, University of Iowa.

He has done pioneering work in cross-cultural counseling, counseling black women, and human relations training. He has had numerous articles published in leading journals.

Dr. Exum is a licensed psychologist, a certified therapist and is a professional member of the American Psychological Association, Association of Black Psychologists, and the American Association for Counseling and Development.

INTRODUCTION

The major objective of this paper, which is essentially a collection of case notes, is to add to the body of literature which is designed to assist Black Americans acquire appropriate belief systems and cognitive coping strategies needed to successfully negotiate the academic environment at high pressure predominantly white research institutions. The major focus of the paper will be a self-help intervention designed to assist Black women combat alienation and loss of esteem on predominantly white campuses. The intervention is based on four major assumptions:

(1) that the stress and general disequilibrium experienced by many Black women at predominantly white institutions are the result of conflicts between their expectations of the academic environment and their actual experiences in academia. They essentially experience culture shock,

(2) that the disequilibrium itself is not necessarily negative, but the adjustments made to the disequilibrium may be negative.

(3) that graduate and professional women are all susceptible to this source of distress and,

(4) that part of the successful resolution of these conflicts can be facilitated through a rational balancing of academic, social/emotional and physical activities.

This paper approaches the disorientation and loss of esteem expressed by Black women on white campuses as a temporary failure of their coping strategies. The goal of the intervention is to increase the woman's sense of personal mastery of the academic environment and to increase her self-efficacy.

Perspectives on Counseling Black Women in Academia

by Dr. Herbert A. Exum

Introduction

From the outset the reader should know that this paper is written from the perspective of a Black American male. It seems prudent to believe that while Black people have had common experiences in America as a result of being Black, the interpretation of these experiences and the behaviors which result from them, have probably been different for Black men and Black women. Consequently, the self-help strategies discussed later in the paper may need to be modified to fit the world views of some Black women. Nonetheless, the basic assumption of this paper is that what worked for the women in this sample may be useful to other Black women in similar settings and situations.

Also the orientation of the intervention is decidedly cognitive-behavioral. The work of Beck (1976), Burns (1981), Ellis (1970), and Meichenbaum (1986) have influenced the design of the intervention. Suffice it to say this paper supports the belief that moods are created by cognitions, and the way a person feels is a function of what a person says to herself about a situation.

SUBJECTS

The findings in this paper are based on a sample of 31 Black female graduate students and new professionals. The data was collected over a five year period at 3 different large Midwestern universities. All the women in this sample were either upper level graduate students, recent graduates of doctoral programs, or entry level professionals, e.g. assistant professors, within the institutions of study. They ranged in age from 26-41 years and came from the same general socio-economic class. All of the subjects had parents holding at least a H.S diploma, and in all cases both parents worked outside the home. In 75% of the cases at least one parent had received a baccalaureate degree. None of the parents of the subjects had completed either the master's or doctoral degree at the time the data was collected.

This sample is relatively small primarily because these observations were not originally part of an ongoing study. They are, in fact, the results of clinical observations. They are case notes. The similarity of experiences shared by these women is striking, however, and helps to make the generalizations made from these notes useful to persons in other settings. All of the subjects in this sample, with one exception, were self-referrals. The one exception was a first year doctoral student who contacted the author at the request of a Black counselor at the institution where she completed her Master's degree. The referral procedure consisted of instructions of "talk to_____if you have any problems." The Black counselor and the author had never met each other.

FINDINGS

The most common presenting problem of the subjects was feeling down, depressed, bad, or otherwise "out of it." The causes of these feelings ranged from low grades to poor social life. The generic issues, however, involved: (1) loss of personal esteem, (2) loss of self confidence, and (3) loss of a sense of feminine beauty. The major source of this stress and personal disequilibrium seemed to have been the result of conflicts between the samples' expectations of the academic environment and their actual experiences in academia.

Three interrelated constructs proved to be useful in providing a conceptual framework from which to understand the feelings and behavior of the women in this sample. These concepts are stress, depression, and culture shock. Each of these concepts will be discussed briefly. Then the relationships between the concepts and the experiences of the women in the sample will be established. The first concept to be reviewed is stress.

OVERVIEW OF STRESS

This concept was first formulated by Cannon (1939) as a characteristic of the physiological system of humans. He defined stress as a disturbance in homeostasis in response to new situations which are perceived to be threatening. Lazarus (1966) defined stress as any event in which internal or external demands tax or exceed the adaptive resources of the individual. More recently, Selye (1975) defined stress as a non-specific response of the body to any demand. While these definitions differ, the common thread is defining stress as a response. Hence, the individual experiencing stress is not the initiator, but is acted upon and then experiences stress in response (Didos-Ritsma, 1982).

Though stress is a response, it is not just one type of response. Several interrelated concepts actually determine the magnitude and subjective experience of stress. These concepts include frustration, threat, conflict, and anxiety. Frustration results when a course of action cannot be carried out or brought to its conclusion for some reason. Threat is the anticipation of some undesirable consequence, and this undesirable consequence is a function of interpretation; it is relative to the person making the judgment. So in essence a person has to learn to be threatened by a situation. Threat depends on what the person believes about the situation, and this knowledge need have no correspondence with objective reality (Exum, 1977).

In threat, harm is anticipated but has not yet occurred, but in frustration the harm has already taken place. In a sense, then, threat is future oriented; while frustration is present and past oriented. Threat requires preventive action, and frustration requires corrective action to be lessened.

The third stress-related concept is called conflict. Conflict is the simultaneous presence of two incompatible goals. The goals are incompatible, because the behavior and attitudes necessary to achieve

92

one goal are opposite those necessary to achieve the other. Conflict makes threat or frustration inevitable, because if one goal is realized, the other will either be blocked or threatened (Exum, 1977).

The final concept, anxiety, like stress itself, has several basic meanings. It is generally viewed as a response and as an intervening variable having its own effects. In this study anxiety is defined as a painful emotional experience which is produced by excitations in the internal organs of the body (Hall, 1970). The pain in the back of the neck, the soreness in the shoulders, or the churning feeling in the stomach experienced when one is under pressure, threatened, or frustrated are all manifestations of anxiety.

RESULTS OF STRESS

The stress experiences by the Black women who comprise the sample in this paper went well beyond minimal levels. The anxiety produced by the stress they experienced was no longer motivating; it was clearly no longer experienced as excitement or exhilaration. The most commonly reported subjective experience of this level of stress was heaviness: an unrelenting physical sensation of being crushed or weighted down. The behavioral manifestations of the results of this chronic stress were essentially those of depression. Table 1 lists some of the common physical complaints presented by the women in this sample. Table 2 lists psychological and emotional symptoms.

Table 1

PERCENTAGE OF SUBJECTS MANIFESTING PHYSICAL AND/OR BEHAVIORAL SYMPTOMS

Symptom	Percentage Experienced
Very late sleeping or insomnia	90%
Loss of appetite or frequent binges	90%
Loss of libido or hypersexuality	65%
Absence of dreaming or excessive dreaming	80%
Agitation or psychomotor retardation	100%
Unusual weight gain or weight loss	75%
Hair loss	80%
Unusual menstrual cycle	50%
Diarrhea	60%
Chest, back, neck, and shoulder pains	100%
Shortness of breath	50%
Excessive shopping or traveling	50%

Table 2

Percentage of Subjects Manifesting Emotional Symptoms

Symptom	Percentage
Mood swings (increased lability of affect)	90%
Impaired short term memory	80%
Impaired attention span	80%
Decreased ability to manage daily living activities	80%
Thoughts of Suicide	75%
Sadness	100%
Free floating anxiety	100%

DEPRESSION

Depression has been called the world's number one public health problem (Burns, 1981). The term depression has come to encompass a broader range of entities, clearly heterogeneous albeit some similarities (Schuyler, 1974). The depressive continuum includes a feeling state familiar to most individuals, a grief reaction experienced by many persons, and a neurotic depressive reaction to stress (Schuyler, 1974). The milder forms of depression comprise about 75% of the depressed population (Greist, et al, 1979).

Chesler (1972), suggested that women in general, have much higher rates of depression than men. She contended that the nature and incidence of mental disorders among women are a reflection of women's secondary status and restricted roles in American society.

Women, in general, and Black women, in particular, are still allowed a very narrow range of appropriate roles and behaviors. When a Black woman does not accept these externally imposed definitions of her being, she poses a threat to those who wish to define her. If her attempts at self-affirmation are ridiculed, ignored, or greeted with contempt, frustration and depression are likely results. This was the case for the majority of the Black women in this paper. Depression was normal.

CULTURE SHOCK

"Culture shock" is usually reserved to describe the emotional reactions of a foreigner in a host country. It nonetheless seems to accurately describe the experiences of this sample of Black women on predominantly white campuses. The experiences of the sample paralleled the five stages of culture shock: incubation, crisis, transition, resolution, and re-entry (Oberg, 1958).

In the first or incubation stage of culture shock, individuals feel genuinely euphoric about the exciting new culture or environment around them. In the academic setting these euphoric feelings are sometimes mixed with pride and heightened esteem for having been admitted to graduate school or for having been hired in a prestigious new job--and therefore becoming, or at least being recognized as, a very highly qualified professional.

Black Americans have a tradition of believing "education is the way." But few who have this belief have attended predominantly white institutions at the graduate level, and fewer still will discuss or can discuss the travail involved in securing a degree from these institutions. It follows logically, then, that those who know education is the way, may not know the way to obtain that education or the pitfalls to be avoided in obtaining it. Accordingly, few Black Americans come to graduate school prepared for the psychological and emotional hurdles which await them.

As Anderson, Fierson, and Lewis (1979), noted, Blacks in predominantly white universities are often deceived into thinking that "in the liberal university atmosphere things are different, everyone gets a fair shake, the doors of opportunity are wide open, and Blacks have only themselves to blame if they do not succeed." Racism is no longer seen as a major problem. Unfortunately, too many Black women believe this mythology. The desire for this state of affairs to be true is often so strong that it blocks accurate assessment of the environment.

The real "shock" in culture shock comes about when individuals come to realize that their expectations of the academic environment are not being met and probably will never be met. This is the crisis stage. As Oberg (1958), described this stage, the individual must learn to deal with a continual series of disruptions in normal daily life activities. The individual experiences feelings of hostility toward those around her for being "unreasonable."

In the academic setting this stage is precipitated when the student's or the new professional's idealistic egalitarian expectations are trampled by reality. Figure 1 contains several of the most common expectations and illusionary beliefs about the academic environment held by the Black women in this sample.

Figure 1

ERRONEOUS AND SELF-DEFEATING BELIEFS ABOUT ACADEMIA

1. Highly educated people would not, (even could not), hold racist attitudes.
2. If people see that I am having a hard time, they will come to my assistance.
3. My advisor/dept. chair should have a personal concern about my feelings and my emotional well-being.
4. All the faculty are vastly superior human beings—omniscient (if not omnipotent as well).
5. I have to suffer in order to do well in graduate school.
6. My dissertation must present a totally new and revolutionary idea. It must be the major contribution to contemporary thought on the subject that I am studying.
7. I cannot understand statistics, and I will do very poorly in that class.
8. If I have an easy time on an exam, it must be because the instructor is patronizing me; they think I can't do "hard" work.
9. Because I have a Ph.D., my colleagues have to accept that I am capable and equal as well.
10. Professionals, especially my colleagues, would not be unethical.
11. If my colleagues see how hard I am working and how much I want to demonstrate my competency, they will reward me...at least through recognition.
12. My ideas are not good enough for publication.
13. If I were really bright, I would not have problems in school.
14. The students who talk a lot in class, (the high participators), have a much stronger knowledge base than I do. They are smarter than I am.
15. It is much more important for me to study every free minute than to take any time out for other things I want to do.

These fifteen statements represent consistent themes found in the belief systems of the women in the sample. Of course these statements are not far-fetched or totally unrealistic; and they do have some degree of "truth" in them. However, it is the rigidity with which these beliefs are held; their absolute nature, which makes them self-defeating. Wanting them to be true does not make them true. Accepting that these beliefs are erroneous and self-defeating is crucial for successful negotiation of the academic environment.

COPING STYLES DURING CRISIS

The second stage seemed to be the crucial point for most of the sample. It is at this stage that many of our most sensitive and competent graduate students and professionals become lost, emotionally, psychologically, even literally, The disequilibrium and depression precipitated by this crisis is generally managed by withdrawal. The withdrawal takes place from the environment and into the self. At a basic level the individual withdraws from participation in class and then withdraws from class altogether. At a deeper level, the individual withdraws from friends, acquaintances, and the academic environment, in general. The person is no longer "in circulation." At the most profound level, the person considers withdrawing from life itself. Unfortunately, suicide is often perceived as the best means of alleviating the hurt, anger, frustration, and indignation experienced by so many Black women during this stage. For most, however, the withdrawal is temporary, and then other coping mechanisms come into play.

The Black women in this sample demonstrated four other primary styles of coping with stressful events. These were denial, isolation, repression, and introjection. These four coping mechanisms seem to be fairly prevalent in Black American culture among all social classes. This particular set of coping mechanisms is exceptionally effective in blocking movement against a threat or against a harming agent. This set causes its users to consistently choose inaction as a means of resolving conflict which, of course, is no resolution at all.

It seems these coping mechanisms have persisted in Black American culture due to a cultural ethic which confuses faith with denial, forgiveness with repression, and humility with introjection. Merging these concepts has been disastrous for Black Americans. In the same way that Black people say education is the way without really knowing what that entails, "forgive and forget," is not always the best way to resolve a problem. Assertive methods of coping are usually more appropriate.

One way Black women have sought to deal with disillusionment is through denying that the anxiety producing event ever occurred. This often happens when a Black professional woman is the target of a racist or sexist statement; especially when directed by a colleague, and she says she didn't hear it. It also happens when obviously less qualified persons receive pay increments or are granted tenure while one's own academic salary and/or rank remain the same. The solution to feeling hurt is to deny these events occurred.

The second coping mechanism used by the women in this sample is isolation. This style of coping operates when the individual avoids recalling or perceiving connections between related events, information, or thought associations which might arouse anxiety. This mechanism is very similar to denial, but here the event itself is not denied. The recurring pattern is denied. One women in the sample reported consistently missing special study groups called by members of her research seminar. Even though she was the only person who "missed" these study sessions, it had not occurred to her that she was the only person other class members consistently "forgot" to tell about the sessions. It is crucial for us to remember that this is not an instance of a woman of low intelligence being duped. This is an example of her not perceiving an obvious pattern of discrimination because of its potency in causing negative feelings. This defense mechanism is, in fact confounded by intelligence. The more intelligent the individual, the more likely she can rationalize the behavior of others through isolation.

The third coping mechanism used by this sample is repression. Repression is essentially the censoring of memories, feelings, or perceptions that have high anxiety producing potential. In repression events are forgotten in the sense that they are not readily accessible to conscious memory. This defense or coping style is extremely powerful, because not only are the instances of discrimination "forgotten," but also attempts by others to uncover this information are met with resentment, dread, and anger, all designed to keep the negative hidden. The therapist's task here is to have the client see a painful event that she would not ordinarily see. Hence, it is reasonable that any attempts to uncover these painful memories would be met with whatever resistance the client could muster.

The fourth and perhaps most destructive coping mechanism used by the sample is introjection. In this coping style the woman defends against disillusionment in others by accepting personal blame or responsibility for the problems, herself. Guilt, loss of esteem, and depression are the inevitable result of this style of coping. This mechanism is so terribly destructive, because the individual actually takes the blame for something she did not do. At a minimal level this is what happens when a graduate student says, "I must have gotten confused about the time for the appointment" when the professor does not come. At a deeper level, this is what happens when the professional comes to believe she is not actually qualified for the promotion she was denied. At the most profound and most oppressive level, this is what happens when the Black woman comes to believe she deserves the discrimination she has to endure: it is her cross to bear.

All of these coping mechanisms, especially introjection, arise from the cultural sets of Black Americans. The values usually taught in Black families, and especially to Black women, center on maintaining relationships, thinking the best about everyone; trying to get along with others, always being ready to forgive transgressors, believing that everyone is a "child of God," and believing that no one is really a "bad" person.

For at least these reasons many Black women unconsciously engage in denial, isolation, repression and introjection when confronted with racism and sexism in academia. The Black woman's capacity for forgiving and her own resilience are used against her. The depression and self-doubt that arise from this stage leaves psychological scars which too often are permanent.

Fortunately, not all women get stuck in this second stage, and not all have to suffer it to the same extent. A major difference between those who are free and those who get stuck is that the former tend to be more analytic, more objective in their approaches to problem-solving, while the latter tend to be more personal-emotional. The former are also less concerned about personal approval from Anglo-Americans. For the latter "equality" means equality with whites, but "competition" means competition with Black women. The former are able to "see it like it is" and adapt, while the latter seem to be so appalled, so disappointed, and accordingly so frustrated, that they cannot extricate themselves from the downward spiral into depression. It is not that they do not comprehend...it is that they do not accept. It is this staunch refusal that lies at the core of their inability to adapt and successfully negotiate the system.

Black women who transcend the second stage of culture shock quickly move through the third, fourth, and fifth stages which are called transition, resolution, and re-entry respectively. In these stages the woman learns to understand the alien aspects of culture of academia, and to accept its contradictions. She learns to take what academia has to offer her and to discard what is irrelevant.

COUNSELING INTERVENTION

The counseling intervention used with this group was designed to reduce the symptoms of stress and depression by changing the client's perception of the environment, increasing her ability to master it, and facilitating her movement through the latter phases of culture shock. Since the majority of the stressors are inherent in the environment, it was important to reduce their level of threat and thereby reduce the degree of anxiety precipitated. Figure 2 illustrates the perceptual model upon which this intervention is based.

Figure 2
COGNITIVE/BEHAVIORAL MODEL OF RESPONSES TO
ENVIRONMENTAL STIMULI

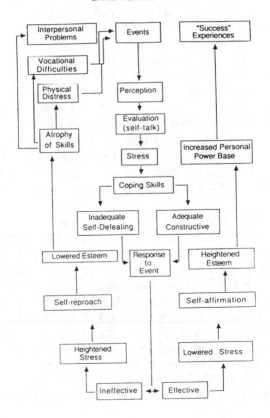

The intervention itself consisted of five steps. These are (1) acceptance of the client's emotional state, (2) affirmation, (3) shifting the client's locus of responsibility, (4) reinforcing the client's present coping skills, and (5) behavioral rehearsals.

The first two steps operate concurrently. They involve showing the client that you do, in fact, believe her subjective experience of reality is true for her. These steps involve demonstrating to the client that she is neither crazy nor hysterical. Challenging the client's belief system too early may add to distrust and/or lessen her esteem even further by suggesting she is not bright enough to see the obvious. Also, immediately offering alternatives to the client does not allow her to fully state her problems, or to state the interrelationships between her (1) expectations of the academic environment and how it has failed to meet them, (2) the coping mechanisms she has at her disposal and (3) her ability to effectively use them.

It is most important at this stage to let the client know that she has the right to feel the way that she does, that the way she feels is not unusual, and that she can still successfully negotiate the system by increasing her knowledge-base and coping skill repertoire. Support and encouragement are most important at this stage.

The next step involves balancing the client's locus of responsibility for her present feelings. Clients typically feel that they are completely responsible for what has happened to them and consequently, for how they feel. Sometimes, too, they feel that they are completely powerless in the situation and doomed to failure. The goal of this step is to have the client realize that, in fact, much of what happens to her is beyond her immediate control; but much more importantly she needs to realize how she **responds** to what happens to her **is** under control. The loss of confidence the client experiences is often the result of her perceived loss of ability to control what happens to her in the academic environment.

The usual one-to-one relationship between doing something and seeing expected results does not seem to exist. Because the client does not accept, denies, or does not actually see the functional relationship between behaviors in the academic environment, she may come to believe the relationships are random. Hence, she believes she cannot actively influence the events of her own life. She feels out of control.

A major goal for the client is to accept that what happens in the academic environment really does happen. She does not have to agree with it, nor does she have to like or justify it; but it is imperative that she acknowledges this is what it is. Any other position is dysfunctional, by definition, because it is a distortion of reality. This acceptance is one of the hardest tasks for most Black women. The hurt, anger, and resentment resulting from having been disrespected, ignored, and forced to exist in one more oppressive system are often nearly overwhelming. Perhaps what is even more frustrating is that even when Black women can vent their feelings, little change in the environment actually materializes.

It is important for the client to realize that the academic

environment operates on a different set of rules than she first thought. But these rules can be learned and used to the client's own advantage.

The final steps of the intervention involve determining how the client presently deals with problems, bolstering her effective problem-solving skills, deleting the self-defeating coping mechanisms, and increasing the client's repertoire of direct-action and cognitive coping strategies. Cormier and Cormier (1980) and Meichenbaum and Turk (1976) have provided an excellent summary of direct-action and cognitive-coping strategies and positive self-statements which would be useful during this phase of the intervention.

The single most important aspect of the final phase of the counseling intervention is, perhaps, behavioral rehearsal. Up to this point, the basic information about the academic environment and cognitive coping strategies would have provided some insight for the client. She certainly knows more, but she still may not act in a more effective manner without practice. Behavioral rehearsals are then designed to have the client practice behaving in a more effective manner in those situations which are particulary stressful for her. She is to practice not only acting differently but also thinking about the situation differently, as she role-plays these new behaviors.

Insight alone, without behavioral rehearsals, seems more useful before the problems associated with chronic stress become severe. Insight is also useful in acute stress reactions to situations. Overall, however, behavioral rehearsals seem to have the widest range of applicability. Knowing how to act in a stressful situation plus having "seen" oneself behave appropriately in the situation are apparently the necessary conditions for consistent stress reduction.

MAINTAINING PERSONAL WELL-BEING

In a very practical sense, in order to restore or to even maintain one's own personal well-being in the academic environment, one must attend equally to the mind, the body, and the spirit. Psychological wellness is maintained through a balance of academic and socio-emotional stimulation. Psychological well-being is maintained through nonabuse of coping mechanisms and through positive friendships held outside academia. It is essential that ideas, values, beliefs, and attitudes which originate outside the institution remain cherished by those in the institution. They form the core of the personal sense of self. Without them the individual becomes lost. Some of the values may need to be expanded to more adequately address the demands of the academic environment, but none should be discarded without very close examination. While everything "the old folks" said is no longer relevant, the majority of what they offered is still useful in some form, and in any case, none of what they said was given maliciously.

Physical well-being is maintained through proper attention to diet and to recreation. It is essential that some form of vigorous physical exercise remain an integral part of one's lifestyle. Exercise not only lessens the somatical aspects of anxiety, but it also helps to maintain physical attractiveness thereby enhancing self-esteem. A poor diet or vitamin deficient diet combined with harsh chemicals in water and soaps, often results in the loss of elasticity in the skin. Excessive amounts of coffee, candy and carbohydrates plus processed foods can change the body chemistry in a dysfunctional manner. One procedure found to be useful with this particular sample of Black women was increasing the amounts of vitamin E, vitamin C, and the B-complex group which were ingested.

Feeling good also means looking good. Attention to physical well-being means more than being well clothed, however. It means having an attitude of beauty--feeling desirable; feeling attractive. It means allowing oneself to be noticed rather than hoping one will be found. Also, while the exact amount of sleep needed varies among individuals, the general notion of about eight hours still seems appropriate. It is not necessary to stay up all night every night to be successful in academia.

Spiritual well-being means feeling oneself connected to forces or powers greater than oneself which serve as the source of one's vital essence and as one's point of connection with the universe. Spiritual well-being may be achieved in many ways. For most Black women it is found through formal Christian religion. For others it may be found in "peak experiences," altered states of awareness, or through other transcendental experiences. Regardless of the exact nature of the experience, this particular component seems to be quite necessary for holistic functioning; but because of its very nature, it is difficult to grasp, and a thorough explanation is well beyond the scope of this paper.

Personal well-being comes from a balance of these three factors in an individual's life. Over attention to any one of these factors also creates imbalance and eventual loss of well-being and health. Over attention distorts reality and creates distress for individuals when their ideas, values, and beliefs are not shared by others in the environment. Personal well-being means balance, flexibility, and direction.

PEER SUPPORT NETWORK

The peer-support network described in this paper is the result of attempting to design a proactive developmental intervention that would prevent some of the emotional/psychological problems that Black women experience on predominantly white campuses.

In the absence of the traditional African-American therapeutic groups, e.g. church, sororities, etc., the problem with many "formal" or student services interventions is that they are actually extensions of the institution. No matter how benign they may seem and no matter how many good intentions back these efforts, they somehow usually end up serving the interest of the institution which funds them. Somehow the students served by these programs never quite "take advantage" of what the program has to offer, and somehow the problems they are designed to address never quite get solved. Somehow they tend to reinforce the ideas that the majority of Black people just are not college, professional, or some other "type of material," and that if they would just conform they would be all right.

In truth, the goals and needs of the research institution are generally not those of the Black students who attend them. Many Black students come to this realization too late. The peer support network is designed to help Black women help themselves in their own best interest.

Figure 3 outlines the basic phases and steps of the peer support network, while Figure 4 outlines a counseling model.

Figure 3

PEER SUPPORT NETWORK

Phase I   Environmental Assessment

What support systems currently exist for Black women?
How adequate are these systems?
To what extent are they utilized?
How accessible are they?
What generic problems and issues exist for Black women in the environment?
What factors negatively affect the quality of life of Black women?
What human resources are available to address these needs?

Goal: to design a peer support system geared to the specific needs of the campus population.

Phase II   Implementation

Part 1. Building trust on a one-to-one basis.
         ("Each one reach one")
Part 2. Consciousness raising: Increasing political awareness.
         ("Each one teach one")
Part 3. Forming the basic peer support unit.
Part 4. Forming the peer support group.
Part 5. Use of the referral network.

Phase III   Evaluation

To what extent have loneliness and alienation been reduced among Black women?
To what extent has political sophistication been facilitated?
To what extent has personal esteem been enhanced?
To what extent has psychological growth and maturity been facilitated?
To what extent has academic achievement been heightened?

103

The intervention proposed here is comprised of both individual and group methods, and it is based on four major assumptions. First, it is assumed that the general disequilibrium experienced by most Black women is the result of conflict between their expectations of the academic environment and their actual experiences in academia. Secondly, it is assumed that the disequilibrium per se is not necessarily negative. Adjustments to it can be very negative, however. Thirdly, it is assumed that undergraduate, graduate, and post-graduate women are all susceptible to this source of stress. Lastly, it is assumed that successful resolution of this conflict can be partially balancing of academic, socio/emotional, and physical stimulation.

Figure 4

INDIVIDUAL COUNSELING INTERVENTION: A COGNITIVE/BEHAVIORAL MODEL

A. Acceptance of the client's emotional state.
B. Affirmation of the client's perception of reality.
C. Adjusting the client's locus of responsibility.
D. Assessing the client's existing coping skills.
   1. Helping the client better use those she has.
   2. Teaching the client new direct-action coping skills.
      a. Collecting objective or factual information about the stressful situation.
      b. Identifying escape routes or general ways to decrease the stress.
      c. Mental-relaxation methods.
      d. Physical-relaxation methods.
   3. Teaching the client new cognitive coping skills.
      a. Self-directed thought stopping.
      b. Self-directed positive reinforcement.
E. Behavioral rehearsal

Generally, then, this intervention approaches disorientation and loss of esteem in Black women on white campuses as a temporary failure of coping strategies. The goal of the intervention is to increase the woman's sense of personal mastery of the academic environment by increasing her repertoire of effective coping and problem-solving skills before she experiences severe difficulties, and by also providing emotional support while she is in crisis until the problem-solving process can be initiated. Accordingly, the intervention is not only crisis oriented, but it is also developmental.

This intervention is not seen to be the responsibility of the institution. On the contrary, it is perceived to be a manifestation of the responsibility of Black people to care for each other. It is intended to be an example of Kujichagulia (self-determination) and Umoja (unity). Also the intervention is not designed to be anti-white or anti-male. This is a pro-Black, proactive intervention designed to enhance the psychological growth, maturity, and personal functioning of Black women. It is offered to Black women for Black women.

GETTING STARTED

Since the number of Black women at each institution varies, and since the number and kinds of existing support systems also varies, it will perhaps be more useful to describe the major elements and procedures of the intervention and then secondly discuss how it might be applied in various settings.

An informal peer support network consists of three or more individuals who voluntarily have formed a coalition designed to increase each other's success experiences. This intentional unit is different from just a group of three friends, because the expressed purpose of this group is the pooling of resources for mutual success. Close friendships may develop but are not necessary for the unit to be successful. The purpose of the unit is to enhance each member's ability to negotiate the system through increased personal power derived from emotional support and accurate information regarding the environment.

Informal peer support networks are traditional in Black American culture. However, the ability to readily form these alliances has apparently been lost. This has happened, perhaps, because many Black Americans have taken them for granted. Secondly, it happens because unfortunately many Black Americans have not been socialized to value this type of behavior. Thirdly, for whatever reasons, many Black Americans have very low levels of trust for each other. Part of this actually comes from Black Americans having limited experiences with other Black Americans. This is obviously a fairly new phenomenon, which could not have existed 30 years ago, but one which is common among undergraduates in predominantly white institutions though not so prevalent among graduate students. It also happens because of the competitive nature of formal education. The high achieving Black woman, especially the one who attends graduate and professional schools, must be competitive. Most often she is competitive with herself and is consistently striving to improve her last performance. This internal sense of competition is usually positive and helpful.

Self-esteem is derived from knowing that she has improved, done better, or in some way progressed. Sometimes she is compelled to receive recognition for having outperformed others in the academic arena. The competition with others for grades extends to other areas such as, attention, approval or whatever else is external. Self-esteem comes from seeing oneself superior to others or by seeing others as inferior to oneself. While this behavior is often modeled in academia and reinforced, it also causes other members of the environment...especially other Black women...to be seen as rivals for the same rewards. The competition itself pulls potential allies apart. This gives rise to the paradoxical situation in which close relationships are sought and simultaneously avoided. The inconsistent communication and nonverbal behavior which arises from this conflict does nothing to promote trust. Much of the bizarre behavior that transpires between Black people at predominantly white campuses is a manifestation of lack of trust and/or fear of rejection.

ESTABLISHING TRUST

Establishing trust is the key procedure of the support network. No trust—no networks. Trust takes both time and commitment to establish. It is cultivated on essentially a one-to-one basis. So the first part of the proposed intervention involves individuals establishing relationships with each other.

Trust is established by verbally and nonverbally greeting other Black people even if the others do not at first return the greeting. Trust cannot be established if the greeter gets angry or otherwise "cops an attitude" because the person who did not speak is suspected of having negative attitudes toward Black people or superiority feelings toward herself. Establishing trust involves patience and a commitment to eliminating irrational suspicion among Black women. At a very basic level, establishing trust means being consistent; It means doing what you say you will do when you say you will do it. It means being reliable.

This first phase of the support network is designed to reduce the unfamiliarity, the alien quality of the new environment. It is designed to let individuals know that their presence has been acknowledged and that they are not invisible.

The second phase of the intervention involves building a basic relationship with other Black women in the environment. It means being careful to notice new faces on campus, taking the time to meet them, and, most importantly, taking the time to assess their basic knowledge of the academic environment with particular emphasis on their knowledge of their own major and/or department.

Important issues to be discussed include: the relationship between student and advisors, the differences between assistant, associate, and full professors, how to select electives, the importance of study groups, relationship between departments or schools, requirements for tenure and promotion, the difference between "hard money" and "soft money," differences between P.A's (project assistants), R.A.'s (research assistants), and T.A.'s (teaching assistants), etc. Those who have been in the environment and who have been successful in negotiating it sometimes forget what and how they felt when they first entered it; and they forget, also, when they did not know what they now know about it. This phase of the support network is designed to increase the woman's problem solving ability by increasing her knowledge base.

The next part of the intervention involves promoting the ideas of self-reliance, self-determination, and mutual support. The goal of this intervention is to facilitate the establishment of cooperative rather than competitive goal structures. This basic peer support unit (three people), increases in size by having each member repeat parts 1, 2, and 3 of phase II of the intervention.

THE PEER SUPPORT GROUP

The first three parts of the implementation phase of the peer support network are more preventive/developmental than remedial. They are organized to prevent the development of problems by providing information that is not systematically taught in academic courses. The goal is to provide Black women with accurate information that will help them make more appropriate plans and life decisions. In this sense it is prevention oriented.

The peer support group is growth, prevention, and, also, remediation oriented. It is prevention oriented in that it is designed to give women support through some of the rough spots in their lives. It is designed to prevent any serious interpersonal or vocational difficulties from being incurred. It facilitates psychological growth and maturity in the sense that it provides participants incentive, support, and motivation to make changes that are in their best interest. Participants are motivated to take actions and maximize their personal power through self-affirming behaviors.

The peer support group is remedial for those women who have been swallowed by the vortex of self-defeating attitudes and behaviors generated in academia. Most of these women could probably extricate themselves at some point without this intervention. However, the peer support group allows them to recover more quickly and with less emotional/psychological damage. Figure 5 illustrates the peer support group model.

Figure 5

PEER SUPPORT NETWORK SELF-HELP GROUP MODEL

Basic Constructs

1. The full potential of the group is awesome.
2. Action resolves problems.
3. Social responsibility maintains behavior.

Group Model

1. Group represents the community.
2. Personal identity is clarified.
3. Problem-network is defined and clarified.
4. Members are related by a common problem.

Leader's Role

1. Models appropriate behaviors.
2. Makes process observations.
3. Encourages total group participation.
4. Summarizes

Techniques

1. Brainstorming
2. Confrontation
3. Problem Census
4. Behavioral Reversal
5. Role Playing

Peer Support Network Self-Help Group Model Continued

Functions of Group Members

1. To generate alternative solutions to each other's problems.
2. To provide feedback to other members.
3. To provide support.
4. To assume leadership role.

Group Members' Goals

1. To gain self-confidence.
2. To gain self-respect through helping others.
3. To develop self-sufficiency.
4. To heighten sense of social responsibility.

The curative factors at work in the peer support group include instillation of hope, orientation to reality catharsis, imparting information, mutual trust, caring, understanding, acceptance, altruism, universality, support, and cohesiveness. While the group is meant to be therapeutic, it does not have to be a therapy group.

REFERRAL SYSTEM

The next portion of the peer support network is called into play when some members are found to be experiencing such levels of distress in their lives that professional help is necessary. The peer support network needs to compile the names of campus and community resource persons skilled in crisis intervention and professional support services for Black people. This information is provided in the same way that all other information is provided. When a support group member uses the referral system, the role of the support group, or of individuals in the support network, is to simply offer their support and to offer whatever help they can offer.

The final part of the intervention involves evaluating how well the network is working. Functionally this means making sure no Black woman has to feel alienated, lonely, abandoned in a hostile environment. Practically, the network will probably not include every Black women on campus or every member will not be involved to the same degree. The network is designed to make sure that Black women know that they have the option to participate and are invited to participate in any way that they can.

One of the basic truths of contemporary black American life is that no one negotiates the academic system in a predominantly white university without undergoing some change. **SOME OF THE CHANGES ARE FOR THE BETTER, AND SOME ARE NOT. IT IS AN ILLUSION, HOWEVER, TO BELIEVE THAT YOU WILL NOT CHANGE.** Even those who have the greatest confidence, ability, and coping skills are affected. The effects of the environment are inescapable. Further, it is chronic rather that acute stress that takes its toll. Accordingly, the sophisticated sojourner must consider how to maintain her own psychological, emotional, and physical well-being as well as how to prevent damage to her psyche. She must actively maintain what she has, as she strives to gain more.

Support is essential for everyone, and the support network has a place for everyone. The stronger help the less strong. The experienced help the new, and all help each other retain their vital qualities: the integrity, creativity, sensitivity, and sense of justice each brings to the environment. This is the way the network functions.

The major curative factor of the support network is community reconstruction. It strengthens the bands of kinship which have traditionally existed among Black people. It provides continuity. It provides a place to be. For many the Black community no longer physically exists. There is no Black neighborhood. But in truth, the Black community exists wherever Black people are actively engaged in self-determination and mutual support, and wherever "Black is beautiful" is felt. If those values have been forgotten or if they were never learned or if they have been misplaced, the peer support network can revive them. The peer support network is not a new idea; it is not a revolutionary idea, but it is an attitude of revolution.

A major conclusion of Noble's (1956) study of the college education of Black women was that their education was substandard.

Four specific themes seemed to run through the recommendations from her respondents. They are:
1. The need for vocational and personal counseling.
2. The need for a more functional "realistic" education.
3. The need for education that develops good human relations.
4. The need for education that promotes self-acceptance.

Dorsey's (1981) replication of Noble's (1956) study revealed similar recommendations: Dorsey's sample expressed a desire for:
1. Improvements in the area of career counseling of Black women.
2. Improvements in the area of personal counseling. (Specifically mentioned was helping women develop self-confidence, independence, and a knowledge of self).
3. More courses related to Black Studies areas. (Specifically mentioned were Black male/female relationships and courses that focus on the social and psychological stress particular to the Black women in the American society.
4. More Black female role models as college professors, counselors, and top level administrators employed by institutions of higher education.

For 30 years Black women have been waiting for institutions of higher education to address their particular needs, and for 30 years they have not been heard. The peer support network is offered as an alternative to waiting another 30 years. We already possess all that is needed to accomplish our goals. The plan exists, and the time for action is now.

References

Anderson, W., Frierson, H., & Lewis, T., (1979), Black Survival in White Academe. **Journal of Negro Education.** 48, 92-102.

Beck, A., (1976), Cognitive Therapy and Emotional Disorders. New York: International University Press.

Burns, D. D., (1981), **Feeling Good: The New Mood Therapy.** New York: Signet Books.

Cannon, W. B., (1939), **The Wisdom of the Body.** New York: Doubleday

Chesler, P., (1972), **Women and Madness.** New York: Doubleday

Cormier, W. H. & Cormier, L. S., (1980), Interviewing Strategies for Helpers: A Guide To Assessment, Treatment, and Evaluation. Monterey, California: Brooks/Cole Publishing Company.

Didos-Ritsma, S., (1982), Effectiveness of Biofeedback Training and Group counseling in the Prevention of Academic Underachievement Due to Stress Induced Anxiety. Unpublished Manuscript, Dept. of Counseling & Guidance, University of Wisconsin-Madison.

Dorsey, R. T., (1981), The Effects of Black Student Protests on Higher Education as Perceived by a Select Group of Black Females. Unpublished Dissertation; School of Education, University of Iowa.

Ellis, A., (1970), **The Essence of Rational Psychotherapy: A Comprehensive Approach to Treatment.** New York: Institute for Rational Living.

Exum, H. A., (1977), **Going to Class Without Going to Pieces.** Minneapolis: St. Mary's Junior College.

Greist, T. H., Eishens, R. R., Klein, M. H. & Faris, T. W., (1979), Antidepressant Running. **Psychiatric Annals.** 9, 134-140.

Lazarus, R. S. (1966) **Psychological Stress and the Coping Process.** New York: McGraw-Hill.

Meichenbaum, D., (1986), Cognitive Behavior Modification. In F.H. Kanfer & A. P. Goldstein, (Eds.) **Helping People Change.** (pp 346-380) New York: Pergamon Press.

Meichenbaum, D. & Turk, D., (1976), The Cognitive Behavioral Management of Anxiety, Anger, and Pain. In P.O. Davidson (Ed.) **The Behavioral Management of Anxiety, Depression and Pain.** New York: Brunner/Mazel.

Noble, T. L., (1956), **The Negro Woman's College Education.** New York: Columbia Teachers College Press.

Oberg, K., (1958), Culture Shock and the Problem of Adjustment to New Cultural Environments. Washington, D.C.: U.S. Dept. of State, Foreign Service Institute.

Schuyler, D., (1974), Counseling Suicide Survivors: Issues and Answers. **Omega: Journal of Death and Dying.** 4, 313-321.

Selye, H., (1975), Stress without Distress. New York: Signet.

Relating to Black Students

Sandra J. Foster, Ph.D.
Grambling State University

ABOUT THE AUTHOR

Dr. Sandra J. Foster is an assistant professor in the School of Social Work at Grambling State University. Dr. Foster is the President of the Faculty Senate at Grambling and was elected as Teacher of the Year for 1985-86 in the School of Social Work. She is the advisor for the Student Association of Black Social Workers and the Nigerian Student Association.

Dr. Foster teaches a weekly seminar on **How to study for success.** The seminar includes information on how to take notes from lectures and in books, how to read faster, vocabulary building, how to study math, how to negotiate with students, professors and professionals, how to make speeches and related subjects.

She received her B.S. from Central State University, Wilberforce, Ohio, her MSSW in Child Welfare and Ph.d in Social Welfare from the University of Wisconsin, Madison.

Dr. Foster has served as an Assistant Professor at Stephen F. Austin State University, as a project assistant at UW-Madison, and as a teacher in several metropolitan school districts. She continues to conduct workshops at professional conferences and writes on a variety of topics.

INTRODUCTION

Although recruitment of Black students appears to be on the increase in the nation's colleges and universities, the retention rate continues to decline. Part of the problem is that many students lack the proper attitudes and values necessary for survival in an academic environment. This article provides some insight into why some students have developed attitudes that keep them from remaining in school and offers strategies for what can be done about it.

RELATING TO BLACK STUDENTS

by Dr. Sandra J. Foster

When teaching, counseling, or advising students, it helps to understand cultural diversity and the effect it has on why people do the things they do. This knowledge is most crucial when the students are Black. Many Black students do not share the same values and beliefs about education as those generally accepted by the dominant society. Although all Black students are not the same, those from the United States share a common historical experience which has strongly influenced their attitudes about attending school. This common experience is slavery.

By understanding the slave experience and the effect it has had on Black students' attitudes towards education, one is better able to help the student identify and eliminate destructive academic behaviors. The task is not to give students excuses for their behavior; it is to help them with constructive methods for securing a strong education.

THE INFLUENCE OF SLAVERY ON BLACK STUDENTS' BEHAVIOR

During slavery blacks were not allowed to read or write. Even though many slaves did learn to read, they did so under the threat of severe punishment. Consequently, Black children were not encouraged to read for their own protection. Parents did not expose their children to reading or writing materials in the home. Bed time and other stories were communicated orally, not written.

This pattern of not encouraging reading and writing remained with Black families long after slavery ended. Many Black families still do not display reading or writing material in their homes, read to their children, or encourage their children to read. Therefore, the children do not develop a positive attitude about reading or writing and the pernicious tradition initiated by the master is perpetuated by the slave. Some Black children become even more apprehensive about reading and writing when they enter school.

Many are turned off by subject matter that lacks clear, positive, exciting examples of Black reality. That is especially true of the child who was not encouraged to read at home before beginning school. Although the images are more positive today than before, Blacks are still not depicted very positively in the average text. Add to this the Black child in the predominantly Black school setting who is forced to read stories about the history of white families and is constantly bombarded with pictures of white families and their achievements. Many students who do read are sometimes not able to comprehend the subject matter. For example, many texts use words, phrases and experiences that are unfamiliar to Black children. References to common foods, furniture, plants, etc., may not be understood. Some common yet unfamiliar terms include artichoke, eggs benedict, bagels, yams, credenza. Although the student may correctly pronounce the word, he or she may not know the meaning; and if that is the case, he or she may be too ashamed to ask. Additionally, some students' comprehension is thwarted by reference to unknown people, places or events. Add this to the unfamiliar words, and it is easy to see why some students give up on reading.

Some of these same students who have given up on reading and writing are entering the university systems. Since slavery and later Jim Crowism and racial segregation prohibited Blacks from entering systems of higher education, many of these students are first generation college students. Therefore, they have not benefited from observing the behavior of parents or other relatives who have already completed college. They do not come to school having seen a parent study at home or go to the library to prepare for tests or assignments. They have not heard their parents or older siblings discuss class materials or the quality of individual instructors. They tend to attend school blindly, groping for the path to a passing grade. They do not understand how to take notes, prepare for class or to negotiate with their instructors. Since many have limited reading and writing skills, they lack the foundation essential for successful achievement.

During slavery Blacks were forced to work but were not allowed to enjoy the benefits of their labor as did other members of society. No matter how skilled their performance, the slaves remained tied to the master for their material well-being. Even after slavery was legally abolished, Blacks still remained dependent on whites for their material existence. While other students attended college in order to enhance their chances of accumulating money, property, freedom of choice and movement, education for Blacks has not resulted in similar opportunities. Unemployment is higher, and the pay scales are lower for Black college graduates than for whites. Additionally, Blacks are not able to live, work, or play where they choose no matter what the education.

These inequities serve as a disincentive for the Black student. The attitude becomes, **"Why work yourself to death trying to get through school when your chances of survival are cut in half before you even begin to compete with your fellow graduates."**

The student with this defeatist attitude, then comes in contact with you, the teacher, counselor, or advisor. What can you do to change this destructive behavior?

ENCOURAGING POSITIVE ACADEMIC BEHAVIOR

The first step is to probe for academic deficiencies and destructive educational attitudes in a very empathetic, non-threatening manner. Realize that the student may have had 12 years of practice hiding his/her shortcomings. Find ways to get the student to write and read out loud. One technique to use, if the class is small enough, is to have each student read a section of the syllabus during the first class meeting. For larger classes, especially those with smaller Lab sections, this individual reading activity can take place in small groups that have been developed to work on a specific activity. You might find some students who claim that they have forgotten their glasses and cannot see the print. For these students you might insist that they read aloud to you when they get their glasses or have them to read material that has been enlarged.

To probe for writing deficiencies during the first class session, have the students write a short paragraph on who they are, why they are enrolled in your particular class, how they think they will benefit from the class, and what they plan to do to receive a passing grade. This will give you an opportunity to determine the effectiveness of the student's grammar, punctuation, sentence structure, and ability to connect ideas. Deficiencies in comprehension can be identified through quizzes that are given within the first two weeks of class. At least two or three short quizzes - one multiple choice, one true false, and one essay within the first two weeks will help you determine how well the student understands the class lectures and reading material.

With the information from the reading activity, the short paragraph, and the early quizzes, you should have a pretty good idea of which students need additional attention. Now you can confront the student with the information you have documented. Talk with him or her about the deficiencies and how it will affect his or her chances in school and in the work setting. Encourage the student to seek help. Do not accept any excuses for why the student doesn't have time to seek help. Remember he or she has had 12 years of practice in not doing. You want the student to practice doing.

After you have referred the students, periodically check with them outside of class to see if the assistance is useful. Don't take their word for it until you are sure it is helping. Ask them again to read out loud, write a paragraph, or verbally quiz them on the class material. Whatever you do, don't give up. A student may not take your advice until after the fifth or sixth time you have given it. Don't give up.

You might find that the student is reluctant to take your advice because he or she is overwhelmed, especially the student who does poorly on two or more of the three measures. For this student you might be introducing too much change at one time. You might need to prioritize the students needs, then break them down to small objectives that can be worked on one at a time. Each time an objective is reached, the student will have more incentive to go forward.

Many first generation students' class behavior is not appropriate for academic success. They may not know when to interrupt the instructor, how to formulate and ask questions, how to take lecture notes, how to behave when the instructor must leave the room, or how to wait their turn during class discussions.

In developing their sense of "somebodyness," the appropriate classroom behaviors were not included. Instead the student may be recognized because he or she is an athlete, musician, fancy dresser, or good looking. Since these qualities have helped them to achieve status, they may not realize the need for a reputation as a scholar.

These students can sometimes create problems in class by being disruptive, encouraging other students to be disruptive, or they may not attend class. When you witness this behavior, it is best to take the student aside and explain the behavior and how it is interfering with their academic success. Help them to channel this behavior to more constructive activities. Convince them that the additional reputation as a scholar can only add to their status and that they might even help influence others. Remember that this advice is best if presented in an empathetic, nonthreatening manner.

In working with Black students it helps to understand why they do what they do. Although we are not able to change the why, we can change what they do by understanding the why. Just like it took time for slavery to have an effect on Black student behavior, it will take time for teachers, counselors, and advisors to effectively change their behavior. We must not get caught up in the TV series syndrome where a problem is developed and solved within an hour long series. It will take time, patience, and plenty of caring and concern. We must be willing to go beyond the traditional methods because we are dealing with nontraditional minds. We must be willing to walk with the students through the library, take them into our homes and guide them through their classes. Only then will they develop the ultimate trust in our personal and professional competence which is necessary for us to help them change their values and behavior.

This does not mean that we should spoon feed black students. Instead we must help them remove self-destructive barriers to their academic success by being firm, yet demonstrating concern about what happens to them and be able to communicate those feelings.

Chapter 6

Elements of a Chicano Student Support Program

Louis Sarabia
New Mexico State University

ABOUT THE AUTHOR

Mr. Louis Sarabia is Director of Chicano Programs at New Mexico State University. He received his B.A. and M.A. degrees from New Mexico Highlands University and is currently working on his Ph.D at Laurence University. For over a decade he has been a leader in establishing successful programs for Chicano students. He has taught at the university level as well as directed a variety of special services programs for students. Mr. Sarabia serves as a resource person on a number of issues related to Chicano concerns.

INTRODUCTION

The author contends that a successful minority support program consists of six basic factors. These are:

(1) a clear definition of the program, its "mission",
(2) proper administrative placement and strong support,
(3) proper staffing,
(4) appropriate functions and flexibility in programming,
(5) good inter-institutional relationships and
(6) an honest evaluation system.

In addition, there should be continuous contact with student organizations, cultural programming, and research to determine program effectiveness. In this paper Mr. Sarabia expands on these factors and shows how they were incorporated into the Chicano student support program at New Mexico State University.

ELEMENTS OF A CHICANO STUDENT SUPPORT PROGRAM

by Louis Sarabia

Mission

Every organization which expects to be successful must have an idea of where it is going, and this is doubly so if the organization or program is directed at ethnic/racial minorities. I would recommend a written statement of "mission." This should be no more than two or three sentences long and should contain the **basic raison d'etre** of the program. What is the purpose of the program?

The purpose or "Mission Statement" of the Chicano Programs Office at New Mexico State University (NMSU) states that **"The Chicano Programs Office serves as an educational advocate for Chicano students and is involved in all areas affecting a student's life. It also provides educational services and experiences which are designed to enable students to successfully achieve their educational goals."** Very simply this tells the institution, the public and our students what we are about.

Next, one should also have a written list of functions. These outline the day-to-day activities with which your program is concerned, and all of these should fit neatly into the "mission" statement. If you are doing something that has nothing to do with your "mission", there is either something seriously wrong with the "mission" or with the office.

Funding

There are three basic approaches to the establishment and funding of a Chicano student support program. First, the program can be entirely institutionally funded. Second, it can be entirely supported by outside funding sources, either private foundations or federal grants, in most cases. Third, it can be funded by a combination of sources.

Administrative Placement and Support

Administratively the program can be structured in a variety of ways. First, and to my way of thinking, best, it can have its own staff and administrators who report directly to either a Vice President or Dean. The key word here is directly. Second, the administrators and staff of the program may have joint appointments, serving part time in the Chicano services program and part time in another segment of the university. This may be in an area of student affairs or in an academic department. The problem with this arrangement is that often the demands placed on an individual are heavy and instead of having a 50-50 working arrangement, it soon becomes a 60-40 or 75-25 situation. This quickly will lead to burnout and frustration, particularly if, as is most often the case, salaries are not commensu-

rate with the work required. Student demands can also bring heavy
pressures; and if the Chicano programs staff is not available, when
the students feel they should be, this can lead to complaints from the
students, under-utilization of services, a perception of non-necessity
by the university community, and eventually dismantling of the
program.

In terms of office placement within the existing structure of the
institution, there is quite a bit of controversy. I have served under
a Dean of Students and a Dean of Arts and Sciences (Wyoming), a
Director of Ethnic Studies (New Mexico Highlands University), an
Academic Vice President and the Vice President of Student Affairs (New
Mexico State University). I have not found my effectiveness seriously
impaired in any of these situations, but this may be a factor of
personality. I know that the original purpose of placing our Chicano
Programs office under the Vice President for Academic Affairs at NMSU
was for protection. At Wyoming we moved from the Dean of Students to
the Dean of Arts and Science because of greater flexibility in
programming and funding. Based on my experience, the key factor seems
to be working with someone who is supportive and willing to be your
advocate.

Functional Responsibilities, Flexibility and Evaluation

At my institution we have broken down functions into four
categories:

1) **Internal Coordinating** functions refer to budgetary and other
administrative functions.

2) **Orienting functions** serve to clarify and facilitate relationships among students, the institution and the community at large.
Orienting functions include, for example, new student orientation,
academic advisement, and serving as a student organizational sponsor.

3) **Supportive** functions provide for the physical and emotional
needs of students to allow maximum utilization of their college
experience. This category consists of serving as a student advocate
with the student government, encouraging students to participate in
co-ed recreational programs, guaranteeing equal access to university
facilities, and in many cases, attempting to change university policies or procedures which have a negative impact on Chicano students.

4) **Educative** functions are those activities which promote learning directly or which improve the formal instructional process. This
area might contain such items as Chicano studies curriculum development, establishment of Chicano studies library, tutorial programs
(though this might also be included in the previous function), a
textbook loan program, and typing service.

Each of these functional areas should have a list of activities
with which the office is concerned. Periodically the list of functional responsibilities should be checked to see if there are changes
which should be made, to delete functions and to add new functions as
needed. This type of organizing allows flexibility and adaptabilty to
changing situations, and to be effective, given today's economy and

the move away from idealism, requires both flexibility and adaptability. For example, in 1974 one of our functions was recruitment of Chicano students. We had approximately 1100 Chicano students on our campus at that time. Today, with over 3000 Chicano students, and considering the fact that the Admissions Office now has Chicano personnel involved in recruitment, our function has changed to **"assisting the Admission Office in recruitment."** This is a subtle change, but it saves us money and time which can be better used elsewhere. At the same time, however, Chicano enrollment is closely monitored on a semester by semester basis, and should enrollment dip, we are in a position to once again become actively involved in recruitment.

Another example is our tutorial program. In 1974 we didn't have one; however, it became evident that we were losing many students who just couldn't handle the academic loads required. This past academic year we spent about 75 per cent of our budget on tutors; we tutored about 250 students and provided an income for about 24 student tutors. (It should also be noted that our institutional drop out rate is about 35 per cent, while the drop out rate for Chicano students is 30 per cent.) In addition, in talking to students who requested tutors we found that many were being poorly advised; and as a result, many were carrying more credit hours than they could properly handle based on their previous academic background. So, our office became involved in working with the academic advising centers.

Evaluation

Having a written document assists in the evaluation of your program. Evaluators, either external or internal, have some place to start their study of your program, and your written functions help in defending your program should anyone question its efficacy. Meanwhile, any weaknesses found can be added to the list of functions. One of the major aspects of having a list of functional responsibilities lies in explaining your program to others, particularly faculty members at your institution. Often they will be surprised to find that you have a "mission" and a way to achieve it. This is surprising, because most academic departments are not as organized, and one thing academics admire, or at least talk about a lot, is organization.

In having your program evaluated, it is wise to indicate to your supervisor that you wish to have it evaluated on a regular basis. Given the amount of resistance to most evaluations, this will be a pleasant surprise to your chief supervisor. The evaluation can be either internal, utilizing staff members of your institution, or it can be external. The key to a good evaluation is in having good evaluators. You should suggest individuals to your supervisor who are knowledgeable in the area of student affairs, empathetic to minority students, and who are scrupulously respected by their colleagues. Any attempt to "load" a committee will be obvious and the results of the evaluation tainted. This applies to external evaluators as well.

Intra-institutional Relationships

Especially important in the organization of a Chicano Programs Office is the establishment of working relationships with other offices. This means that if your mission and functions require you to work with the housing, admissions, health center, placement and counseling centers, and financial aids, you had best know who the key people are in each of these areas. You should know them by name and you should know as much as possible about what they do and their procedures for doing things. In understanding how other offices operate, you become aware of problems which may affect the students whom you seek to serve. For example, the deadline for financial aid applications at our institution is March 1. Approximately 50% of our Chicano students fail to submit their applications on time, and one of our major problems is the student who hasn't received financial aid. We have been working to overcome this problem with our students, and at the same time we have tried to establish good working relationships with the financial aids office which allows us to help these late applicants.

You should also be prepared to offer these offices assistance. My office staff assists with the New Student Orientation programs. As a result, we make early contact with incoming and transfer Chicano students, we receive updated training on student advisement, and we learn how the system is operating. In addition, this provides us with the further opportunity of suggesting ways to improve new student services and thus better serve our students.

As another example, several years go we "loaned" our Ballet Folklorico to the Housing Department for a regional conference which they were hosting. Our group provided entertainment and was well received by the visitors. A year or two later, we hosted the National Association of Ballet Folkloricos' conference; approximately 375 people attended. When we approached the housing office for assistance in housing the participants, they were extremely helpful. They provided us with special housing rates, staff at sign-in time, and also provided meeting rooms within the dorms. As a result, most of the conference participants were more than pleased with their accommodations, and were favorably impressed by our office and its institutional support.

It has also been my experience that getting to know secretaries and custodians can sure make life easier. In most cases, a departmental secretary knows as much about the department as does the department head and usually is more available. Send your favorite secretary a card and a flower during National Secretarys' Week and you'll have a very helpful friend. Custodians can be of tremendous help when you need something moved, cleaned, extra paper towels because you're making posters and need clean-up materials, and when you're working late and don't want to be disturbed. We usually have a potluck dinner once or twice a year and our building custodians are always invited or a special plate is left for them to heat up in the office microwave.

All too often directors of minority programs are isolated from the rest of the "academic world." You should make it a point to serve on as many committees as possible; and when you get on a committee, do your share of the work! The inside information which you will gather in committee meetings is invaluable and can often provide clues as to changes or shifts in institutional thinking and policies. You will also become acquainted with individuals whom you might otherwise not meet. This past year, my staff and I have been involved in formulating an alcohol policy for the university, looking at procedures for chartering student organizations, serving on the committee planning the university's centennial celebration, and have participated in decisions affecting the computerization of the Student Affairs Division as well as the North Central Accreditation task force. While it can be argued that these activities have little to do with Chicano students, indirectly or directly, they will have an impact on our program and our ability to serve our students.

Retention

In today's economic and academic environment, **RETENTION,** is the name of the game. Any program, new or established, on any college campus must have retention at its core, or it will soon be facing serious problems in terms of attacks from academic programs which see their budgets being frozen or cut and are out looking for new funding. Many minority programs were not popular with administrators and faculty to begin with, and often they will find any excuse to either diminish or eliminate the programs. However, if a program is doing a good job of retention, that program will likely be spared any undue hardship. Retention means much more that just more tuition to the institution; each student who comes to college and stays spends money for dorm rooms, meals, books, t-shirts, records, etc. For example, if we assume a student provides $5000 to the institution each year, the loss of 100 students means a loss in revenue of $500,000. Particularly hard hit will be the housing and food services areas which usually employ large numbers of people. A loss of 500 students is a loss of two and one quarter of a million dollars! If you can develop a program aimed at keeping students in school, then you are helping the institution make money; and education is a business!

One of the obvious retention devices is a tutorial program. Our office pays for tutors for students who apply for assistance. The tutee pays no fee. We have identified four or five areas which appear to be most requested and we concentrate on providing tutors in those areas. If your program doesn't have enough of a budget to provide such a program, there are alternate sources of funding. There are federal programs which provide funding for support programs. In addition, many businesses and corporations which recruit students graduating from your institution often will support programs which help minority students, especially if there is a direct link to the type of student they are recruiting. An example is providing math tutors for minority engineering students. The student government is another source of funding, although in this case the tutorial program might have to be open to all students. (In this case you are helping your perception as a segment of the institution, and in most cases Chicano programs, in fact all minority programs, need all the good public relations they can get).

If you have, as we do, organizations based on academic disciplines, (Engineering, Education, Business), you can often find free tutorial help within the organization. Local professional organizations such as the Chicano Bar Association, the Hispanic Chamber of Commerce, and the Society of Hispanic Professional Engineers or Mexican American Engineering Society might also provide support. You need to be creative in approaching funding matters.

In addition to having a tutorial program, you should also keep meticulous records regarding the number of requests, number being served, and final results in terms of the grade received by the tutee in the class in which the student was tutored. Comparisons should be made from one semester to the next and over a period of time as well.

Other student retention programs on campus should be heavily utilized as well. We make referrals to our Learning Assistance Center, to other tutorial programs and to the Special Student Services program. Again, it is vital that one establish good working relationships with these offices to insure that your clientele is served properly and to facilitate follow-up.

Student Organizations

Student organizations can provide a number of benefits. Student organizations and their activities keep your program in the public's eye. Our students sponsor a homecoming queen candidate each year as well as a homecoming float, always with a cultural "difference." They are also active in blood drives, food drives, and coordinated efforts this past year to assist the victims of Mexico City's earthquake. Student organizations also provide you with an opportunity to develop leadership, and this is something which our community of **raza** desperately needs.

Cultural Activities

Each spring we sponsor a full week of cultural activities. This year marked our fifteenth Chicano Week. We have found the state film library can provide quality films at extremely low cost and the student activities office provides funds for speakers, musical concerts, comedians, **teatro**, panel discussions, and any other number of activities. Our week has also tried to include activities which involve the entire community and, in particular, family participation.

This past year we had a Spanish language festival for junior high and high school students, had folk dancers from an elementary school, provided shuttles for the elderly from local senior citizens centers, and had a classical guitar concert and lecture which attracted many non-Chicanos. We also had two panel discussions; one focused on U.S.

policy **vis-a-vis** Central America and the other on **la Chicana** and **machismo.** No week can be termed a success without a dance, and don't forget **la marcha!**

Research

Research is important in any institution, and research based on minority students is usually in short supply. The results of retention studies, shifts in enrollment patterns, shifts in admissions status, changes in preferred academic majors and so on, are important areas for institutional planning. In addition, many faculty members may be involved in research which could have an impact on Chicano students. You may be able to provide input into research design, provide publicity for the research being undertaken, and possibly provide research subjects. By either conducting or participating in research studies, your office should be better able to tailor its program to real needs and keep on top of the latest research being conducted. Having the results of such research can also assist in requesting additional staff or budget items.

Conclusion

There is no doubt that the number of Chicano students coming of college age is on the increase, and thus institutions of higher education will have to respond to the needs of these students. But, there is also no doubt that directors of Chicano programs will have to provide services which those students need. In addition, directors will have to assume their rightful place as administrators within the institution. Any attempt to remain apart from the institution leaves one vulnerable and suspect. A successful program is not only a Chicano program, but an institutional program.

Additional Reading

Anderson, E. C. "An Equal Opportunity Program Retention Design." College and University, 1976, 51, 692-699.

Educational Standards, Testing, and Access: Proceedings of the 1984 ETS Invitational Conference. Educational Testing Service, Princeton, N.J., 1985.

Minorities in Higher Education: The Changing Southwest. West interstate Commission for Higher Education, 5 Vols., Boulder, CO., 1985.

New Directions for Student Services: Reducing the Dropout Rate. Jossey-Bass, Inc., San Francisco, 1978.

New Directions for Student Services: Evaluating Program Effectiveness. Jossey-Bass, Inc., San Francisco, 1978.

Noel, L. "College Student Retention--A Campus Wide Responsibility." National ACAC Journal, 1976, 21 (1), 33-36.

The State of Hispanic America. 2 Vols. The National Hispanic Center for Advanced Studies and Policy Analysis, National Hispanic Center/BABEL, Oakland, 1982.

Helping Students Prepare for the Workplace

Bettye I. Latimer, President
Latimer Associates, Green Bay, Wisconsin

About the Author

Bettye I. Latimer brings over twenty years in corporate and government work with such industry giants as Procter & Gamble, World Bank, Green Bay Packers, major universities, and community based organizations. She has served as an affirmative action officer for a major metropolitan city and is considered an expert in personnel related issues. Today she runs her own management consulting firm. Her insight is revealing because it's based on real experience. She knows the ins and outs of the corporate culture.

Introduction

In this article, Ms. Latimer discusses the major factors students need to be aware of while job hunting. She helps students prepare for the work place. She discusses the myths surrounding the world of work, while giving students practical advice that should prove to be very beneficial. She asks the right questions and challenges students to take a critical look when preparing their resumes. Her discussion of professionalism is worth noting, and it soon becomes obvious that she is quite familiar with the corporate culture.

Her observations leave little to chance. Her advice is specific, probing and informative. Students are encouraged to work smarter, not harder.

Helping Students Prepare for the Workplace

by Bettye I. Latimer

GETTING A NEW JOB IS NOT EASY

Whether you're a first time job hunter or thinking about changing jobs, getting a new job is not easy. Job-hunting is a job in itself. If you're unemployed and want a job, spend full time at job-hunting-not 3 hours a week or 3 hours per day-full time. If you're employed and want to change jobs, reduce your priorities with your present job and your personal/family responsibilities, and make room to seriously look for a new job. To help facilitate your task, let me divide the world of job-hunting into **MYTHS and FACTS:**

MYTH #1: A good resume will get you a job.

Fact #1: Resumes, for the most part, screen people out. I'll take the risk and say that no one has ever gotten a job through a resume only. There are exceptions, but mighty few. Some professional jobs require a resume for consideration, but people don't hire resumes. They hire people. Do not rely on a resume to get you a job. The screening of resumes is what is known as a first cut. Personnel people use resumes to determine who they do not want.

FACT #2: An interview gets you a job. People do not hire strangers. They hire people they like--people who have the right "chemistry", people who have the talents they need, and people who come at the right price. They hire people in that order. In other words, people are hired by "chemistry" first, talent second and price third. Your major goal in job-hunting is to get an interview with the person who has the authority to hire. Just as you wouldn't hire a stranger for your business, no one else will either. Recall your past experiences. Have you ever gotten a job without an interview? That would happen only if the person knew you ahead of time.

People hire people they like and they know. An interview is a way of getting to know you. Would you hire somebody you didn't like, respect, or felt "weird" about, or didn't know? This is to say that the interview is the most important part of your job-hunting work.

MYTH #2: Newspaper ads are a good source of potential jobs.

FACT #3: Newspaper ads or any other kind of ad are the poorest sources.

Eighty percent of the jobs available are never advertised openly. Your best chances of getting a job are through people you know, people already working in a job that interests you and people inside a company. If you have ever worked for a medium or large size organization, you have discovered that many people are cousins, in-laws, brothers, sisters, sons, and/or daughters. Chances are that they got the scoop on job openings inside the company from a relative who knew the company was "looking for somebody." Word-of-mouth news is a gold mine for job openings.

A personal recommendation by someone inside the company is better than ten gold-tipped resumes. If you read the Wall Street Journal lately, you know that a Morton Erhlich was making a 6-figure salary at Eastern Airlines. When he didn't get the presidency as anticipated, he started looking. He eschewed sending out resumes in favor of telephoning folks he knew. Morton Erhlich's three months of contact finally paid off with a job offer from the TWA president in an interview at a posh New York restaurant. The TWA president and Morton simply met for lunch, but Morton knew it was an interview to "test the chemistry"--to see if the president liked him. I doubt if the TWA president ever reviewed Morton's resume.

Talk to people you know. Tell them of your interest. Call people who are actively working. Let them know you want to change jobs. Talk to people you don't know but who work in a job that you'd like to have. Call them up. Introduce yourself as a stranger if necessary. Ask if you can come to talk with them about their field.

YOUR RESUME: DOES IT REALLY SHOW HOW HARD YOU HAVE WORKED?

What have you been doing the past two years of your life- the past five?-the past 10?-the past 15? That's a formidable question and yet your resume must show how hard you have worked during those years.

Your resume should be confined to one page, and no more than two pages. Busy bosses do not have time to read chapter after chapter of your life's history. You must be skilled enough to summarize your work history in a couple of pages with plenty of white space and wide margins.

I don't want to hear the excuse that you can't write. You know better than anyone else what you have done and you can write about that. Writing a resume is not like writing a 600 page book on the history of the Roman empire.

I find that most people err in making their resume too long or too bulky with unimportant details. (Who needs to know whether you're divorced or married or shacking up?) They also err in being able to distill the essence of their work history. We tend to give details of our daily tasks rather than a summation of results. A resume should present a picture of what you have accomplished as a result of having a job, not merely the fact that you were provided with a means of making a living. You should ask yourself, **"As a result of my being in a certain position for a certain length of time, what changed? What did I manage? What did I accomplish that impacted the business? What goals did I achieve? What was different as a result of my being there? How did I use my talent? my education? my past experience? my skills? my knowledge?"**

Numbers are impressive. If you were responsible for a budget, state how much. If you served customers, how many? If you managed a territory, how large? If you produced widgets, how many? If you supervised people, how many? If you brought in dollars, how many? If you reduced costs, by how much?   If you were a janitor and received a compliment for a safety change, tell about that. If you trained people, were they beginners or advanced? In other words, what was distinctive about what you did?

Let's review some segments from three real-life resumes which I have seen and let's see how they can be revised to better reflect real talents, skills, or accomplishments.

First draft: I sold insurance for Midwestern Insurance Co. and worked in the home office until transferred to a branch office for the past year.

Revision: I sold insurance for Midwestern Insurance Co. and fourteen out of twenty one months exceeded the departmental goal. I increased sales in four territories by 68%, increased renewals by 35%, and opened up two previously unsolicited markets.

First draft: I own, operate and maintain a rental housing unit.

Revision: I own a rental housing unit grossing $60,000 annually, have reduced maintenance costs consecutively by 4% over the past 3 years, and have reduced tenant turnover by 10%.

First draft: I am a legal secretary with duties such as typing various pleadings and legal documents from written drafts, dictaphone and dictation, photocopying, scheduling meetings, relieving receptionist when necessary and miscellaneous other duties as assigned by legal administrator.

Revision: I am a legal secretary with a typing skill of 85 wpm. I have operated 3 types of dictaphones; scheduled meetings for staff of 7, typed documents, statistical and financial records. In addition I have reorganized and instituted a new filing system for two lawyers.

In talking with this person, I found out that she typed 85 wpm—an exceptional skill! She also said that she did a lot of statistical papers and some accounting reports. She told me what a mess the files were in when she came and how she spent several weeks reorganizing them. In her first draft she concentrated on the ordinary tasks common to every legal secretary. A legal secretary is expected to type "pleadings and legal documents and do photocopying." We all have had to "relieve" someone else and answer the telephone. This is no big deal. Furthermore, "miscellaneous other duties" etc. merely takes takes up space.

Both descriptions have the same number of words; but the revision, partly by using numbers, describes three unmentioned skills, shows her unique contributions to that office and is separated into sections to emphasize a distinct accomplishment with the files.

By revising the description of her job, her real skills, her productivity and her versatility were emphasized. Each revision above keys in on something which is measurable and gives prospective employers a better idea of the scope of that person's talents, experience and hard work.

Let numbers do the talking for you. If you have worked hard, let people know it. Look over your resume tonight and see what you have left out, what you can summarize in measurable terms and how you can give a better picture of your hard work.

Professionalism

Professionalism is a word which you hear as often as motherhood and apple pie. What do people mean when they speak of professionalism? How do you distinguish a non-professional from a professional? What are the nuances of meaning behind professional behavior? After you graduate from college, you will encounter the word professionalism time and time again. By virtue of having a college degree you will be considered a professional – until you prove otherwise. The first rule of professionalism is the image you portray of taking your work and your discipline seriously. You must always be about the business of learning more. You must keep up with the state of the art. You must project that you have studied a subject matter for several years and that you have insight into that field.

When people inquire about your major, say what your major is with pride. Don't "mumble jumble" about it. Don't disparage it. Don't give excuses for your choice. A similar attitude should be portrayed about the school from which you graduate. It is true that some schools are superior to others. However, all schools have a history as well as heavy monetary investment in professors and curriculum. Be respectful of your school. You received benefits from that school that you wouldn't have gotten anywhere else.

In the world of work, professionalism is paramount. It begins with the job interview. Prospective employers want problem solvers more than any other attribute. Regardless of your major, your college education has expanded your ability to solve problems. The principal benefit of a college education is learning to think, to see relationships, to solve problems, to innovate with a blend of old and new ideas. In your job interviews and on the job be a problem solver, not a critic. Isolate a problem and begin work on it. Be a problem solver, not an excuse-maker. As soon as you graduate from college, you should join a professional association relevant to your major. This reinforces your professionalism, is a positive attribute on your resume and enables you to keep up with changes in your field.

Next I want to summarize some of the most common criticisms which I hear about us. Us means Black people. Some of the criticisms come from us and some come from them. The fact is that I hear these criticisms consistently across the board and they negate our professionalism.

Criticism No. 1: Lateness

They expect us to be late and we expect each other to be late. If we go to a Black program which starts at 8:20 instead of the announced time of 8:00, we laugh and say that it's "CP" (Colored People) time. Operating on "CP" time is death in the white world. They have a fetish about time. Don't go to work 5 minutes late. It detracts from your professionalism. They won't notice what you do after that time anyway.

Criticism No. 2: Bad Manners

We have a tendency to "tell it like it is." In doing so, the impression is that we are rude and abrupt. Slow down. Say thank you.

133

Listen. Repeat what the other person says, and disagree without being sarcastic. These tips may sound mundane, but from experience I know that people like to hear thank you for even small gestures. I also know that when I disagree with people, I am seen as unprofessional if I attack them or the subject matter under discussion. I dislike Reagan, but instead of saying he is a fool, I am more professional if I say, "In my opinion Reagan has mismanaged the country as well as worked against Black people and the poor."

Criticism No. 3: Language

Some of the best of us split verbs, leave "s's" and other endings from words, and mispronounce common words. "Mines", meaning belonging to me is a word we often use, but there is no such word in the dictionary. This makes us sound not only unprofessional but illiterate. The problem is that our speech habits seem normal when we are around people who have similar speech patterns. However, in the world of work, where the larger culture prevails, poor speech habits work against us. People who split verbs generally do not recognize this. Just to make sure, ask a friend whom you trust and admire to give you feedback on your speech habits. Ask that person if you split verbs or talk poorly (ungrammatically). Don't get defensive. Listen and map out a program for improvement. I know that you can grow. I know that you can contribute to your field. I know that you can make money. I know that you can improve your professionalism.

In the scheme of things, most people want to be recognized as a professional. This is human nature because recognition as a professional awards you status and promotes self-esteem. Professionals know that they have done extra preparation for their field of work. They also are rewarded with better pay in the organization than non-professionals. Depending on rank, the organization may give them certain "perks." Perks are extras. They supposedly are a catalyst for better performance. A designated parking place is a perk. So is a bonus, or stock dividends, or an office, or special furniture in your office, or even a nameplate on the desk or door. A common perk in the sales field is a car, paid for by the company. So if you have elected to be a professional, you had better act like one.

Professionals are noted for their commitment. Deliver on the date and at the time you say you will. No excuses, no apologies, no procrastination. Commitment is the hallmark of a professional.

We tend to think of delivery in terms of products. But delivering can be as fundamental as getting back to a person if this is what you promised. Delivering is following up your phone calls in a timely matter. Delivering is going to the meeting at the scheduled time, although you would rather be at the beach. The worse thing that can be said about a professional is that "you can't depend on him/her".

Following closely on the heels of commitment is time management. All the stagnant professionals I know work overtime. That statement may shock a lot of people. If you find yourself consistently working overtime, going to the office on weekends, working to catch up on holidays—I bet you are not managing your time effectively. You either are trying to do too many things or not delegating effectively, or not prioritizing. Exceptions are special projects that are time-limited, such as conference preparation or a custom product. In the corporate world, working overtime is called "OE"- overengineering. Overengineering is designing a Cadillac when the car needed is a Ford.

If you are doing too many things, you probably are doing someone else's work. Give it back to them. If you are not delegating effectively, delegate. The phrase "that's not my job" is misused most of the time. In production areas that statement is commonly used to avoid doing work, especially when there are stringent or crazy union rules. But as a professional, ask yourself: can someone else do this task better than I can? Swallow your pride and delegate. Can someone else do this task quicker than I can? Give it to them and then give them credit. A professional is a specialist, not a jack of all trades. Can someone else do this task cheaper than I can, based on my professional worth? Take your hourly earnings and multiply by the time involved in doing the task; use the same formula for transferring the task to another resource. Consider both internal and external resources. Then compare the actual difference. When you can save time, money, or delay due to lack of know-how, do so.

Learn to work smarter, not harder.

Failure to prioritize is a guarantee that you will waste most of your time. Not all things are equal. A solid professional knows how to prioritize and what to prioritize. Successful professionals do prioritize. Ask them. Anyone who starts their work day without having an agenda or goals for that day should not be at work. You shouldn't get up in the morning to go to work. You should get up to accomplish specific tasks. Key your tasks A, B, C. Do the A's first. Do the B's after the A's are completed. Ignore the C's. Try this for a day. An alternate method is to first do the difficult or "I don't want to do that" tasks and the fun or easy tasks later.

A guideline for determining A's is to determine what would happen if this task were not done one year from today's date. In sales marketing is the priority. In social work areas, keeping client records is the priority. As a top manager, maintaining cash flow or adhering to a budget and keeping the organization goals in focus is the priority. In design engineering finishing the blueprint is the priority. In teaching knowing what you will teach the next week is the priority. As a professional managing your time in the real work world will give you an A for excellence, or a C for mediocrity or a D for flunking out. As an Afro-American, you were born to be excellent.

Packaging Yourself For A Job

Have you ever walked into a business place fully intending to make a purchase, and suddenly you walked out because it didn't feel right, look right, smell right? Have you ever looked at two products? One was crumpled, and slightly soiled, with washed out colors. Did you choose the cleaner looking one? This is exactly what happens when you go for a job interview. While your appearance may not immediately get you a job, your appearance (your packaging) can be the cause of immediate rejection. The buying process begins the moment you have your first contact with prospective employers. They begin sizing prospects up very early in the game. Early means the way you fill out an application blank, your punctuality, your tone of voice over the phone, and your physical appearance at the interview.

Prospective employers are in the market for buying a product, you – for a salary. As a buyer, they control the market. As a buyer, they are looking over several products – you and people competing with you. As a buyer, they will choose the best looking product that fits their needs. While your appearance, your punctuality, your phone voice, your paper application may not immediately get you a job, these factors can eliminate you. People hire other people largely for emotional reasons with a little rationale thrown in to substantiate the hire. Judging a person on the clothes he/she is wearing is an emotional response. Maybe it shouldn't be like that, but it is reality.

While working at a client organization recently, I overheard the supervisors discussing the scheduling of interviews. The organization happened to be a civil service agency, which theoretically, has enough regulations and standards to be objective. However, the supervisors had already rejected one person because of two factors. First of all he didn't fill in all the blanks on the application. One comment was, "If he can't fill out an application, he certainly can't do our work." Another comment was "I wouldn't hire him in the next ten years."

These were white folks talking about white folks. Guess what happens if we slip up. Secondly, he called explaining that he had forgotten the time of the interview. That question further sealed his fate. This prospect will be interviewed because he qualifies highly according to the civil service rules and his test scores. But he has been rejected prior to the final interview-subjectively rejected. His interview will be perfectly meaningless. I don't know how the candidate inquired about his interview appointment. I only know that had I been in his situation, I hope I would have found the right words to ask about "confirming" my appointment rather than asking for its exact time. While we don't have control over other people's subjective responses, we do have control over how we look and how we present ourselves. College students wear jeans and sweats and beat up shoes. While perfect for the campus, these are not interview clothes. But it goes beyond that. You should forego wearing your most expensive suit if it is a little too big or, heaven forbid, a little too tight. First of all, you will be uncomfortable.

Secondly, your interviewers won't know your suit is expensive; they will only know that it doesn't fit right on you. College students have to make a conscious effort to look their best for an interview because, so far as I can observe, college students are not in the habit of looking spiffy everyday. Runs in stockings, unshined shoes, dirty fingernails, unpressed trousers, missing buttons, dirty cuffs, ravels. Check yourself before you go for an interview that is important to you. Be on time or ahead of time. Five minutes late is too late. Mainstream people are paranoid about time in my opinion. But they run a good deal of the world. They have control of a lot of the available jobs. For minority women, be careful about jewelry, head rags, and large pocketbooks. In general, I think we have a creativity for wearing those kind of accessories, but I also know that those things are scary to many folks. Take a shower. Tone down the fragrance. Wear what your Aunt Mattie would consider "good church clothes."

Your attitude - mental and spiritual - is the other plus that you must carry with you. Remember that the way you package yourself will deny or confirm that you are right for the job. First impressions do count.

Your Job Hunt and AA

Your job hunting efforts depend a lot on AA. In fact, your success can be measured by your AA. Your AA is the most potent force in getting the kind of job you want. There is a job existing in the next 30 days if your AA is working for you. AA does not stand for Alcoholics Anonymous nor Affirmative Action. It is **ATTITUDE ANALYSIS.** Your job hunting success, no matter whether for your first or tenth job depends on ATTITUDE ANALYSIS.

ATTITUDE ANALYSIS is reflected in terms of whether you are motivated or procrastinating, optimistic or pessimistic, confident or fearful, positive or negative, energetic or lethargic. As the cliche goes, "if you think you can, you can; if you think you can't, you can't." Think about that cliche for a moment. Olympic champions never enter the race believing that they cannot win. Babies do not attempt to walk assuming that walking is impossible. Frederick Douglass didn't devote his life to the abolition of slavery believing that slavery was unconquerable. Successful millionaires have not taken the risks by thinking "poverty". Jack Johnson publisher of **EBONY** magazine believed that the time was ripe for a Black oriented magazine and that he had the business talent to pull it off. No one has worked for and secured a job which they believed they did not deserve.

Getting the job you want begins with believing that your job exists, that you are deserving of the job and that you can be successful in securing it. When you learn about the job you really want, go to the interview with gusto! Radiate. Ask for the job. Make your prospective boss think that you are the only person in the world suitable for that job.

Prepare your ATTITUDE ANALYSIS. Think positive. Act positive. Believe. The laws of logic say that if you think negatively and act negatively, you will get negative rewards. The process of negative thinking produces excuses, rationalizations, defenses, lack of self-confidence, blindness to opportunity, paralysis. Positive thinking enables you to see opportunities that you did not think existed, opens up new horizons, generates new resources, prepares you to see roses on the thorns instead of thorns on the roses. The positive attitude which you bring to the interview can be the most important asset in getting the job you want.

Put Your Best Foot Forward

After the tumultuous excitement of graduation rituals, saying goodbye to friends and having Mom and Dad overload the car, the world of reality thunderbolts into your life. If you haven't already started job hunting, you must do so now. Job searching after your May graduation is your only job.

There are 3 ways of getting a job: INTERVIEW, INTERVIEW, INTERVIEW! As I have said previously, people do not hire strangers. All prospective employers like to talk with you before they invest money in you. Employers want to see and hear the product they potentially will invest in. Before you interview, I hope you have done these things:

1. Invested in a typed resume on good quality paper, which has generous margins. In the trade, it's called "white space." People are more likely to read attractive looking documents rather than something that looks formidable and crowded.

2. Invested in an attractive hair style and clothes that enhance your natural looks. First impressions won't get you a job, but if an interviewer's first impression is that you don't look right, the remainder of the interview is null and void.

The more conservative an organization the less they will approve of trendy hair style, obvious hair coloring, and men who wear earrings. For the interview, wear your all-American clothes and accessories.

The Interview: Questions to Prepare For

Be prepared to answer any or all of the following questions for each interview. consider each job prospect unique:
1. Tell me about yourself.
2. Why do you want this job?
3. What qualifications do you have that make you outstanding?
4. What are your strengths?
5. What are your weaknesses? (Usually the interviewer is trying   to ascertain two things: are you aware of your shortcomings, and how well you get along with people)?
6. When can you start? (This question reflects that the interviewer is strongly considering you.)
7. What problem did you solve on your last job (or while in school) that you feel good about? What techniques did you use?
8. Where do you see yourself five years from now? In two years?
9. Be alert for any "people managing" questions. They appear in various forms. The interviewer may ask about conflict-managing

138

techniques, things that upset you , how other people perceive you, etc.

10. What can you offer the company besides a college degree? Be sure you have taken an inventory of your job experiences and your personal qualities.

The Interview: Questions You Can Ask

Prepare a list of questions ahead of time which you would like to ask. The more formal the interview, the more likely the interviewer will ask you if you have any questions. Be sure to ask something. By all means do not say, "No, I don't have any at this time." Show an interest in the company. Recall what the interviewer has asked you and ask a related question. You can always ask these "generic" questions.

1. How will I learn my job? Do you have a formal training program? Who will train me to learn your procedures and policies correctly? What is the length of the training?

2. What will you expect of me? How will you measure your expectations?

3. What are my opportunities if I do well? How will I advance?

4. What has traditionally been your turn-over for this position? (The answer will alert you to companies that have "revolving door" practices and a low rate of retention.)

5. How soon do you expect to fill this position?

6. How many candidates are you looking at?

7. Is this a newly created position?

8. When can I expect to hear from you?

9. Are there things which I need to clarify further for you?

Such questions will give you more information as to the quality of the job, what you can expect, your competition, and the interviewer's timetable. Any one of these questions will give you more than a "yes/no" answer and prepare you for the next interview, in case you or the prospective employer declines. Keep your best foot forward and persist in getting interviews until you find the organization that is right for you.

Chapter 7

Activities to Get Students to Interact - Human Relation Type Activities

Introduce Your Partner

* Have each participant pair up with another person, ideally someone he/she doesn't know at all. This process can be speeded up by asking them to count off one, two, one, two, ...
(This can also be varied by sex or race by having women be all ones and men all twos and pairing off and having whites be all ones and minorities all twos and pairing off).

* Give all persons a 5 by 8 inch card and have them interview each other for five minutes. Give them the following items to be included in the interview:
-name, and/or nickname, ethnic/racial background, job, school, travel, hobbies/interest
-experiences with different racial groups
-why they came
-what they hope to get out of this activity
-one thing (activity, food, leisure . .) they like and one thing they dislike.

* When the time is up have everyone form a circle. Give each person 2-3 minutes to introduce his or her partner to the total group. Members of the group can ask additional questions or clarify questions of the person being introduced.

* The facilitator should participate in this exercise as well to emphasize a community atmosphere.

Greet to the Beat

This is a fun way to loosen participants up and have them meet each other. Have the group form a Soul Train line (two lines facing each other). With medium to fast paced music playing in the background, have two people at a time walk or dance down the line introducing themselves. Both lines should sway to the music. When the two people reach the end of the line they reverse positions and go back up the opposite line and introduce themselves to people in that line. When the couple reaches the top of the line the entire group shouts welcome Tom & Mary (whatever their names may be and applauds). Then the next couple starts. This process is repeated until everyone has had a chance to go down and up the Soul Train line. Encourage participants to be creative when they go up and down the line.

Mingle and Meet

Give each person in the group a 3" by 5" index card. Have them record the following information on the card:
1) their name, 2) their astrological sign and, 3) finish the sentence "I am here because . . ".

Have them tape or pin the card to their clothing in such a way that participants can read their cards. Tell participants they have two minutes to walk around the room, read as many cards as they can and introduce themselves. This exercise works well in getting people to talk about themselves. It helps put people at ease since everyone has to answer the same questions and talk about their astrological sign.

Additional Introductory/Orientation Exercises

1. Have participants tell their names. Next have them pass an object such as a ball and have them say something using the word ball as they pass it around. Only the person with the ball can speak.

2. Have the participants repeat their names and use an adjective describing how they feel.

3. Have persons get together according to zodiac signs, states, birth, etc. and introduce themselves to the group members.

4. Have participants pile name tags on the floor and have each person grab a name tag other than his/her own and find the owner introducing him/herself in the process.

5. Make up cards with numerous things for the participants to do, say, or pantomime and have each one select a card and do whatever the card says.

6. Have participants pile their left shoes in a pile and have each person grab a shoe that's not his/her own and put the shoe on the owner's foot and introduce themselves.

Warm Up Activities

Finger Match

Have participants form groups of three forming a small circle. When the facilitator says ready, set, go using one hand only, each group is to try to extend exactly ten fingers out. (of course there can be no talking among group members). If one person extends say 5 fingers and someone else four and the third person two, obviously they have extended more than ten fingers. The facilitator repeats the instructions ready, set, go until one group has extended exactly ten fingers. This game usually generates enthusiasm and participants normally shout or applaud loudly when they've succeeded in getting ten fingers. This activity can be stopped after the first group extends ten fingers or groups can take their seats after they reach ten through a process of elimination. Either way this makes for a fun energizer that can help get the day off on a good foot.

Multi-cultural Groups

This activity should take place in a wide open space. All chairs, tables, etc. should be moved out of the way because participants will need to move around with their eyes closed in this exercise. Have participants form groups of four. (If there are an equal number of whites and minorities present each group should have two white and two minority members); otherwise base your mix on a percentage of the number in attendance.

Before participants form their groups inform them they are not to talk in the exercise, nor open their eyes. Their goal is to create a multi-cultural circle consisting of four people. Half of the group is to be white members and the other half, members of a racial minority group. As you might suspect since participants can't talk or look in this activity, it gets very exciting. Expect a lot of touching and laughter. Allow participants about 5-10 minutes to form their groups. After the time is up ask them how they were able to form a multi-cultural group. If they were unsuccessful ask them to explain why. This activity is a perfect lead in to a discussion about cultural differences, stereotypes, "color blindness", etc. Spend some time discussing this activity.

Puzzle Game

Write fun messages or instructions on several sheets of paper (For example: Shake hands with everyone in your group, Feel the heads of all bald-headed persons, Hug all the males in your group, etc.). Cut the messages up so no more than two or three words appear on the paper. Mix all the parts of messages up and distribute randomly among the participants. Inform them that their words form a message when joined together with other words. They are to find the other words, complete the message and do whatever the message says. This activity can end when the first group completes its puzzle or continue until all groups have completed their puzzles.

Confrontation Exercises

Racial Fact Sheets

A. 1. Divide participants along racial lines.
   2. Next have participants spend about 30 minutes compiling a one page "fact sheet" they would give an alien about Whites, Asians, Blacks, Indians and Hispanics. Emphasize the need for honesty as opposed to tact.

3. Also have each racial group create a fact sheet about themselves.
4. Have each group select a spokesperson.
5 Bring the groups back together and have the spokespersons read their fact sheets. Allow ample time for discussion, clarification and confrontation.
6. Conclude by having the group brainstorm what should be included on a fact sheet when describing a human being.
B. 1. Have participants discuss these statements:
    a. All whites are racists!
    b. Minorities should quit blaming whites for their problems and do something about it themselves!
    c. I would not want to be an **Indian** (substitute any ethnic group) because......
    d. I would not marry a **Asian** person (substitute any ethnic group) because......

Encourage participants to be honest about their feelings.

BREAKING IN

1. Have participants form a seven to nine person circle. Designate the circle as a white neighborhood.
2. Next designate someone as a black person to physically break into the circle.
3. Have the circle designated as a neighborhood lock arms and physically keep the black person out. (Since this exercise is a physical one and gets rough at times, remind the participants to show restraint).
4. After the black person has tried to break in, discuss this activity. Discuss what the white neighborhood must do to keep blacks out? How does it feel to have to force one's way into the neighborhood? etc...

Cultural Exploration

Divide the participants along racial lines into groups of three. Tell the groups they are to spend about thirty minutes planning an activity they feel would interest someone of a different racial group. (Ideally this activity should be something that could actually be carried out). Tell them to write out (1-2 pages) why they selected this particular activity and why they feel someone who is racially different would enjoy it. After each group has finished writing their cross-cultural activity exchange papers and have the group the event was planned for evaluate the activity in terms of strengths/weaknesses, stereotypes and make suggestions as to how the affected group would have planned the activity differently.

Allow ample time for discussions. This exercise reveals a lot about participants values, sensitivities and perceptions of others. Another option is to allow the groups to actually conduct the activity during their free time and then discuss it afterwards.

This activity normally reveals the need to include impacted groups when planning cross cultural events. The various factors that must be considered usually surface during the discussion in a manner that illustrates the need for better communication and understanding. This is a good exercise to help participants reflect on their feelings about others who are culturally different.

Black Cultural Card Game

INSTRUCTIONS

Introduction

The **Black Culture Card Game** is designed to introduce participants to selected aspects of black slang the **Fun Way.** This game is ideal for a classroom setting or any audience up to fifty people. This game can be used alone or in conjunction with a broader discussion of black culture. It should be pointed out to participants that this game is only a very small part of black culture and it does not attempt to substitute for the richness and diversity that make up the **Black Cultural Heritage.**

Rules

Write or type the 50 cultural (slang) messages on index cards. Have each participant select a card and read the cultural message out loud. Whatever the message says, the reader has to do. If the reader is not able to understand the message have them guess. Finally, explain the correct meaning to the reader. Feel free to discuss each message in greater depth after reading. Conclude with a general discussion of black culture and black cultural differences. Have Fun!

BLACK CULTURE CARD GAME (SLANG DEFINITIONS)

Card	Cultural Message	Meaning
1	Sell some wolf tickets	To bluff and boast about how tough one is, in a disguised effort to avoid a confrontation
2	Pretend you are clean	Dressed real nice. Your Sunday "best."
3	Pretend you are a down person	A person that's cool and has his/her act together
4	Pretend you are GQ	A person that is clean, stylish and chic

144

5	Describe "jammin" the box	Playing the stereo loud
6	Pretend you are going to raise	Getting up to leave
7	Define Bo-guard	To force one's will or way upon another
8	Describe or show a pick	A hair comb shaped like a minature pitchfork
9	Define T.C.B.	Taking care of business
10	Describe pleather	Fake or cheap leather
11	Describe a Deuce and a Quarter	It is a Buick Electra 225 (car)
12	Give someone five on the black hand side	Slap someone's hand with the palm facing up
13	Pimp across the room	Walk cool, strutting across the room
14	Pretend you are a bad person	Cool, all-right
15	Define a ride	A car or other means of transportation
16	Define "The Man"	Usually a white male in a position of authority, (ie, cop, boss, etc.)
17	Describe going to the crib	Going home or to the apartment
18	Pretend you are in a soul train line	Two dancing lines with individuals or couples dancing down the middle. The lines rotate to the music
19	Pretend you're in your 'chine	In your car
20	Describe yourself getting off	Deeply into your music, dance or whatever turns you on (jamming)

Black Culture Card Game Continued

Card	Cultural Message	Meaning
21	Play the dozens	Verbal word game that includes talking about someone's mother in a negative sexual way. The dozens often use phrases that rhyme.
22	Imitate a person who has the Holy Ghost	This applies to a religious person in a fundamentalist church that's been filled with the Holy spirit and jumps up shouting and dancing.
23	Give an example of getting over on somebody	Taking advantage of someone to get what you want
24	Shoot some game to someone	Try to sweet talk a person
25	Do the bump	Do a dance where you bump your partner.
26	Pretend you are a player	A playboy, Lover and/or playgirl
27	Show your kicks	Show your shoes
28	Pretend that you have your heat with you and draw	Draw your gun or weapon
29	Run your hands up and down someone's threads	Feel someone's clothes
30	Croon anything you want	Sing a song
31	Give someone chump change	The loose change men have in their pockets or women have in their purses, small amount of coins
32	Describe "pullin" a piece	Drawing your gun or weapon
33	Step for the people in the room	A fraternity or sorority dance step
34	Pretend you're counting your long green	Counting your money

146

35	Talk some jive to the group	Talk a lot of bull
36	Feel someone's blowout	Feel someone's Afro hair style
37	Pretend you're on your gig and see if the participants can guess what it is.	Gig means job (pantomime this)
38	Describe corn killers	Very tight shoes (a size too small)
39	Run a game on someone	Try to take advantage of someone
40	Fire up a short	Light up a cigarette
41	Finish Richard Pryor's famous line "Money talks and _____"	Bullshit walks
42	Define Cop	Get or obtain
43	Describe the difference between a set and after set	A set is a party and an after set is the party after the first party
44	Take someone's sky piece off	Take someone's hat off
45	Pretend you are flooding	Your pants legs are too short, exposing your socks
46	Define flunkying	Working
47	Describe someone about to to "raise"	Getting ready to leave,
48	Describe an oreo	Said to be a person that's black on the outside but white on the inside
49	Define "crib"	House or home
50	Describe someone cooling out	Laid back

Values Clarification Exercise

No Place to Study

Directions: Read the following to the participants. Have them discuss the values and assumptions that are implied in the story.

The setting is a college student union. Ralph is a black student, who is concerned that no black studies courses are offered in his subject area. He goes through the regular procedures to obtain funds, approval, and a faculty member for a black studies course. Twenty black students sign up. Ralph goes to the student union director and asks if they can use the movie room on Thursday nights since that is the only time the professor is free. The movie room is the only room in the union with audio-visual equipment. The student union director approves the request.

Thursday night arrives. The black students go to the movie room and find a group of white students watching Animal House. A heated discussion occurs. Charlie, a white student, yells out, "you damn niggers don't belong on this campus anyway." Tom, a white student, believes that the black students should be allowed to use the movie room since it is the only place they have to meet. He does not say anything, however. The black students leave. Ralph later goes to the student union director to explain what happened. The director replies, "I made a mistake. The movie room really serves a need for all students. Since there are only 20 students, find another place."

The next Thursday night the black students go to the movie room early and begin class. A fight breaks out; there are injuries and several hundred dollars worth of damage done to the movie room.

Discuss who is at fault? How should the situation have been handled? You can use the following values and assumptions to stimulate the discussion.

Values

* Black studies have a low priority-why do you think this is so ?
* Black studies mean violence
* White people can't be forced to integrate
* Black needs are unimportant
* It's a White problem

Assumptions

* Inconsistencies
* Lack of understanding
* Denial of responsibility
* Minorities receiving special privileges
* Ignorance of legitimate minority demands

What's your choice?

This exercise is designed to help participants clarify their values. Read the statements below and allow ample time for discussion. To be successful in your discussions help participants realize that to clarify their values they have to understand how they came to prize their beliefs and behaviors, how they selected their beliefs and behaviors and how to act on their beliefs.

1. If you had to be born over, which would you rather be?
   An American Black, An African Black, or a European Black.
2. Which death is the greatest loss?
   Martin Luther King Jr., Jesus Christ, John F. Kennedy, Malcolm X.
3. Which would you have the easiest time introducing to your parents?
   A homosexual friend, an interracial date, or a Nazi member?
4. Which would you prefer as a neighbor if there was only one house available in your neighborhood?
   A white couple, a minority couple, or a foreign couple?
5. If it was your decision to make, what funds would you cut first?
   Welfare, defense, or funds for education?
6. Who should get the longest sentence?
   A robber, a murderer, or a rapist?
7. If you had to legalize a drug which would you choose?
   Marijuana, Cocaine, or heroin?

The Fatal Choice

After their ship sank in heavy seas, eight survivors found themselves on a rubber raft that was gradually sinking because it could support only six adults. The eight survivors included a 65 year old white man, a Jewish doctor, a 25 year old blond woman, a black baby boy and his mother, a white sailor, a young black minister, and a convicted Indian murderer who was prior to the shipwreck, being transported to jail to serve a life sentence.

They all knew the raft would sink within a half hour if their weight wasn't reduced. Because they had been blown out of the main shipping lanes, there was almost no chance of being rescued for two or three days. Two people would have to be removed from the raft. The survivors talked it over, but no one would volunteer to jump overboard. Who should be forcibly removed from the raft? Why?

Stereotyping

Time required: 45 minutes - 2 hours

This activity should start off with a definition of stereotyping. Next the facilitator explains to the participants that the activity they will be engaging in will help determine whether they have any stereotypes at work. The facilitator continues by saying: "I will read some paragraphs and you stop me as soon as you get a mental picture of the people you think I am describing. Tell me who you see." The facilitator may want to start with the descriptions below:

1. A group of people are gathered around a table. They are having a great time, drinking wine and laughing loudly. The music playing in the background sounds like an opera. The robust mother yells in an accented voice at her son for dropping spaghetti on the carpet. What ethnic group am I talking about?

2. Walking down the city street, I observed some people sitting in front of a housing project listening to loud music and doing fancy dance steps ever so often. A Cadillac pulls up, a good looking woman gets out and I hear someone say, "What's happening momma?" What ethnic group do you see?

3. I'm sitting in the living room of a family. The children are well behaved and polite. They bow when they greet the grandfather. The tell me they are having rice for dinner and ask whether I prefer chopsticks or a fork. What ethnic group do you see?

4. While stopping to fill my car with gas, a pick up truck stops near the tank across from mine. I can't help but notice the gun in the window and the confederate flag in full display. A thin hairy man with a tatoo on his arm and a "pot gut" gets out of the truck and says, "Hey boy fill'er up!" What do you see?

The participants will probably identify the examples mentioned as follows: Example #1, Italians, #2 Blacks, #3 Asians and #4 Red neck/poor white.

The facilitator should then lead the group into a discussion of stereotypes. The questions listed can be used to stimulate the discussion.
1. Could these examples apply to other groups than the ones you've identified?
2. What did you find out about your stereotypes?
3. Would your stereotype determine how you might treat people?
4. How do you think you acquired your stereotypes?
5. What do you plan to do about your stereotypes?

As a follow up have the participants write a paragraph on a stereotype they may have. Have them read it out loud and discuss why it is a stereotype. Continue the discussion.

Sensitivity Exercises

The Blind Sensitivity Game

1. Have the group pair off in teams of two.
   Have one member close his/her eyes while being led around the room by the partner. This exercise is to build up a certain level of trust, to talk about dependency and to experience blindness for a brief period.
2. Repeat the exercise having the pairs trot around the room. Discuss.
3. Have everyone close their eyes and walk to the other side of the room. Discuss.

Blind Communication

1. Have the participants form two circles.
2. Have each circle count off beginnings with 1, 2, 3, etc.
3. Next have each circle mix the numbers up so they will be out of order. (See example below)
4. Then have both circles close their eyes, not speak and pretend that they can't hear.
5. Finally, when you say go, have both circles try to get back in numerical order with out talking, speaking, or looking.
6. Have them clap their hands when they feel they are back in order.
7. Then announce the winner.
8. Discuss this activity.

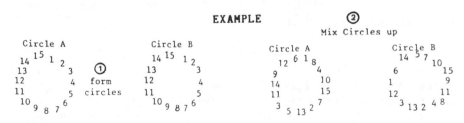

EXAMPLE

③ Then have circles get back in correct order:

Jokes as Put Downs

Specific Learning Objective:
For the participants to recognize racial, sexist, and ethnic jokes as hurtful put downs.

Procedure:
1. Begin activity by asking questions below. Discuss these orally:
   a) What is a joke?
   b) Should a joke put down individuals or groups of people?
   c) In what ways might a joke put down individuals or groups of people? Give some examples.
   d) Have you ever been the butt of a joke? How did you feel in that situation? (Good, bad, dumb, or indifferent)?
2. Give participants a handout of three to six jokes. (see jokes in this section).
3. Have participants answer the following questions about the jokes provided them on the handout.
   a) Who are the characters or individuals who are represented?
   b) What did the joke say negatively or positively about the individual or group?
   c) What emotions might the individual/group that is the brunt of the joke feel? Try to put yourself into that individual/group person's shoes.
4. Have participants tell one ethnic joke that they've heard.
5. As a culminating activity offer the following suggestions about how to check out a joke: Whenever you are about to tell a joke instead of using Jews, Blacks, or Polish people, women, native people, etc., as the character(s) in your joke, substitute "I" and/or "we" or "My friends" and "I" and/or "my family" to see whether you like what you heard about yourself or those that you care about. Try to refrain from telling ethnic jokes.

"Jokes"

1. Q: Why are poor whites found by trash cans?
   A: Because that's where they go window shopping.
2. Q: Why was a black man the only male survivor of the Titanic?
   A: He was the only one that could use his lips as a raft.
3. Do you know how Chinese select names for their kids? No, How? By dropping coins onto a metal floor and listening to the sounds! Ding-Dang, Twang Twong ....
4. Q: What does a tongueless female dog have in common with a Blond?
   A: They're both dumb bitches.

Are You Six Feet Tall?

Specific Learning Objective:

This activity will show how the groups to which you belong help to define who you are.

Procedure:

1. Split participants up into two groups: those who are six feet tall, and those who are under six feet.
2. For the purpose of this activity, pretend that all short people have the following traits:
   a) ignorant
   b) homely looking
   c) boring
   d) clumsy
3. The two groups should meet separately for 10-15 minutes. The tall people must decide how to treat the others. The short people must decide how they expect to be treated by the people over six feet. They must also decide how they will respond to that treatment.
4. For about 30 minutes tall people must treat the short people in the way they decided. The short people must respond to that treatment in whatever way they feel is appropriate and realistic.
5. Talk about what happened and how you felt about it.
   a) How did it feel to be a member of your group?
   b) How realistic do you think your group experience was?
   c) How do you think your group helped you to define who you are?
6. What are the advantages and disadvantages of the group you belong to in real life.

Indian Cultural Differences Test

True and False

    T   F

1) ___ ___ Scalping was a common Indian practice.

2) ___ ___ The Political leaders of Indian Nations were known to their people as "Chief".

3) ___ ___ The BIA was once a branch of the War Department.

4) ___ ___ Indians were primarily nomadic people.

5) ___ ___ Prior to the European invasion, cancer, syphilis, and tooth decay were virtually unknown on the North American continent.

6) ___ ___ IHS stands for the Indian Health Service.

7) ___ ___ Individual States are authorized to enter into treaties with Indian Nations by a special constitutional amendment.

8) ___ ___ The Native American Church worships mescalito, the spirit god of peyote.

9) ___ ___ A "snowsnake" is a reptile indigenous to cold climates.

10) ___ ___ Gambling was first introduced to Indians in 1803 near Las Vegas, Nevada.

11) ___ ___ AIM refers to "Allied Indian Manufacturers".

12) ___ ___ Tuberculosis is virtually unknown in the U.S. today.

13) ___ ___ Chicle, the chewy ingredient in bubble gum, was first introduced by Indians.

14) ___ ___ "Manifest Destiny" is the belief that white men are ordained by god to own and control the North American Continent.

15) ___ ___ Of the 371 major treaties signed by the U.S. and Indian Nations, 371 have been broken.

154

Indian Cultural Differences Test Continued

Multiple Guess

1) Which of the following is not an Indian invention?
   ___ Canoe
   ___ Kayak
   ___ Parka
   ___ Tomahawk

2) Of the four main staples in world food, which of the following two were first domesticated by Indians?
   ___ Rice
   ___ Corn
   ___ Wheat
   ___ Potatoes

3) The Words "Kemo Sabe", popularized by the Lone Ranger's sidekick Tonto, means:
   ___ White Friend
   ___ Blue Eyes
   ___ Honky
   ___ Nothing at all

4) The phrase "The only good Indian is a dead Indian" is attributed to:
   ___ Gen. Philip Sheridan
   ___ Gen. Wm. T. Sherman
   ___ Col. Henry B. Carrington
   ___ Lt. Col. Geo. A. Custer

5) Which of the following was not a member of the League of Six Nations (Iroquois Confederacy)?
   ___ Oneida
   ___ Seneca
   ___ Kiowa
   ___ Onondaga

6) Which of the Following major colleges was first instituted primarily to educate Indians?
   ___ Yale
   ___ Harvard
   ___ Dartmouth
   ___ Princeton

Match

___	Geronimo	A	Iroquois prophet
___	Wovoka	B	Hunkpapa Sioux Medicine Man
___	Clarence Tinker	C	Osage: General, U.S. Air Force
___	Oshkosh	D	Sac & Fox: 1912 Olympic Decathlon Champ
___	Dekanawida	E	Kaw-Osage: Vice-President, 1928-33
___	Jim Thorpe	F	Chiricahua Apache Medicine Man
___	Eli S. Parker	G	Menominee Chief
___	Charles Curtis	H	Seneca: 1st Indian BIA Commissioner 1869-71
___	Sitting Bull	I	Paiut Medicine Man

Tribe   **Region**

___	Seminole	A	Eastern Woodlands
___	Miami	B	Southeast
___	Yakima	C	Great Plains
___	Pawnee	D	Northwest
___	Arapaho	E	Southwest
___	Apache		
___	Potawatomi		
___	Creek		
___	Hopi		
___	Salish		

Date   **Event**

___	1492	A	Discovery of Columbus in Caribbean
___	1754	B	Dawes General Allotment Act
___	1838	C	Wounded Knee I
___	1864	D	Indian Reorganization Act
___	1870	E	Sand Creek Massacre
___	1887	F	Little Big Horn Victory
___	1890	G	Termination Act
___	1934	H	French & Indian Wars
___	1953	I	Trail of Tears
___	1972	J	Self-Determination Act

True & False (Answers to Indian Cultural Differences Test)

F   1)   Scalping was instituted by the Dutch in the 17th century. Settlers were paid a bounty on all scalps brought in; male scalps generally were paid more than female or children's scalps.

F   2)   "Chief" is an Anglo-European Term. Many Indian Tribes have accommodated this word.

T   3)   The BIA was transferred from the War Dept. to the Dept. of Interior in 1849.

156

F   4)   Many Plains Indians followed the migrating animals upon
         which they depended, but all Tribes have clearly defined
         territories, and most were permanently settled in towns
         and villages.

T   5)   Pre-15th century North America was relatively free of
         these serious diseases.

T   6)   The BIA controlled health services until 1955, when IHS
         was transferred to the Public Health Service under DHEW.
         No substantial changes were made, unfortunately.

F   7)   The U.S. Government reserves sole right to enter into
         treaties; any State-Indian Tribe treaties are supposedly
         invalid. (1790 Non-Intercourse Act).

F   8)   The Native American Church uses peyote as an aid to
         inducing visions, from where its individual members
         then derive names and direction.

F   9)   A snowsnake is a game played by the Iroquois. The
         snowsnake itself is a long, narrow piece of wood, round-
         ed at the front and tapering toward the rear.

F   10) Many Indian Tribes had a highly developed system of
         gambling.

F   11) AIM is the American Indian Movement, a political pres-
         sure group of militant young warriors.

F   12) Tuberculosis is the second major killer of Indians li-
         ving on reservations, according to IHS statistics.

T   13) Chicle was used by South American Indians many centu-
         ries before Wrigley patented it.

T   14) Manifest Destiny was the handiest justification for
         land acquisition and westward expansion.

T   15) Not one single documented treaty between the U.S. and
         Indians has ever been fully honored. "They made us
         many promises, more than I can remember, but they
         never kept but one; they promised to take our land,
         and they took it"-anonymous Indian.

Multiple Guess   (Answers to Indian Cultural Differences Test)

1) The tomahawk was a french invention later copied and used extensively by Indians.

2) Corn and Potatoes

3) No one knows where this phrase comes from; there are no known languages that this can be traced to-another Hollywood gimmick.

4) Gen. Sheridan's direct quote: "The only good Indians I ever saw were dead." The phrase was later simplified for layman's use.

5) The Six Nations were composed of:Oneida, Seneca, Tuscorora, Ononodaga, Cayuga, and Mohawk.

6) Dartmouth

Match

Name	Tribe - Region	Date - Event
1 - F	1 - B	1 - A
2 - I	2 - A	2 - H
3 - C	3 - D	3 - I
4 - G	4 - C	4 - E
5 - A	5 - C	5 - F
6 - D	6 - E	6 - B
7 - H	7 - A	7 - C
8 - E	8 - B	8 - D
9 - B	9 - E	9 - G
	10 - D	10 - J

Black Cultural Difference Test

True Or False (4 pts. each)

____ 1. A deuce and a quarter is a term used by blacks to describe a poker bet.

____ 2. "What it is" is a form of greeting used by blacks usually meaning "what's happening or what's going on."

____ 3. There is a "national" handshake used by most blacks (primarily males) when greeting one another.

____ 4. A grey broad is slang for a black woman.

____ 5. When a brother is crooning he is dancing.

____ 6. Ice Berg Slim is a preacher well known in the ghetto for his fiery sermons.

____ 7. A "hog" is the kind of car the stereotype says most blacks drive.

____ 8. A pressing comb is slang for an iron.

____ 9. The spook in "The Spook Who Sat By The Door" referred to a ghost.

___ 10. A process is a hair slickening and straightening technique that formerly included lye and potatoes as ingredients in the mixture applied to the scalp.

Multiple Choice (2 pts. each)

11. The statement "She was cruising in her "chine"" refers to:

___a. Using her laundromat

___b. Riding in her car

___c. On a float trip

___d. None of the above.

12. Long green refers to:

___a. Plenty land

___b. A golf game

___c. A naive person

___d. Plenty money

13. The spank is a contemporary

___a. Dance

___b. Rock group

___c. Cult hero

___d. Way of rapidly placing one's hand on a child's behind

14. Money talks and bullshit walks as a quote was made popular by:

___a. Richard Nixon

___b. Richard Pryor

___c. Billy Carter

___d. Big Daddy George Watson

15. The majority of blacks living today were born in the:

___a. North

___b. East

___c. West

___d. South

16. Who said, blacks can only win their freedom through the "Ballot or the Bullet".

___a. Martin Luther King Jr.

___b. Marcus Garvey

___c. Huey Newton

___d. Malcolm X

17. A "Cooling Board" (still referred to in black fundamentalist prayers) is :

___a. The paddle whites used to beat blacks with during slavery

___b. The slab of wood blacks were buried on during slavery

___c. Ice rack used on the plantations to preserve food

18. James Weldon Johnson was a:

___a. Poet

___b. Baseball player

___c. Dancer

___d. All of the above

19. "Jumping de broom" was a slave phrase that meant:

___a. Running away

___b. Harvest time

___c. Getting married

___d. None of the above

20. The north star was so valuable to black slaves because it:

___a. Provided the northerly direction when black slaves needed to escape

___b. Became the name of a newspaper Frederick Douglass founded

___c. Both A & B

___d. None of the above

Translate This

Dig, I'm trying to cop a gig. I went to the man and this sister was flunkying. I tried to shoot game and she dug where I was coming from. She hipped me to the happening thing at her cut. I slid over to her crib and jammed back.

Matching

____ Cop	a. cool
____ Heat	b. beautiful
____ Jive	c. get or obtain
____ Grey-Broad	d. Gun or weapon
____ Scope	e. #1 woman
____ Threads	f. Sister
____ Game	g. White Woman
____ Boo-Koo	h. Phony or full of bull
____ Main Squeeze	i. Check out or look over
____ Hog	j. Shoes
	k. Money
	l. Clothes
	m. Heavy or deep rap
	n. Plenty or deep
	o. Cadillac

Answers to Black Cultural Differences Test

Answer Key for True/False

False 1. A deuce and a quarter is a term blacks use to describe a car:(a Buick Electra 225)

True 2.

True 3.

False 4. A grey broad is slang for white woman

False 5. He is singing

False 6. He was a pimp known for his ruthlessness

True 7. A hog is a Cadillac

False 8. A pressing comb is a metal comb when heated is used to "press" and straighten black hair

False 9. Referred to a black person

True 10. In the 50's and early 60's the process received wide acceptance from entertainers and inner city residents. In the mid 60's and 70's it gave way to the Afro, the Blow out and other hair styles. It's still a popular hair style among some inner city residents.

Multiple Choice

11. b	16. d
12. d	17. b
13. a	18. a
14. b	19. c
15. d	20. c

Translation:

Listen, I'm trying to get a job. I went to the boss and this black woman was working. I tried to sweet talk her and she liked what I was saying. She told me what was going on at her place. I went over to her house and partied.

Answers to matching

<u>c</u> Cop   <u>l</u> threads

<u>d</u> heat   <u>m</u> game

<u>h</u> jive   <u>n</u> boo-koo

<u>g</u> grey-broad   <u>e</u> main squeeze

<u>i</u> scope   <u>o</u> hog

How did you score?

90-100 You should be leading a session on black slang/culture

80-89 What's happening blood!

70-79 You know just enough black culture to get beat up

0-69 You need help!

Chicano Cultural Differences Test

What Is Your Chicano Culture Quotient?
Taking this test should give you some idea of how much or how little you know about Chicano Culture and History. (Circle your answers)

1. The term "Chicano" refers to:
   a. "Militant" Mexican Americans
   b. Latinos who reject their culture
   c. Mexican Americans who desire the benefit of two cultures

2. The treaty of Guadalupe Hildago ceded to the United States what is now known as:
   a. the state of Texas
   b. the state of New Mexico
   c. the state of California
   d. the southwestern United States

3. Cinco de Mayo is a Mexican holiday which commemorates:
   a. Mexico's independence from France
   b. the battle of Puebla
   c. the death of the Frito Bandito
   d. the decline of the Diaz regime

4. Mexican culture has been influenced by which of the following cultures?
   a. Aztec
   b. Spanish
   c. Inca
   d. Indian
   e. all of the above

5. The first "wetbacks" crossed into America:
   a. at Ciudad Juarez in 1846
   b. at Tiajuana in 1922
   c. at Plymouth Rock in 1620
   d. at Nuevo Laredo in 1882

6. The Chicano equivalent of a "ghetto" is:
   a. el gato
   b. el barrio
   c. el rancho grande
   d. la tierra

7. A frajo is a:
   a. short handled hoe
   b. car
   c. cigarette
   d. pachuco

8. Chicanos in the United States average_____years of education.
    a. 9.3
    b. 5.0
    c. 12.2

9. Mysticism is used in Chicano culture to control behavior of children:
    a. hardly at all
    b. to a large degree
    c. never

10. A curandera is a:
    a. healer
    b. witch
    c. curious person

11. La Llorona and El Coco are recognized by almost all Chicano children to be
    a. benevolent persons
    b. animals
    c. bad persons

12. The 12th of December is:
    a. Cesar Chavez's Birthday
    b. The day of the Virgin of Guadalupe
    c. The anniversary of "pachuco" riots

13. La jura refers to:
    a. an Anglo jury
    b. a judge
    c. the cops
    d. a lawyer

14. To Chicanos their term Carnal means:
    a. brother
    b. butcher
    c. sports car
    d. enemy

15. Macho refers to:
    a. being chauvinistic
    b. being manly and honorable
    c. being a disloyal person
    d. being courteous

16. A tio taco is a:
    a. Mexican dish
    b. individual who rejects his culture
    c. Cuban
    d. an uncle from Spain

17. The most valued institution in Chicano Culture is:
   a. the educational institution
   b. the religious institution
   c. the political institution
   d. the family

18. The Chicano family is usually comprised of:
   a. parents and children
   b. parents, children, and relatives
   c. parents, children, and grandparents
   d. parents, children, relatives, and friends

19. Many Chicano parents feel their children will be severely handicapped by:
   a. erratic school attendance
   b. knowing and speaking spanish
   c. influences of Chicano culture
   d. learning both English and Spanish

20. Some teachers view the major handicap to be overcome by Chicano students as:
   a. culture conflicts
   b. lack of English-speaking ability
   c. short attention spans
   d. innate stupidity

Answers To Chicano Cultural Differences Test

1. c The term Chicano is a concept which many Mexican Americans identify with because it gives them a feeling of pride. It identifies them as being proud of their cultural heritage.

2. d The treaty of Guadalupe Hildago was signed by the United States and Mexico in 1848. With this treaty, Mexico accepted the RIO Grande as the Texas border and ceded the Southwest (which incorporates the present day states of Arizona, California, New Mexico, Utah, Nevada, and parts of Colorado) to the U.S. in return for $15 million.

3. b This celebration is in reference to a battle in which a small Mexican Army defeated a French Army Battalion. Cinco de Mayo celebrations are still commemorated in Mexico and all over the United States where there are a significant number of Chicanos.

4. e The Mexican heritage is one that is often referred to as Mestizo or "mixed". A number of different people have influenced what is known as "Mexican Culture" today.

5. c The term "wetback" is often used to refer to illegal Mexican aliens entering the United States. However, from the Chicano's

167

point of view, the first "wetbacks" to enter this country were the pilgrims who crossed over on the May Flower.

6. b To Chicanos their neighborhood is known as el barrio.

7. c The term frajo is a slang word for cigarette which is commonly used in the barrio.

8. a This is a fluctuating figure that rises and falls from year to year. However, it should be stressed that Chicanos have the highest drop-out rate and the lowest educational level achievement of all groups of people in the United States.

9. b Traditionally, Chicano culture is very superstitious and parents utilize this belief to control their children.

10. a The curandera is a person who is able to relieve people of their physical sickness. Many elderly Chicano people do not believe in the "doctor" as they are known in this country. They prefer to be attended by the curandera or healer.

11. c La Llorona and El Coco are a couple of the superstitious characters utilized by parents to control the behavior of their children.

12. b Chicanos are a very religious people. The 12th of December is the day of the most patron saint of the Chicano people -The day of the virgin of Guadalupe.
%% Answers to Chicano Cultural Differences Test Continued %%

13. c La jura is a slang term for "the cop" which every Chicano who resides in el barrio is well aware.

14. a Carnal simply means brother. It is usually used as a greeting between males.

15. b In Mexican culture to be Macho is to be manly and honorable. It incorporates a quite different meaning than is associated with the term here in the U.S.

16. b Many individuals reject their culture due to the educational system in this country. Chicanos have been taught that their culture is inferior and that the Anglo American culture is superior. Therefore, many Mexican Americans (especially second and third generations) cannot identify with their cultural heritage and the term Chicano.

17. d Chicano families are traditionally very, very close. The total Chicano existence revolves around the family.

18. d The Chicano family encompasses the extended type of family lifestyle which incorporates close friends. These close friends are usually referred to as "compadres" and "comadres".

19. b Many Chicano parents believe that their children will be handicapped if they are allowed to learn and speak spanish. Many Chicano parents want their children to succeed in school and they believe that knowing and speaking spanish will hinder rather than enhance their children's education.

20. b Many teachers are not aware of the cultural conflicts that Chicano children are confronted with when they first enter the educational system in this country. The children are accustomed to a particular lifestyle and when exposed to the "white middle class" surroundings they become disorganized and must try and adjust to their new environment. Teachers must become aware that it is more than just language conflicts that hinder Chicano children from learning —it is the entire culture differences.

How did you score? For each correct answer give yourself 5 points.
Scale 90-100 You are probably a Chicano.
80-89   You are very aware of Chicano culture.
70-79   Contact your nearest Multicultural Education Center.
0-69   You are culturally deprived.

Asian Cultural Difference Test

True/False

___ 1. The internment of Japanese Americans during World War II was supported by president Franklin D. Roosevelt.

___ 2. Chinese Americans make up the largest Asian American group in the U.S..

___ 3. There was a Japanese settlement in California as early as 1869.

___ 4. The first Chinese immigrants who came to the U.S. did not work on the railroads.

___ 5. To the Chinese New Year represents everyone's birthday.

___ 6. The Chinese New Year usually begins anytime between March 20th and April 15th.

___ 7. Feng-shui is the belief in giving a packet of good luck money wrapped in red paper.

___ 8. Most Christian religions are not found in Asian cultures.

___ 9. The traditional Chinese Temple is found in almost every Chinese settlement.

___ 10. Buddhism is not a formal religion with priests, prayer, images and a vast array of gods.

___ 11. Chinese were reported in the U.S. as early as 1820.

___ 12. The Chinese almost single-handedly built the Pacific portion of the transcontinental railroad.

___ 13. In the 1974 Supreme Court Decision, Lau vs Nichols, the Chinese opposed bilingual education.

___ 14. When congress passed the Chinese Exclusion Act in 1882 it was the first time the U.S. denied entry based on national origin.

___ 15. Asian Culture did not stress secret societies and self reliance.

___ 16. The Nisei are known as the last generation of Americans of Japanese ancestry.

___ 17. Asian Americans are often referred to as "Model" minorities.

___ 18. Sukiyaki is a Japanese word meaning, how are you?

___ 19. Most Japanese Americans who are Buddhist belong to the Jodo Shinshu Sect.

___ 20. Hanamatsuri is the day on which Buddhists celebrate the birth of Buddha.

Multiple Choice

1. Buddha-Dharma is ____
   (a) the teachings of Judo
   (b) the practice of oriental cooking
   (c) the teaching of the Buddha
   (d) the wife of the Buddha

2. The art of bonsai refers to ____
   (a) Japanese silk screening
   (b) Chinese wrestling
   (c) the growing of trees to exact replicas of large trees which grow in the forest
   (d) none of the above

3. The Koto is ____
   (a) a Korean word for house
   (b) a 13 string instrument used in Japan for many years
   (c) the newest Oriental dance to hit the west coast
   (d) the Vietnamese national anthem

4. This word sometimes means a japanese ghetto____
   (a) Nihon machi
   (b) Sakana
   (c) Kanji
   (d) ghettuloheli

5. Third generation Japanese are called____
   (a) Issei
   (b) Nisei
   (c) Yonsei
   (d) Sansei

Answer Key for Asian Cultural Difference Test

True/False

1. True
2. False
3. True
4. True
5. True
6. False
7. False
8. False
9. True
10. False

11. True
12. True
13. False
14. True
15. False
16. False
17. True
18. False
19. True
20. True

Multiple Choice

1. c
2. c
3. b
4. a
5. d

Exclusion/Discrimination

A. Objective: The participants will be helped to understand the impact that exclusion has on individuals who are not allowed to participate.

Time required: 25 minutes

Activity and Discussion

Tell the participants they are eligible to earn three privileges if they qualify for the rules you have established. The three privileges are: (Feel free to create your own privileges)

1. They can leave class early for one day.
2. They can be excused from one homework assignment.
3. They can work on another class project during your class time for one day.

The rules they must qualify for are:

1. Be taller than 5'5"
2. Possess a driver's license
3. Be a male

After the class learns what it takes to qualify for the privileges, you can expect a lot of dissension and charges of being unfair (i.e., discrimination). This should lead into a lively discussion of what it means to be left out for reasons people have little control over. This activity also allows for role playing having the students who qualify for the privileges defend their selection. The discussion can be enlarged to include other forms of discrimination.

B. Objective: The students should be able to determine appropriate ways to handle discriminatory situations.

Time required: 30 minutes

Situations--

1. Tom Stanley has just been hired as a rental agent to rent apartments in a large apartment complex. On his desk he finds a policy manual that lists policy #1 as follows: DO NOT rent any apartments to "Hippies." What should he do?

2. Mary Tolen gets beaten up by a neighborhood gang for having a Black friend over to visit. What should she do?

3. Charlie Goldberg wants to join a fraternity but it discriminates against Jews. He's Jewish. What should he do?

4. Susan Harris wants to try out for the boys basketball team but her parents are opposed to this. The coach wants her to try out but the boys resent it. What should she do?

5. Harold Tyler is really attracted to Jan Lockman and wants very badly to take her out on a date. The problem is that he is Black and she is White and their parents don't approve. What should they do?

C. Objective: The students should be able to think through the myriad of issues city planners and concerned citizens must address to resolve housing problems.

Time required: 2-3 hours

Break the class up into small groups of between 5-7 people. Give each group the following written assignment:

Your group has just been appointed by the mayor as an advisory council to the City Planning Department. The Mayor expects you to come up with several sites for the city to consider in building low income housing.

The city is divided into four areas. Area A is considered the poor section of the city. Mostly Blacks and Hispanics live there. Most people call it a ghetto. Area B is the working class neighborhood. Blue collar whites and a few Minorities live in this section. Area C is where the professional class lives and Area D is where the wealthy live. Area D is totally opposed to low income housing and will fight against any effort to locate sites in their area. Area C, although not opposed to low income housing, will support it only if it is located in areas A and B.

Area B residents feel their neighborhood is already deteriorating and they believe if additional low income units are built their property values will go down. They also feel these houses are being built at their expense so they are opposed to low income housing. Area A residents want low income housing units badly but want them built in another area because the ghetto is too crowded. They understand the opposition from other segments of the city but vow to do whatever is necessary to get out of the overcrowded conditions.

What will you recommend to the mayor and the City Planning Department? What issues must be considered before you make your recommendation? Allow the groups about forty-five minutes to discuss the issues. Have each group select a spokesperson to share with the entire class what site that group will recommend to the mayor.

After each group has reported, have a general discussion about the issues raised by the students.

Tips For Working With Culturally Different Students

Working with culturally different students is a challenge that requires sensitivity and vulnerability. Because of the potential for mixed signals, suspicion and misunderstanding it's important that care be given to how this interaction is to be structured. While do's and don'ts are clearly out of place it is important to acknowledge some broad generalizations that may prove helpful when working with racial minorities. If these guidelines are followed you stand a better chance of creating positive interactions.

* Avoid the tendency to lump all minorities together or view them as the same.
* Stress cultural pluralism and celebrate diversity while discarding the notion of the U.S. as a melting pot.
* Watch for stereotyping in language, roles, media and in institutional practices.
* Recognize that by treating everyone the "same" does not mean that everyone is being treated fairly.
* Become familiar with different historical world views that each minority group represents. Although George Washington might be considered an American hero to whites, since he owned slaves he may be considered just the opposite by blacks.
* Develop a contemporary perspective about race and culture. Read minority publications and listen to it's leadership.
* Be more accepting of minority descriptions and perceptions of their life experiences in America.
* Take some risks. Attend activities and events that are sponsored by individuals outside your ethnic group.
* Participate in workshops, conferences and classes that deal with race and culture.
* Involve minorities in the planning of programs.

Chapter 8

Fact Sheets on Celebrating Minority Holidays

ASIAN AMERICAN HOLIDAYS:

> Boon Hok Nam
> Chinese New Year
> Hmong New Year
> Vietnamese New Years Day

BLACK AMERICAN HOLIDAYS:

> Black History Month
> Juneteenth Day
> Kwanzaa
> Martin Luther King Jr.'s Birthday

HISPANIC AMERICAN HOLIDAYS:

> Cinco De Mayo
> Mexican Independence Day

NATIVE AMERICAN HOLIDAYS:

> American Indian Day/Week
> Feast of Thanksgiving

BOON HOK NAM

What is Boon Hok Nam?

It is the Laotian New Year, a time of joy and happiness with which many traditions are associated and observed by the Lao people.

When does Boon Hok Nam Occur?

Boon Hok Nam occurs on the 12th day of the Lao fifth month. That day is called **Muc Sangkhan Khuen** which is the day the spirit of the New Year arrives; usually around April 13th or 14th and lasts five days.

The Ceremonies

The morning of the first day people go to the temple to take the Buddha statues down and the ritual of cleaning and washing of the images of Lord Buddha occurs. The afternoon of the first day charcoal and dirt are used to paint some people's faces. An individual who has their face painted may ask another if he or she may wash him or her and then they will throw water on his or her back. When someone wants to throw water to the other for the first time they must say "excuse me" before they can throw the water to bring good luck. This holiday is used to symbolize the washing away of all evil. Normally, there is no school or work for five days.

The second day people celebrate at their own houses and invite others to enjoy with them. They often invite monks to come and **Sia Kho** (drive away the past year's wickedness and evil spirits). Others will have this service performed by their own **Maw Pawn** who will chant the prayers. It is customary to visit parents and employers to **Baci** (wish) them happiness for the following year.

People usually buy fish, turtles, snails and crabs and take them to the ponds and rivers to free them. Pigeons and small birds are released from their cages. This ensures good luck for the coming year because the reincarnated souls, in being freed, will have a good influence on the lives of their benefactors.

For additional information on specific rituals see the fact sheets in this section on the **Vietnamese TET** and the **Chinese New Year.** Many rituals included in these fact sheets are generally observed throughout the Southeast Asian area.

CHINESE NEW YEAR

When Observed?

Chinese New Year's falls on the first new moon after the sun has left the sign of Capricorn and entered Aquarius. In non-zodiac terminology, this means sometime between January 21st and February 20th. The traditional Chinese calendar is lunar. This calendar was established in 104 B.C. with only minor modifications thereafter up until today.

How is it Celebrated?

China is made up of more than 50 nationalities and her territory is larger than Europe. In addition there are Chinese settlements overseas (i.e. in Southeast Asia and the U.S.- Chinatowns). Each has developed its own way of celebrating the New Year. None the less there are some general principles by which the New Year is celebrated throughout the world. The Chinese still practice rituals designed to pay homage to the Gods and the ancestors of the world beyond, and customs formed for the living, such as getting the house ready, settling all accounts, making clothes and foods, and preparing festivities for bidding farewell to the Old Year and welcoming the arrival of the New Year.*

New Year's Eve:

New Year's Eve is a special night during the celebrations. Even today many traditional Chinese believe that during this night deities return to earth and the spirits of the ancestors come back for the family reunion. As a result New Year's Eve is often viewed as being sacred; so sacred that everything one thinks, says and does could cause serious consequences for the New Year and even the future of an individual or family. Therefore, every precaution is taken to avoid bad luck and insure the good. That is why there are so many symbols for good omens.

---

* In recent years God-worshiping has diminished, however ancestor-veneration is still practiced by many Chinese using various styles. For additional information on specific rituals see the fact sheet on the Vietnamese TET which is patterned after the Chinese New Year Celebration.

The Celebration:

Longevity, happiness and prosperity are New Year's wishes. Oranges and fish are often given as New Year's gifts. During the celebration one may find a large hanging or just a piece of red paper with the word "fu" which means happiness" (can also mean blessings and good fortune) on doors, walls, shops, restaurants and homes.

There are many taboos during the celebration also. Words like death, finished and the like are avoided lest bad luck befall the family in the New Year.

Highlights of the Celebration:

The 15th of the first lunar month is a high point. This is the Lantern Festival. Many shapes, forms and colors of lanterns are on display everywhere. During the Lantern Festival the Fire Dragon Dance may take place. The special food for this feast is yuanxiao which are small balls made of glutinous rice flour with sweetened fruits or bean paste stuffing inside, and can be eaten boiled or deep fried.

Red firecrackers are always a part of the celebration. They are used to ward off evil spirits. It was believed that the color red was dreaded by monsters and evil spirits.

ADDITIONAL FACTS ABOUT THE CHINESE NEW YEAR

* Each Chinese year is named after one of the twelve animal symbols of the zodiac: rat, ox, tiger, rabbit, dragon, snake, horse, sheep, monkey, rooster, dog and pig.
* The celebration lasts several days, beginning with private observances and ending with the gala festivities which hundreds of thousands of Americans enjoy from New York to San Francisco.
* Many of the activities are dominated by the symbols of the Taoist religion, especially the Yang and the Yin. These are the balanced opposites in the world--the male and female, the positive and negative principles, the rebirth of Spring and the dormancy of winter--life and death.
* Noise and light are always present during the celebration to route the evil spirits.
* The Golden Dragon is almost always featured and represents one of four Divine Creatures to the Chinese. The others are the Phoenix, the Unicorn and the Tortoise. They all are used to dispel bad spirits but the dragon is honored as ruler of rivers, lakes and seas. The dragon combines the head of a camel, horns of a deer, neck of a snake, claws of a hawk, belly of a frog and scales of a fish.
* The Golden Dragon of San Francisco is over 100 feet long and is handmade of Chinese silk and velvet. It weaves through the streets with bright lights performing the classic dragon dance. (A full performance of the ritual can take up to four hours).

*   The Chinese wish each other a happy new year with these words: Kung Hsi Fa Tsai (say Kung-Sha-Fah-Tsye).
*   Many people decorate the house or apartment with red paper, a symbol of good luck.
*   "Lucky money", usually wrapped in red paper, is given to the children.
*   On the Chinese New Year it is everyone's birthday and it is from that date that age is recorded regardless of the actual day the individual was born.

Praxis Publications wishes to acknowledge Professor Clara S.Y. Sun, Council on Chinese Studies, UW-Madison, Madison, Wisconsin 53706 for her assistance in compiling this fact sheet.

HMONG NEW YEAR

When does the Hmong New Year Occur?

Unlike other Asian New Year celebrations, the Hmong lunar calendar year usually begins somewhere in mid-November to December, depending on the rhythm of nature itself. The Hmong calendar months always have 30 days rather than irregular patterns like the Western calendar.

History of the Hmong New Year

The Hmong are an ethnic group from the highlands in Laos. Hmong means "free man". Many recently have migrated to the U.S. at the end of the Vietnam war. Historically their way of life has centered in working the land and supporting an agricultural based economy. Since their livelihood depended on a successful harvest, the Hmong place great importance on the growing season. As a result, their new year generally falls at the completion of the growing season. The Hmong New Year has been called the most exciting and meaningful celebration of the year. The festivities include parties, food and games, not unlike the American new year.

Celebrating the Hmong New Year

Preparation for the New Year celebration usually begins with a private ceremony performed by each household or family lineage. For those inclined, offerings are made to one's ancestors and spirits to insure good fortune for the coming year. One such ceremony consists of cutting a small tree in the forest and bringing it to the house. A rope braided from reeds is attached to the tree and held by a member of the house. All members encircle the tree and walk around it three times in one direction and four times in the opposite direction to confuse the spirits. If a family member is absent, a piece of his/her clothing is held by another member during the ritual.

Next the head of the lineage or household ceremoniously sacrifices a chicken while reciting a special chant. The chant asks that all the evil and ill fortune of the family be transferred to the tree. The feet of the chicken are examined to see if the ceremony was successful. The tree is then carefully wrapped in red, white and green paper and hidden away from the family. In this way the family is cleansed of evil spirits for the coming year.

In another ceremony, females rush to the mountain streams in order to fetch the first pail of water. This ritual is called "Haus Dlej Tshab" or scrambling for new water, as a way to obtain good luck.

The first two days of the new year celebration are reserved for family activities and to pay homage and respect to the elderly. Family members bring gifts, food and drink and ask blessings from the elders in return. After the family activities, the fun begins. Traditionally horse exhibits, bull fights and ball games are to be found. In the ball games, teams consisting of marriageable males compete against marriageable females. This event provides both sexes with an opportunity to meet each other and plan for possible future marriages. Since coming to America, the Hmong have had to modify their new year celebration. As they begin to attend America's campuses it's important that universities permit them to celebrate their cultural heritage, both as a reminder of their roots and to familiarize Americans with Hmong culture.

VIETNAMESE NEW YEAR'S DAY

When does TET Occur?

TET NGUYEN DAN, or the Vietnamese New Year's Day, begins the first day of the first month of the lunar year and continues for three or more days. Since TET normally occurs at the end of January or early February, the celebrants also celebrate the return of spring during the TET festivities.

In Vietnam the holidays and festivals are determined by the lunar calendar in which the months are regulated by the moon. That's why the dates of TET may vary from year to year.

History of TET

Although the exact date of TET's beginning is unclear, many Vietnamese historians credit the Ly dynasty (1010-1224 A.D.) as originating TET. During this period the Chinese customs were introduced into Vietnam. Ever since then TET has been considered the most solemn festival by the Vietnamese.

Preparing for TET

TET has been described by westerners as Thanksgiving, Christmas, Memorial Day and 4th of July all rolled into one. Therefore, preparations for TET are elaborate and take many days. Families save money throughout the year specifically for the TET festivities. Wishes for prosperity, happiness and longevity are displayed everywhere on scarlet paper and banners. Many Vietnamese buddhists put up bamboo poles in front of their houses and hang talismans and musical stones on them to drive away evil spirits. Flags are also hung to attract the spirits of the ancestors. Altars are set up in many homes and candlesticks and incense burners are made ready for use. People visit their ancestors' gravesites to clean and decorate them. New clothes are bought and special meals are prepared. People that live away from home try to return for a reunion with their families.

On the 23rd day of the 12th lunar month the farewell to the Kitchen God ceremony takes place. It is believed that this god lives in the kitchen and records everything that happens on earth during the year. On the 23rd the God has to report to the heavens all that he has observed during the past year. The Vietnamese have a special ceremony to send the god off on his heavenly journey.

Holy Night of TET

This is a most spiritual time. The people wait to welcome the "Giao Thua". Giao means to give, Thua means to receive: The God of the old year is leaving and is transferring authority to the God of the new year who receives it.

All the business activities and most shops close at noon

preceding the beginning of the holiday. Bamboo poles are placed in front of houses to ward off evil spirits and to win the good will of genii. Debts are paid off, quarrels are forgotten and people try to start off with a clean-slate. People take their last bath to start the New Year off right. As night approaches some people go to a Buddhist or village temple to ask for blessings on their house and families. In a special ceremony the ancestors are welcomed back to share the festivities with the living. When the clock strikes midnight, fire crackers are set off to welcome in the New Year.

Celebrating TET

The celebration begins the first day of the first month of the lunar year and continues for three days. Great importance is attached to the first visitor to one's home. Since many Vietnamese believe that the first visitor may determine what type of year they will have, they often ask a selected person to "Xong dat" (Step in on the land of one's property).

On the first day of TET people get up early to pay respect to the eldest person in the house. Wishes for a happy and prosperous New Year are exchanged as well as red envelopes containing money. One more year is added to everyone's age in a ceremony called Mung Tuoi.

On the second day the wife's family is visited and/or the children return to their mother's home place. On the third day of TET a visit is paid to the teacher(s). The teacher-student relationship in Vietnam is very close.

Throughout the TET festivities the staple meal consists of Banh Day (round cake of glutinous rice that is soft and sticky) and Banh Chung (a square cake wrapped in banana leaves and tied with lacings of flexible bamboo slivers). The insides contain a bean paste filling with small pieces of pork). The cakes are available at every meal along with another staple, pickled onions and marinated fish.

The Unicorn dance is performed. The Unicorn symbolizes kindness and wisdom in Vietnam mythology. The ceremonial unicorn is made of cloth and paper stretched over a bamboo frame. TET is unthinkable without beautiful flowers. Flowers that signal spring are usually displayed throughout the ceremony. The most famous flowers used are the Narcissus which are carefully tended indoors in an effort to make them bloom on the first day of TET.

After the third day of TET the Vietnamese believe their ancestors return to their heavenly abode and life returns to its normalcy. Vietnamese Americas are encouraged to maintain the TET tradition.

BLACK HISTORY MONTH

FOUNDER:Carter G. Woodson (1875-1950); known as the father of Black history study. He was born on December 19, 1875 in New Canton, Virginia. Woodson received his education at Berea College, in Kentucky, the University of Chicago, Harvard and the Sorbonne in Paris. He authored many books including **The Education of the Negro Prior to 1861,** (1915); **A Century of Negro Migration** (1918); **The Negro in Our History** (1922) and **The Rural Negro** (1930). Woodson died in Washington, D.C. on April 3, 1950.

BLACK HISTORY MONTH

Today Black history month is an accepted national event celebrating the contribution of black people to the progress of humanity, in general, and to the development of the United States, in particular. However, Black history month has its "roots" also. In 1915 Carter Woodson founded and became the director of the "Association for the Study of Negro Life and History". In 1926 he introduced Negro History Week as a reaction to American racism and to highlight the role blacks played in the development of civilization. Negro History Week was introduced in February because Woodson wanted it scheduled as close as possible to the birthdays of Frederick Douglass and Abraham Lincoln.

Why did Dr. Woodson and the Association for the Study of Negro Life consider it necessary to set aside a time to reflect on the meaning of Black History? The answer may lie in the social conditions of the times when the issues were raised. White historians have characterized the 1920's as the "gay twenties" but for Blacks there is much evidence to suggest that times were anything but gay. Jim Crow laws and terrorist attacks by the KKK were the conditions that many Blacks were facing. The society was deeply segregated. In spite of this bleak picture, Dr. Woodson, Dr. W.E.B. Dubois and other black historians and social scientists systematically proved that blacks played an integral part of human history. Black historians went beyond the accepted elitist history which was mainly centered on the heroic deeds of exceptional men and women. They demonstrated that the heroic deeds of individuals were interdependent with the actions of the unknown millions and that denying the contribution of black people to the progress of humanity represented the denial of true human history. Over the years, Negro History Week has undergone a redefinition of terminology. Today this national observance has been expanded to encompass the entire month of February and is now referred to as black or Afro-American History month. Generally black history month is observed with speeches, lectures, films, presentations, theatrical performances, exhibits and historical information.

Every year the national theme for black history month is selected by the association that Woodson founded. For additional information on black history month, we encourage you to write or call the: Association for the Study of Afro-American Life and History, 1401 14th St., NW; Washington, D.C. 20005; (202) 667-2822.

JUNETEENTH DAY

When Does Juneteenth Day Occur?

The Emancipation Proclamation of January 1, 1863, had little impact in Texas because so little of the state was occupied by Northern troops. Most plantations in Texas were still intact and a quarter of a million Black people were still working as slaves. It was not until June 19, 1865, when Major General George Granger landed in Galveston to issue the order that "all the slaves are free," were the slaves actually freed. June 19, therefore became the day of Independence for thousands of Blacks.

Today, it is still a day for festivities in communities throughout Texas. Its observance has depended solely on the perpetuation of strong traditions among Blacks in the southwest--Arkansas, Louisiana, Texas and Oklahoma--and particularly in eastern Texas. However, in recent years Juneteenth Day (now know as the Black person's 4th of July) has caught on in northern and eastern cities as well. Milwaukee, Wisconsin has over 75,000 people in attendance at its street festival each year.

The Celebrations

Historically, people celebrating the 19th would begin on the evening of the 18th when they would get together to prepare the food. It would be a night of storytelling and the exchanging of tall tales about the past. On the morning of the 19th families often had ice cream and custard. In addition to ice cream, the traditional strawberry soda, which became known as "June 19th soda" was served as an extra treat. Games were held after dinner, with baseball being the main attraction. Today elaborate parades, exhibits, music, speeches, games and fairs are commonplace.

By World War II, a number of cultural and social forces began to undermine the tradition of the 19th. Economic forces were a threat as well. The Depression, the inability to make a living farming and the subsequent migration of people to the cities disrupted families and older ways of life. Many people went to places like the west coast where no one observed the 19th. Even those who went to cities like Dallas and Houston found opposition to the holiday among urban employers. In spite of these problems, the celebration never died out. Throughout East Texas, there have been groups of Black people who managed to keep the 19th alive in their communities. One group is the 19th of June organization in Anderson, Texas. It was started in 1938, by a group of Black men who were landowners.

One of the first things the organization did was establish an annual rodeo. Many Black men in Texas made a living as cowboys. But fees and racial discrimination made it almost impossible for Blacks to ride in White rodeo circuits of that day. Anderson's 19th of June rodeo became one of the few public opportunities for Black cowboys to exhibit their skills as horsemen.

Since the early 70s, with the emergence of Black nationalism, there has been a renewal of public concern about the preservation of June 19th in Texas and other places throughout America. The 1972 Texas House of Representatives passed a resolution recognizing "Juneteenth as an annual, though unofficial, holiday of significance to all Texans and particularly to Blacks of Texas, for whom this date symbolizes freedom from slavery." In Wisconsin, the Governor issues a proclamation proclaiming June 19 as Juneteenth Day each year. Perhaps no other day symbolizes Black pride as does Juneteenth Day.

References: 1. Negro Digest, February 1976, p.15
2. William H. Wiggins, "Free at Last!: A Study of Afro-American Emancipation Day Celebration"
3. General Orders, No.3, Galveston June 19, 1865, Vol.48
4. Dallas Morning News, June 20, 1972, p.10
5. Wendy Watriss, "Celebrate Freedom Juneteenth" Southern Exposure, Vol. 5 (1977)

KWANZAA

What is Kwanzaa?

Kwanzaa has its roots in Africa although it was founded in America by Ron Karenga an activist known for his Civil rights efforts. Kwanzaa means first. Traditionally it signifies the first fruits. In Africa, harvesting the first fruit crops has always been the cause of much celebration. Based on the traditional African holiday, Kwanzaa is a time in which the people of the community come together to give thanks and celebrate being together after working, struggling and building together. During the 60's many blacks in America embraced Kwanzaa as an alternative to "commercial" Christmas. Because Kwanzaa emphasizes humanistic and cooperative values, many blacks have made the seven principals which comprise it, part of the new black value system.

When is Kwanzaa Celebrated?

Kwanzaa is celebrated annually from December 26 through January 1, for a total of seven days.

Why is Kwanzaa Celebrated?

Celebrating Kwanzaa demonstrates pride in African heritage through participation in meaningful African customs and expands the African family and nation by strengthening the foundation and including new members in the universal black nation. Each year the celebration of Kwanzaa teaches black children that the values which Kwanzaa emphasizes have deep meaning and should be reflected in the things they do. As the children mature, they will hopefully be molded by these values and carry on black traditions.

How is the Kwanzaa Celebration Performed?

The Kwanzaa ritual is very symbolic and involves everyone in the household. Although Kwanzaa does not begin until December 26, many families gather all the items needed for the celebration earlier. Families take great care in preparing the symbols of Kwanzaa. The symbols are the MKEKA, the KINARA, the MUHINDI, the ZAWADI and the MSHUMAA. The MKEKA is a large straw mat on which all other symbols are placed. It symbolizes tradition as the foundation on which everything rests. The KINARA is a candle holder which holds seven candles. It represents black ancestors, black origin and symbolizes the black will and ability to continue the reproduction of the black nation. The MUHINDI are ears of corn, one for each child in the family. They are placed on the mat around the candles. They symbolize the ability of each child to become **stalks**, insuring the immortality of the nation. Every house should have at least one ear of corn to recognize the potential even when no children are present in the family. The ZAWADI are presents. They too are placed around the candles and corn or wherever there is room. They symbolize the fruits of the labor of the parents and the rewards for good acts and deeds sown by the children and the parents.

The MSHUMAA are the seven candles which represent the seven principals NGUZO SABA. As families prepare the MSHUMAA, they teach their children the meanings and significances of all the things that are part of the celebration. Each day during KWANZAA, a candle (MSHUMAA) is lit and one of the seven principles NGUZO SABA is explained. On the first day **Umoja** (unity) is explained.
On the second day **Kujichaquila** (self-determination) is explained. On the third day **Ujima** (collective work and responsibility) is explained. On the fourth day **Ujamaa** (cooperative economics) is explained. On the fifth day **Nia** (purpose) is explained. On the sixth day **Kuumba** (creativity) is explained. On the seventh day **Imani** (faith) is explained.

During the week of Kwanzaa (beginning December 26) the **Kinara** is brought to the dinner table each evening. During the first day of Kwanzaa each family member says "Umoja" when given the traditional greeting, "Harbarigani". Normally one responds by answering "Njema", which means well.

On the second day, members of the family ask Harbarigani of one another and answer "Kujichaquila". This continues throughout the seven days. For the adults, the "Karamu" or feast takes place on the night of December 31. It normally lasts all night. The feast is eaten African style without European utensils while sitting on pillows on the floor. African music should be played during the feast.

All present during the "Karamu" drink from the "Kilomble" (unity cup) and say **Harambee** which means, let's all pull together. Later that evening each person announces his/her commitment for the new year based on the **Nguzo Saba.**

On January 1, the final day of Kwanzaa, the **Zawadi** (presents) are opened after the children's commitments for the coming year are heard.

All of the special foods that have been prepared are served and the **Karamu** continues with food, drink, music, dance, laughter and conversation.

As a footnote, many black families decorate their homes in black, red and green. The black symbolizes the black nation. The red is a symbol of the blood that blacks have shed in their quest for liberation. The green is the symbol of the land on which the black nation will be built. Some families also decorate their tables using black, red and green tablecloths. Then they place baskets of fruits on the tablecloths to symbolize strength and nourishment.

DR. MARTIN LUTHER KING DAY; NATIONAL HOLIDAY

When is Dr. Martin Luther King, Jr.'s Birthday?

Dr. King had a dream - "that one day this nation will live out the true meaning of its creed: that all men (and women) are created equal." King was born on January 15, 1929 in Atlanta, Georgia. He devoted his life to trying to make this dream into reality.

History of Dr. Martin Luther King, Jr.

The son of Martin Luther King, Sr., the pastor of the Ebenezer Baptist Church in Atlanta, Georgia, he attended public schools in that city, and he went to Atlanta's Morehouse College. During his junior year there he decided on a career in the ministry. He was ordained in his father's church in 1947.

After his graduation from Morehouse in 1948, King continued his studies at Crozer Theological Seminary in Chester, Pennsylvania. He was the first Black in the history of the school to be elected class president. He received the B.D. degree and won a fellowship for further study. In 1951, King began his doctoral studies in theology at Boston University. There he met Coretta Scott, a graduate student in music, and in 1953 they were married. In 1958, King was awarded a Ph.D degree, but in the meantime his work in the civil rights movement had brought him national prominence.

On December 1, 1955, Rosa Parks, a Black seamstress in Montgomery, Alabama, refused to obey a bus driver's order to give up her seat to a white male passenger. Mrs. Parks's defiance resulted in her being fined $14. Of greater significance, however, it marked the beginning of a citywide bus boycott by Montgomery's Black residents. King was chosen to lead the campaign. The boycott drew national attention and gave King an opportunity to implement his belief in non-violent civil disobedience. In the course of the boycott, King was arrested and even when his home was bombed he did not abandon his belief in peaceful protest. The Supreme Court ruled on November 13, 1956 that segregation on buses was unconstitutional and integrated bus service began in Montgomery on December 21, 1956. As a result Dr. King emerged as the undisputed leader in the civil rights movement.

In 1957 King helped found and was chosen to head the Southern Christian Leadership Conference, and in 1958 he helped in establishing the Student Non-violent Coordinating Committee. In April 1963, King started a daring civil rights campaign in Birmingham, Alabama. For several weeks, Black citizens participated in protest marches and "sit-ins" at lunch counters where they historically had been denied service, and they picketed stores that practiced segregation.

Dogs and firehoses were used on the demonstrators. White supremacists bombed a Black church, which killed four young Black girls. Dr. King was arrested and spent five days in jail, where he wrote his famous letter from Birmingham, condemning the white moderate's concern for order rather than for justice.

190

The event that climaxed the campaign for civil rights was the march on Washington that took place on August 28, 1963. More than 200,000 Blacks and whites gathered in the nation's capitol to demand justice and, in the shadow of the Lincoln Memorial, this great mass heard Martin Luther King deliver his famous speech, "I have a Dream." In 1965, Dr. King led demonstrations against unfair and unreasonable voting requirements in Selma, Alabama. Hundreds of Blacks were arrested. King himself was beaten and kicked, but after the drive ended 25,000 persons marched from Selma to Montgomery.

Dr. King was an outspoken opponent of U.S. involvement in Vietnam, arguing that the war effort used resources that might otherwise have gone to the nation's poor. And he sought to draw attention to the plight of the underprivileged with a Poor People's campaign that was scheduled to begin in Washington, D.C., on April 22, 1968. As planned, thousands of Black Americans encamped in the nation's capitol in the summer of 1968 to demonstrate to Congress the need for legislation that would provide better economic opportunities for the nation's poor. But King was not with them.

On April 3, 1968, Dr. King had gone to Memphis, Tennessee, to help organize a strike of the city's predominantly Black sanitation workers. There, on the 4th of April, 1968, he was assassinated. The shot ended his life, but not his dream.

During his life's journey, King was honored by many nations and he received the Nobel Peace Prize. In 1968, Senator Edward W. Brooke of Massachusetts, the first Black to sit in the U.S. Senate since Reconstruction days, introduced a resolution to have January 15, King's birthday, set aside as a federal holiday. This effort failed when the 91st Congress adjourned without acting on Brook's resolution.

Many organizations, local and state governments have taken steps to pay tribute to his memory. A growing number of states have made King's birthday a legal holiday. Many cities have special proclamations calling for observance of January 15 as Martin Luther King Day. Even Montgomery, Alabama where King was jailed for his earliest civil rights activity as a leader, proclaimed his birthday, Martin Luther King Day in 1975. On November 3, 1983, the law was enacted declaring January 15 as a national holiday; effective January 1985.

How it is Commemorated?

In many communities across the U.S. observances on January 15 are likely to include memorial church services, rallies, musical and film tributes. In Atlanta, where King is buried, throngs gather to commemorate the day: a wreath is customarily placed on his grave and an overflow crowd fills the Ebenezer Baptist Church, where memorial services are held, and distinguished guests speak. The Martin Luther King, Jr. Center for Social Change, located in Atlanta, serves as a lasting memorial to this civil rights giant. Thousands visit the center annually.

The accomplishments in King's brief life are far too numerous to list and certainly no list could ever measure the extent to which

Martin Luther King will determine the future course of this nation's and the world's quest for freedom for all oppressed persons. His message was not confined by geographical limits and although he was only 39 years old when he died, the spirit of his message is timeless.

CINCO DE MAYO

When Does Cinco de Mayo Occur?

Cinco de Mayo or fifth of May is when the day is celebrated.

What is Cinco de Mayo?

One of the greatest days in Mexican history is known as Cinco de Mayo (fifth of May). It is the anniversary of the 1892 battle of Puebla, in which Mexican forces, against overwhelming odds, defeated French invaders. The battle was only a temporary setback for French troops, nevertheless, it appealed to the imagination of the Mexicans and gave them the moral confidence to win in the run long. This battle demonstrated to the world Mexico's willingness to fight for its independence. Some historians speculate that had Mexico failed to oust French foreign control, France and England would have supported the Confederacy in the U.S. Civil War.

Where is it Celebrated?

May 5 is a national holiday in Mexico; therefore it is celebrated with festivities by Mexicans both at home and in foreign countries. In the United States the anniversary is observed especially in the southwestern states of Texas, Arizona, and California, land that once belonged to Mexico. By no means is the celebration limited to those states, it is national in scope.

Cause of the Much Celebrated Battle

During the period of political change, known in Mexican history as La Reforma (The Reform), the Conservatives were ousted from power. The Liberal party sought to implement a system of government that would abolish special privileges held by the landholders, the church and the army. In protest, the Conservatives initiated a war that wracked Mexico for three years. They were eventually defeated. Some fled overseas where they enlisted the aid of France, England and Spain to help them regain power. The three countries agreed but needed an excuse to intervene. The excuse was provided by the Liberal party when it declared a two year suspension of payments on Mexico's large foreign debt. An arrangement was made by the three European countries to make a joint naval demonstration against Mexico in order to compel payment to bondholders. It was announced that there was no intention of conquering Mexico and that nothing was desired but a settlement of just claims. A conference was arranged with Mexican representatives and a preliminary agreement was reached. British and Spanish fleets sailed home in April, 1892. The French, however, had other plans. French emperor Napoleon III, eager to establish a centralized monarchy under French control in Mexico, as a means of achieving hegemony in Spanish America, started a war of conquest.

When he attacked the forts of Laredo and Guadalupe near Puebla on May 5, 1892, two thousand Mexican soldiers under General Ignacio Zaragoza drove back 6,000 French soldiers with serious losses and finally won the day. Cinco de Mayo inspires Hispanics everywhere because it symbolizes victory against overwhelming odds. It represents the classic tale of David and Goliath.

How is it Celebrated?

Puebla, Mexico is the scene of a fiesta and a reenactment of the famous battle annually on May 5. The city's celebration includes a military parade usually attended by the president of the republic, and a **comate de flores**, (battle of flowers) in the evening.

In the United States, Mexican social clubs and organizations generally sponsor a variety of events, such as parades, patriotic speeches, and beauty contests. In San Antonio, Texas for example, there are festive gatherings in two city parks with such features as a chicken barbecue, dances and music. In Los Angeles an official observance complete with orchestras and bands, banners and flags, visiting dignitaries, speeches, and Mexican dances takes place.

MEXICAN INDEPENDENCE DAY

When Does the Celebration Occur?

Mexican Independence Day is celebrated on September 16, but its commemoration really begins on September 15, which is the "Dia del Grito de la Independencia" (Day of the Cry for Independence).

History of Mexican Independence Day

The people of Mexico are descendants of the Aztec and Mayan civilizations. Their heritable traditions remain an integral part of the Mexican culture to this day. In fact, most Mexican holidays are religious observances of their cultural ancestry. However, Mexican Independence Day has become for them one of the most important national celebrations. It marks the end of the Mexican slavery era which began with the Spanish Inquisition.

The first Spanish conquistadores arrived in Mexico soon after Cristobal Colon (Christopher Columbus) "discovered" the "new world" on October 12, 1492. They were first confused for tribal gods because of their lighter skin color, advanced technology and strange looking animals they had brought with them. Little did the Mexican tribes suspect that the Spaniards would soon occupy Mexico and rob them of their freedom, religion, mineral and natural resources. The Spanish conquerors, unlike their Pilgrim counterparts, had crossed the Atlantic in search of gold and new Roman Catholic converts. They brought along weapons, horses, soldiers and missionaries. The Spaniards took advantage of this "warm welcome" and quickly mastered the Mexicans, turning them into their slaves. They also took the Mexican women and satisfied their sexual desires with them. The Spaniards had not brought any females with them. The new "half-breeds" later became known as the "mestizos". This situation became increasingly unbearable and reached its climax in the early 19th Century when the Mexican indigents launched a revolution against the Spaniards. By then, the abuses had sharply worsened and a new generation of slavery was not to be tolerated. The war lasted eleven years and was instigated and led by a Mexican Catholic priest named Don Miguel Hidalgo y Costilla. He was later to become known as the "Padre de la Patria" (Father of the Land).

Don Miguel Hidalgo y Costilla, the organizer and principal leader of the Mexican rebellion against the Spanish ruling class, was born and raised in poverty. The Mexican people readily identified with him. Besides being one of them, he was also a priest. By that time most of the Mexican people had been forced to become Roman Catholic. They had been trained to serve the church without questioning their authority. In addition to expressing loyalty to the church, the indigent people really liked Don Miguel Hidalgo y Costilla. He is known to have been very intelligent, learning to read at a very early age and having thoroughly studied many disciplines. It is also written about him that he was committed to the poor and loved them as much as he despised their enslaved condition. Don Miguel Hidalgo y Costilla started a practice in his young years of taking time each day to visit people working in the fields. This practice made him well-known as he matured. He later began training his people for combat and, from the rectory of his church office in Guanajuato, he issued every order, including the coup d'etat which would win the independence of Mexico. On September 15, 1810, he rang the bells of his church to signal the last massive attack against the Spaniards. As he rang the church bells, he cried out, "MEXICANOS, VIVA MEXICO! --- VIVA LA INDEPENDENCIA!---VIVA LA LIBERTAD!". His cries were echoed throughout the land by everyone who partook in this last winning battle.

The Celebration

American citizens of Mexican ancestry begin to commemorate Mexican Independence Day on September 15, as it is traditionally done in Mexico. It is the "Dia del Grito de la Independencia" (Day of the Cry of Independence). Following the commemoration exercises, there are a variable number of folkloric activities which take place. These include pageant parades, folk dances, contests and other cultural awareness activities.

In some communities, especially those along the southern U.S.-Mexican border, individuals may celebrate for an entire week. Some commercialize the occasion, while others keep the celebration simple and solemn. In either case, with the 20% growth among Hispanic Americans across the U.S over the last census period, it is very likely that the celebration of Mexican Independence Day will become more popular. This has already become evident with the **National Proclamation of Hispanic Heritage Week,** the second week of September.

Praxis Publications Inc. acknowledges Tomas Gomez, for his authorship of this Fact Sheet.

AMERICAN INDIAN DAY
and
AMERICAN INDIAN WEEK

When Does American Indian Day Occur?

American Indian Day is not a perfect tribute because it is not observed in all states and those that celebrate it do not agree on the choice of a date. American Indian Day is celebrated on the fourth Friday in September by most states, although some states prefer the second Saturday in May.

History of American Indian Day

Although American Indian Day was observed by the Boy Scouts in 1912, it was only through the efforts of Red Fox James that the day obtained national prominence. In 1914 Red Fox James, a member of the Blackfoot Nation of Montana, rode more than 4,000 miles on horseback, to solicit aid in having a national American Indian Day proclaimed, from state governors and other influential individuals. His reception was almost always favorable, and on December 14, 1914 he presented his plea and approval of twenty-four governors at the White House. The idea probably would have stopped there if it had not been taken up by the annual assembly of the American Indian Association which met in 1915. The meeting was held in Lawrence, Kansas. Well over a thousand Indians, representing over a hundred tribes, were present and after discussing a proposal for an annual Indian Day, voted their approval. The president of the association, Reverend Sherman Coolidge, of the Arapaho tribe, issued the first formal proclamation on September 28, 1915, which said in part the following:

...**We do invite every American who loves his country and would uphold its honor and dignity, to celebrate this day and consider our early philosophy, our love of freedom, our social institutions, and our history in full light of truth and the balances of justice, in honest comparison with the annals of other races, and to draw from them those noble things that we believe are worthy of emulation....** (He went on to suggest that the date be the second Saturday in May.)

The plea for justice and recognition was made at a time when most Indians were still denied such basic rights as American citizenship and the vote. Nevertheless, the idea of American Indian Day struck a spark and was first observed in 1916 in New York State.

The Ceremonies

There are not festive but rather solemn activities that occur on this holiday. Its purpose is to pay tribute to the hundreds of thousands of Indians that have been killed in wars over the centuries. The day also reflects on the contributions that Indians made to "America as a whole", even though the contributions may not be truly recognized.

American Indian Week

American Indian Week is similar to American Indian Day in that it is observed by only some tribes and states and the dates on which it falls vary. There are no standard festivities during that week among the Indians. Different tribes celebrate the week in a variety of ways. There are usually pow wows, dances, speeches and religious ceremonies. Indians have their own celebrations within their tribes all through the year to celebrate changes of seasons and other things. In many states Indians do not observe this week. The governor of Wisconsin for example declares the dates of American Indian Week each year. If you are interested in determining American Indian Day/Week in your state, it is suggested that you contact the U.S. Department of Interior, Bureau of Indian Affairs, Washington, D.C. Other contacts might be made with your state's Office of the Governor, State Historical Society, Indian Organizations in your area, or the Tribal Chairperson of any tribes which might be in your region.

FEAST OF THANKSGIVING
FROM THE INDIAN PERSPECTIVE

Was the first Thanksgiving a collective giving of thanks to God or just a festive gathering? Was the first Thanksgiving actually started because the Pilgrims wanted to give thanks for their massacre of Indian people in 1637? Did the first Thanksgiving really happen as we celebrate it today?

These questions cry out for historical clarification. But only until we get at their roots will we understand why so many Indian people today, especially those on the east coast call Thanksgiving a "Day of Mourning." The historical record provides reasons to believe that there never was a "First Thanksgiving", similar to the one that Americans re-enact annually in classrooms, with Pilgrims and Indians feasting on turkey, pumpkins and cranberry sauce. William Bradford, the second governor of Plymouth Colony, whose journal is the most reliable primary source for the colony's history, never mentions it. One of the first recorded events that could be considered a day of thanks occurred in 1637, when the European settlers celebrated the murders of approximately 700 Pequot Indians at Mystic Fort, near what is now Groton, Connecticut.

Even if the "First Thanksgiving" had really taken place at Plymouth, Massachusetts, the traditional way of celebrating it is a source of pain to Indians. For them Thanksgiving symbolizes something other than the beginning of a mutually beneficial relationship as portrayed in the legend; it serves as a reminder of the first foot hold Europeans got on the continent. What followed was genocide and a trail of tears.

If the "First Thanksgiving" really did take place, the Indians probably invited the Pilgrims to celebrate it rather than the other way around. The food that was supposed to have been served was exclusively indigenous to Indians. Indians showed the starving, displaced Europeans what they knew about housing, the growing of food and the procuring of game.

Historically, Indians had what could be considered a Feast of Thanksgiving. They held an annual autumn celebration of the harvest in which feasting and performing of the green corn dance were combined with praise for the land and the creatures that had made the bounty possible. It would seem more logical to believe that the Indians had invited the settlers to take part in their feast.

Praxis Publications Inc. would like to thank Dr. Ruth Gudinas, Curriculum Specialist for the Madison, Wisconsin's Department of Human Relations and Dorothy Davids (Stockbridge-Munsee Band of Mohicans) for their assistance in the preparation of this Fact Sheet.

Chapter 9

A Workshop on Minority Student Leadership

Charles A. Taylor

Introduction

The following chapter represents an actual workshop conducted by Charles Taylor at several midwestern campuses. It is complete with examples, activities and structured in a manner that allows the reader to use it in his/her programming. College administrators are free to duplicate any of the examples presented as long as proper credit is given. All activities and examples mentioned are listed at the end of this chapter for your perusal.

Minority Student Leadership

Good morning,

I want to thank the planning committee for inviting me to share some of my experiences with you. I think the topic we will be dealing with is very timely and necessary. I applaud your being concerned with preparing students to assume leadership roles because too often we take for granted that new leadership will automatically spring up.

You in this room represent the next generation of ethnic leadership and being a leader represents a tremendous responsibility. Your presence here today tells me you take this leadership responsibility seriously. You see your university can benefit from your involvement. I want to offer you some ideas that will hopefully stimulate your involvement and help you influence some of the decisions that are being made on this campus so that the rights of blacks and minority students are always protected. I plan to do this through a series of activities and dialogue and not with a long flowery speech. I hope to help you come up with ways that you can make your student organizations more productive and establish the kinds of goals you feel are important.

I'm really pleased that you asked me to conduct a workshop as opposed to giving a speech because from working with student groups, I've found that it's important from time to time to emphasize developmental skills; self improvement techniques that you will be able to use throughout your academic career.

We're going to be moving around and working in groups. In this workshop I depend on your involvement and your feedback. What I will do is show you how to create a process so that any issue your student organization has to address, you can use this process to deal with it. This process is a form of evaluation. It is not a process of fault finding, but rather a well rounded analysis of what works and what needs improvement. I think we grow by reinforcing our strengths and minimizing our weaknesses. If we focus only on how far we need to go, without acknowledging how far we've already come, we'll always feel overwhelmed and frustrated.

Before I go further into this workshop I would like to hear from several of you. Please tell me your name, what concerns you feel need to be addressed and what you hope to get out of this workshop.

Thank you. I sense your perceptions are right on target and I'll try to expand on them as we go along. Take a look at my agenda for a minute.

MINORITY STUDENT LEADERSHIP AGENDA

I Getting and Maintaining Feedback
II Determining Your Leadership Styles
III Topics that Leadership Training should cover
IV Getting and Keeping Members
V Holding Productive Meetings
VI Evaluating Your Organization

I Getting and Maintaining Feedback

As you see, the first item on the agenda is **Getting Feedback** and the technique I just used is the technique used by most leaders of organizations. You have the president or the leader up front asking people what they think. Sometimes this technique may not be the most appropriate. What usually happens is that a few people will talk and dominate the conversation. You get a few opinions but you may not know what others in the group really feel. Just because someone is silent doesn't mean they necessarily agree with what's being said. I would recommend that from time to time you try another technique that allows you to find out what others in the group are thinking and to get everyone's opinion.

Look at the signs I've placed in the four corners of the room. (**Definitely right, Definitely wrong, Possibly right and Possibly wrong**). I will read a statement and I'd like for you to move behind the sign that more closely matches your true feelings.

Statement # 1

The reason more minorities don't get involved in campus activities is because they feel alienated here. [Students moved behind the sign and discussed why they did so - See Rights & Wrongs Activity at the end of this chapter.] Let me cut off the discussion briefly and read another statement. Again I'd like for you to move behind the sign that expresses your feelings.

Statement # 2

The best way to relate to minority students is to treat them the same, like all other students. I hate to break off such an interesting discussion but I want to read one more statement.

Statement # 3

Minority student organizations should make an effort to involve white students in their activities. As you can see this technique allows the president to understand where his/her members are coming from. It also changes his role to that of a facilitator. Everyone's opinion can be ascertained. This technique doesn't take long; it prevents a few people from dominating the meeting, it involves everyone and it won't divide the group as long as you agree on a basic rule that I will be discussing a little later on.

Another technique to get people's feedback is to have them finish a sentence. It goes like this. People should know that Black women face special problems on predominantly white campuses, problems like

_____.

Next I want to divide you up into small groups and have you participate in an activity that will help you determine your leadership styles.

I'll give each group a handout entitled, **The setting is a college student union** [located at end of this chapter]. Take about 15 minutes to discuss this situation. Decide as a group who's at fault; how the situation described should have been handled and as the group's leader what should Ralph have done. Select a spokesperson to speak for your group.

II Determining Your Leadership Style

OK, we've had a chance to listen to how each of your groups would respond to this hypothetical situation. Now let's talk about leadership styles. There are five types I'd like to discuss with you.

Type # 1-Competing

This style is usually uncompromising. An individual pursues his or her own concerns at the expense of the other person. He wants it and he's going to get it and damn anyone that gets in his way. One uses whatever power seems appropriate to win one's own position. Are there times on campus where this style is more effective? Very few, I would say only if there's a clear act of racism or violation of someone's human rights, obviously drastic measures may need to be taken.

Type # 2-Accommodating

This style is usually operating when a person just goes along with the group even though sometimes she doesn't want to. This person is unassertive and appears cooperative. This person sooner or later feels terrible inside. As leaders you will need to be aware of others' true feelings and make sure you understand their real opinions before taking action.

Type # 3-Collaborating

This is the style I prefer to use to resolve conflicts because you're trying to reach an agreement that everyone can live with. This style is both assertive and cooperative. It make take the form of exploring a disagreement to learn from each other's insights, concluding to resolve some condition which would otherwise have you competing for resources. There are probably few situations on campus that can't be resolved using this leadership style.

Type # 4-Compromising

This is like when you want soft candles and quite music and your date wants to go out dancing. You end up sending out for Chinese food and watching TV in the dorm. You may not have gotten what you asked for, but you can live with the alternative. Compromising falls on a middle ground between competing and accommodating. It usually means splitting the difference, exchanging concessions. We all compromise but we have to learn to do it in a way that we don't sell ourselves or the people we're supposed to be representing out.

Type # 5–Avoiding

This person does not address conflict. The avoidance may take the form of diplomatically sidestepping an issue, postponing an issue or simply withdrawing from an uncomfortable situation. You know the best way to get rid of a pest. Lend him/her some money. When he sees you coming he'll cross over on the other side of the street. That's what is meant by avoidance, simply being unwilling to face up to the issue. **"There's no racism here!"** You know a complete denial of the problem. This is perhaps the hardest style to deal with because you have to spend a lot of time educating people who are awfully backward about going forward.

These leadership styles should give you an indication of how your group approached the incident in the student union. How many of you would handle things differently in light of this discussion?

III What topics to include in leadership training

Next I want to talk about the areas I believe should be included when talking about leadership training. Some we'll cover in greater detail than others. However all of them are important. Collectively they offer the kinds of skills student leaders should possess.

Parliamentary Procedure

An effective leadership training workshop should emphasize group dynamics and teach participants how to hold effective group meetings, how to set up an agenda, and how to use parliamentary procedure. It should answer questions like, what is my responsibility as a chairperson, as a secretary, as a member?

There are some good books and films on the use and practices of parliamentary procedure. Perhaps the most popular book on parliamentary procedure is **Robert's Rules of Order.** Too many of us get intimidated by parliamentary procedure. All it is, is a way to conduct a meeting in an orderly manner. You won't need to know a complicated version but rather an adapted version so that your meetings can proceed in an efficient manner. When we talk about creating an agenda a little later on, you'll see that all that is needed is a general knowledge of it. However if student government or similar bodies require a working knowledge of it, you should invest some time in getting more familiar with it. Although we won't be getting into it today I mentioned it here because it should be included as part of any leadership training program.

Establishing Campus Contacts

Believe it or not, although the campus may appear to be a maze, it is actually a highly organized institution. You have your board of regents, your chancellor, or president, vice-presidents, deans, department chairs, directors and so on. Your student organization should have a flow chart so that you know who does what and who reports to who. Then you won't waste your precious time going to this chair who sends you to this dean, who sends you back to this director. After one or two run-arounds like that you don't feel like talking but swinging. Well all of that can be avoided. Sarah Ford, a former administrator at Marquette used to sponsor an annual **Minority Student Leadership** conference and she would give students an actual assignment, say to sponsor an International dinner. Students would then have to go to the International office, to the SAGA food director, to the Dean of Students office, to the director of Public Relations office, to anyone that had to be contacted in order for the International dinner to be a success. In this way students learned first hand how to establish contacts. I would encourage your organization to consider a similar activity.

Creative Programming for Minority Students

This is an important topic because let's face it, people have to have a social outlet. The challenge is to help students use social outlets for creative and productive purposes. There's nothing more frustrating than to plan a big event, spend hundreds of dollars and have only a handful of people show up. Creative programming can help alleviate such a situation but it still takes careful planning to produce successful programs.

To draw students your program should be interesting and presented in a manner that lets students know it directly involves them. Don't be afraid to experiment. Some students who were trying to get black students to donate blood dressed up like Count Dracula. It worked! Other students concerned about the high rate of heart attacks in the minority community sponsored body building and conditioning clinics to get folks to take care of their bodies. On one campus students put up flyers inside the bathroom stalls. What else is there to read while you're in there, right. I'm talking about advertising that works. In the pamphlet we've put together (see chapter 4 on **Increasing Minority Student Participation on Campus for pamphlet contents**), we've listed dozens of programming ideas. You can use them to brainstorm other ideas.

Survey minority students here. Get their direct input before you start programming. Emphasize what students can get out of attending activities. As someone once said, there is no danger of developing eyestrain by looking on the bright side of things. I know it is difficult to get students involved but experience also tells me it's not impossible. True, we have too many students majoring in alibiology. Well I gotta listen to my new jam, or I have to get my hair done, you name it—they've got some alibi, and even after they attend, they're often not satisfied. It's just like those who have free seats in a theater. They always complain the loudest. However appealing that explanation may sound, the lack of minority student involvement is not quite that simplistic. Because I believe strongly that minority students should get involved in every aspect of campus life, I'm going to come back to this discussion and share some examples of ways to increase involvement by using electrifying titles to announce your meetings, a little later on.

Minority Women on Predominantly White Campuses

Next allow me to speak briefly about an issue that needs to receive a great deal of attention. I want to say right up front that I believe women will play a significant role in providing leadership in the 80's and beyond. I think any leadership training should include workshops that address the needs and concerns of minority women. During my travels across the country, I find women always outnumber the men in coming to programs like these and supporting student organizations. Women are actively seeking leadership training and self-empowering skills so it's easy to predict who the next leaders will be.

One of the workshops that I'm asked to conduct from time to time is called the **Circle of Understanding** (located at end of chapter) where participants are asked to explore the schism that is supposed to exist between men and women. I tell you, this activity really gives people an opportunity to express their gut level feelings. I mention that to say that minority women do experience a different set of expectations on white campuses and do have different needs and we men have to be conscious of that and may just have to listen and hear what our sisters are saying if we are going to ever improve relationships. So make sure the concerns of women are dealt with in any leadership conference you decide to sponsor.

Time Management

I often wondered how people like Dick Gregory could make hundreds of speeches a year, write several books, do T.V. appearances, fast and still have time to pursue his own personal interests. There are only so many hours in the day but Dick is a perfect example of someone who knows how to manage his time wisely. Someone once calculated that if we live to be about 65, over a third of our life would have been spent sleeping so in between naps it's important that we learn how to use that other two thirds productively.

A simple but effective exercise I ask students to do is make up a daily and weekly schedule by hours. For example list what you do from 7am to 8am and so on through bed time. Then monitor your schedule to see when and how you're spending the majority of your time. Old habits are hard to break but if you begin to establish new priorities you'll be amazed at the amount of things you'll be able to accomplish.

You will then be in a position to make time work to your advantage. Once you learn to control your time, you may find that you even have enough for party time.

Rational Decision Making

Leadership must direct and lead. It must do more than agitate, it must advocate. It must do more than point out the problems, it must provide the solutions. Campus administrators are no longer interested in rhetoric. They've heard it all before and I guess I get sort of disappointed with student groups who make a lot of noise and have no information to back up their claims. I'm reminded of the old Negro civil rights leader response when the white power broker asked, **"Now what do you Nigras want?"** He snapped back, **"Well what yall got!"** We should be past that stage by now. Do your homework. I mean if you're going after, say a new center on campus or more faculty or more financial aid, do your homework, because just because you say you want it doesn't guarantee that you'll get it. You have to sell more than just your rap. As a friend of mine says, how do you expect to run a nation if you can't run an organization.

As you see this is a very important part of leadership training, learning how to make rational decisions; learning how to use data and statistics to your advantage. You have more credibility if you can meet with the president and say, although we make up only 3% of the student body we represent 25% of the dropouts, 15% of those who take longer to graduate, etc., and that's why we need more minority counselors and staff. To plan does not spoil the trip. If you acquire solid rational decision making skills you can learn to be very diplomatic. After all a diplomat is a person who can tell you where to go in such a way that you look forward to going there.

Cross Cultural Communication

It goes without saying that the world in which we live is multicultural. If anything we need more communication between ethnic groups. Many misunderstandings we face are cultural rather than racial. When we fail to appreciate cultural differences we encourage cultural conflict. Although there is no guarantee that increased contact among diverse groups of people will make people like each other, we can say with some degree of certainty that without some form of interaction chances are that suspicions and misunderstandings will grow. American society is becoming increasingly ethnic. These so called minorities will be the new majority in the not so distant future. If Jesse Jackson's concept of "rainbow" is to become a reality, then genuine communication will have to be a top priority. People of color bring new perspectives, and different historical experiences. They have forced institutions of higher education to recognize the idea of many cultures. That is universities can no longer deal carte blanche with minority students. As a result educational policies have been compelled to be sensitive to the cultural dynamic.

As student leaders it's critical that you understand that culture is the glue that holds all communities together. The respect that you seek for your own cultural practices must be extended outward as well. When I take student leaders on cultural retreats, one activity that is mandatory requires students to spend half of their free time during the weekend with a person of a different ethnic group. Students are expected to take risks in expressing their opinions and ideas through honest self-disclosure. What I found is that there are few better methods to break down racial barriers, and dispute myths than to get students in an isolated setting that allows them to experience a different cultural perspective. Long after the retreat new friendships are cemented and communication across cultures is enhanced greatly as a result of this activity.

Assertiveness Training

The last topic I want to discuss before moving to another agenda item is assertiveness training. Being a leader means being in the spotlight-on front street so to speak. It means being willing to go out on a limb. But why not go out on a limb. Isn't that where the fruit is? The challenge is to learn to be assertive without being abusive or overly aggressive.

I realize that some of you may be shy but you can learn to confront your shyness so it doesn't prohibit you from sharing your vision and making the kinds of contributions you know you're capable of making. Suppose you were permitted to go on a shopping spree in the largest store in this city and help yourself to anything (diamonds, jewelry, etc.), the only limit being what you could carry away. Only a fool would say, **"Guess I'll just take some paper clips and a pencil eraser".** Then consider people who pay for a college education which entitles them, to the limit of their capacity to absorb the accumulated wisdom of the ages, who are contented with just getting by, remaining silent and not participating. Any leadership training should provide training to help students learn about themselves.

Social skills can be acquired that will allow you to orally and nonverbally communicate your feelings without being overly anxious and without intruding on the rights of others. This training can help you take responsibility for what happens in your life. It should help you be a friend with yourself letting you know you have certain rights and beliefs that you need not lose. Assertiveness training should help you protect yourself from being victimized and unfairly taken advantage of.

It is not aggression training whereby other people's rights are violated, rather what makes the training effective is that it's built upon respect, respect for oneself, for others and for one's own belief system. Assertiveness training still is quite popular today and there are lots of books and workshops offered that provide people with practical advice on how they can change certain behaviors enabling them to protect their own space.

Earlier we talked about various leadership styles, competing,

208

accommodating and so on. Returning to a couple of these styles can help us understand assertive behavior better. Take accommodating for example. People who exhibit this behavioral style show a lack of respect for their own needs and values. They are non-assertive. **"Do whatever you want, it's all right with me—Excuse me for breathing."**

Competing behavior on the other hand is just as bad. The person demonstrating this behavior tends to overpower others. In slang it's call "bo-guard" when one gets his way and everybody else better move out of the way. The assertive person stands up for her own space without mistreating or dominating others. Let me illustrate this by showing you a transparency with some examples. You tell me which response is assertive, competing or accommodating. [See assertiveness activity at end of this chapter].

As you can see from the discussion acquiring assertive behavioral skills involves change, taking some risks-even confrontation. On a deeper level it requires us to closer examine our own values. That's why good training is required. This training should give you the skills to work with groups. When an opportunity arises to speak before a group, take it. Use your student organizations to create leadership opportunities for members. Get in the habit of speaking out for those things you believe in and each time you do, it'll get easier. And please don't walk around with your head hanging all down.

Most of all remember, there are three things you just don't do: You don't spit into the wind; you don't tug on superman's cape and you don't walk around with your head hanging down. Stand tall and walk proudly. We need you to be assertive.

IV Getting and Keeping Members

I've just given you the various components that I believe any leadership conference should cover. Now I want to move to the next item on the agenda-**Getting and Keeping Members.**

Personal Approach-There's no other technique that's more effective, not free tickets, door prizes, or other similar gimmicks. Nothing beats yourself or another member of your organization going in person and inviting people to attend your organization's meetings. You have to take some risks.

Make your organization stand for something. Be clear on what your purpose is. **We sponsor parties or We raise funds for Africa's hungry** are much clearer than saying, "We do different things".

Establish Incentives-Black students at the University of Kentucky stressed academics by implementing an incentive plan that provided cash awards to students who excelled academically. They created four categories of awards, greek, freshman, upper class and most improved. **Sponsor campus involvement contests. Use creative titles to announce your meetings.** For example look at the titles I've listed on the blackboard. Which attracts your attention? Why?

Creative Titles

Alienation among Black students   vs   Why do I as a Black student
                                                feel so alone here?

Ramifications of budget cuts   vs   Can minority students afford
on minority students   college next year?

Implications of housing   vs   Places where minorities
discrimination for minorities   can't live in this city

Low Hispanic student turnout   vs   Hispanics can't get together

The right title can help spell the difference between an empty house and standing room only. **Get to know your members**—I tell you, this will cut down on frustration more than anything else. Since it's so commonsensical we tend to take it for granted. A leader can't walk around acting like he or she is god's gift to humankind. If you keep your head in the clouds don't be surprised if you get struck by lightning.

I'm reminded of one student leader who wanted his organization to march on the president's office to protest the rise in tuition and what that would do to black student enrollment. He took for granted his members would go along with him, and he made announcements about the march but when he brought it up at the meeting the students recommended he use other tactics. He had to step down from his position as a result. He never took the time to get to know how his members felt. He didn't know whether his members considered themselves conservative, liberal, radical or what.

If I asked you right now how many of you know where the majority of your members stand politically how many could tell me? Well here's an activity that can help you find out. If you look in the four corners of the room you'll see signs that say **Conservative, Moderate, Liberal or Radical.** Would you move to the sign that closely matches your own political beliefs. After I give you the instructions you'll have about twenty minutes to carry them out. Were you surprised at the results? After listening to the discussion how many would change signs? Are there times when each of us are conservative or radical? What does this say about labels? What does this say about understanding members' political beliefs? [See, What is your political belief at end of this chapter.] **Share an intimate experience**—I'm not talking about that type of intimacy. At least once a year take your group on a retreat or sponsor some activities just for group members to get to know each other better; activities that really require you to communicate and share feelings. Let me demonstrate a couple of fun activities you can use to spicen up your meetings or use to get members to feel comfortable around one another. They're good icebreakers. [see giving and receiving affection; and the blind communication exercise at the end of this chapter].

V. HOLDING PRODUCTIVE MEETINGS

The next item on the agenda, I want to discuss is holding productive meetings.

Agenda

Every meeting your organization conducts should be guided by an agenda. An agenda adds structure to the meeting. It includes all those items that will be dealt with at the meeting. When possible hand it out in advance. Also set aside an agreed upon date so that any member who wants to add an agenda item can do so. For example, if your meetings are held every Wednesday, then students should have until Monday to put an item on the agenda.

I would recommend that your agenda be simplified into two categories. I think you'll find everything that your group discusses can fit under these two categories.
1. **Items for Decision and**
2. **Items of information**

Any item that requires discussion and/or membership approval would go under category one, while announcements, reports, and similar items would go under category two. [see black student union agenda at the end of this chapter].

Seating Arrangements

Take a look at your seating arrangements. Ask yourself one question. Does this arrangement encourage participation or discourage it? If you notice my overhead I've provided examples of other seating arrangements you might consider. [see example of seating arrangements located at the end of this chapter].

Approving Decisions

Perhaps the area that causes the greatest conflict in many organizations is how decisions are made. What turns people off the most is for some members to treat the organization like a private club. Everyone's input is important and should be valued. Everyone's vote is equal. Of course you should have an agreement in your bylaws whereby the majority vote rules. Allow for ample discussion before the vote is taken. Make it clear that after all the arguments have been made pro or con about an issue, and the vote has been cast, that everyone is expected to support the majority's decision. This is the rule I referred to earlier that everyone must support.

If people are allowed to participate then it's unfair for them to bad mouth the group, just because they didn't win the vote. However, if they are not allowed to participate, then the group is fair game for bad mouthing.

Establish Goals

There are three type of goals that I encourage student groups to establish: 1) social/cultural, 2) political and 3) educational. These will give purpose and meaning to your organization, establish direction and increase your overall effectiveness on campus. [see organizational goals at the end of this chapter].

Take Minutes

Minutes are the records of your meetings. They are the official notice of what was done or said at the meetings. Great care should be given to their preparation. Future students should be able to use them to get a historical perspective of the organization as well as learn about the intricacies of the group.

Write them so that anyone who wasn't there could read them and understand clearly what took place. Make sure they follow your agenda. Send them out to people you think might be interested in your group and to people whom you're trying to attract as members. Do this on a regular basis. You'll find this one little practice of sending out minutes will increase your membership and support for your organization greatly in the course of a year.

VI. Evaluating Your Organization

The last agenda item I want to talk about is evaluating your organization. I'm going to share with you the process I mentioned at the beginning of my presentation that you can use to improve your organization. It's called a quality circle. The concept came from the Japanese. It involves group participation. It works like this. You divide your organization into small working groups, no more than five people per group. Every group discusses the same problem using the same procedures I will explain to you now. [see quality circle assignment at the end of this chapter].

Conclusion

Are there any final questions about anything I've discussed today. Let me quickly summarize what I've tried to cover. We discussed ways of getting feedback, using creative titles to attract students to your meetings, shared leadership training topics, shared ways to put together an agenda, talked about the importance of taking good minutes, holding productive meetings and showed you how to use the quality circle as a process to address issues your group has to deal with. These are all developmental skills if you began to use them will in the long run make your organization more effective.

Again I applaud your sponsorship of activities like these designed to give students the skills they need to actively participate on campus. We're in need of new voices, new ideas, and new leaders.

As I say goodbye to you, I have reason to be optimistic. You've

recharged my battery and restored my faith. Just remember that great
leaders are remembered not for what they know but by what they share.
I wish you much success. Thank you for inviting me.

Activities Used in the Leadership Workshop

Rights and Wrongs

Label each of the four corners of the room with a sign identifying a place where students will move to show their answers to a
series of statements you will read to them. One corner should be
labeled **Definitely right,** another **Definitely wrong,** another **Possibly
right and the last Possibly wrong.**

Instruct your students to think about the feelings they hold
about each statement you read to them and then to go to the corner
which best reflects their opinion about how right or wrong a statement
is. Tell them not to depend on how others respond or what others
might think about their responses.

Read a statement and ask their answers. Do not debate which
answers are most correct; rather ask the students to discuss why they
moved to the corners they did. Some examples of statements that might
be used are: (Feel free to create your own statements).

* Homosexuals should be allowed to teach in the elementary schools.
* Affirmative action should be abolished because it leads to reverse
  discrimination.
* Whites should marry whites and blacks should marry blacks.
* Marijuana should be legalized.
* Minorities should be given preferential treatment until racism
  ends.
* The equal rights amendment should never be passed because it will
  destroy the family.
* More nuclear weapons will help prevent war.
* A man has a right to steal food to feed his starving family.
* Only religion can save the world.

The Setting is a College Student Union

Ralph is a black student, who is concerned that no black studies
courses are offered in his subject area. He goes through the regular
procedures to obtain funds, approval, and a faculty member for a black
studies course. Twenty black students sign up. Ralph goes to the
student union director and asks if they can use the movie room on
Thursday nights since that is the only time the professor is free.
The movie room is the only room in the union with audiovisual equipment.

The union director approves the request. Thursday night arrives.
The black students go to the movie room and find a group of white
students watching **Animal House.** A heated discussion occurs. Charlie,
a white student yells out, "you damn niggers don't belong on this
campus anyway."

Tom, another white student, believes that the black students
should be allowed to use the movie room since it is the only place
they have to meet. He does not say anything, however. The black

214

students leave. Ralph later goes to the student union director to explain what happened. The director replies, "I made a mistake. The movie room really serves a need for all students. Since you only have 20 students, find another place."

The next Thursday night the black students go to the movie room early and begin class. A fight breaks out, there are injuries and several hundred dollars worth of damage is done to the movie room.

Discuss who is at fault. How should this situation have been handled to begin with? What assumptions are explicit in this activity? As the group's leader what should Ralph have done?

Circle of Understanding

Objective: To heighten awareness of own sex role, develop empathy for the opposite sex role, to break through traditional stereotyped ways of conceptualizing sex roles, and to improve relationships between males and females.

Time required: 1-2 hours

To begin this exercise have all women sit in a circle. Males form an outer circle, also sitting facing the women. Only the outer circle can ask questions. The inner circle can only answer.

Begin by saying, "There is talk of a growing schism between men and women. In this activity we'll talk about that schism. The facilitator should start off with the following questions.
What do you feel is the ideal relationship that should exist between women and men? (Allow ample time for every woman to answer and if desired answers can be recorded on a flip chart).
Name something you think men could do to improve male/female relationships.
Finish this sentence. I would not want to be a man because....(Have each woman respond to this question).
Next ask the women to respond to any of the following:
a) Men tend to treat us as second class citizens
b) Men are responsible for sexism
c) Feminism is good for everybody
Now the males (outer circle) are free to ask questions, once the facilitator has asked the above questions. By now a lively discussion should be occurring. Continue for about 15 minutes.
Next have each circle exchange places. It's time for the women to question and the men to answer honestly.
The facilitator might ask:
What do you feel should be the ideal relationship between males and females? (Allow ample time for each male to answer).
Name something women should do to improve male/female relationships.
Finish this sentence, I would not want to be a woman because....
(Have each male respond to the question).

215

Next have the males respond to any of the following statements.
a) Women tend to lump all men as the same, treating them like objects.
b) Women are advantaged because of their sex. They get by with more and less is expected of them.
c) Women want to be equal in everything except for the military. That's unfair.

The facilitator should feel free to interject at any time other controversial issues such as abortion, the equal rights amendment, interracial marriage, etc,. The goal is to create an atmosphere where honest confrontation and dialogue can occur. It's ok to let the discussion become heated but not abusive.

After allowing plenty of time for people to speak their mind have everyone stand and form a circle, male standing next to female holding hands. Go around the circle and have each person respond to this sentence individually. This year, I will work to improve male/female relationships because.......

Finally have everyone hug each other.

Assertiveness Activity

Read the examples and responses below. Ask participants to decide which response is accommodating, competing or assertive. Discuss.

Example # 1

You paid your last ten dollars to take your date to see a movie. The people next to you keep talking in a very loud voice making it impossible for you to hear and enjoy the movie. Because the theater is packed you can't change seats.

Response A-You wish they would shut up but you don't say anything about it, other than to suffer in silence.

Response B-You've had enough of their loud talking so you turn around and shout, "Either you shut up or I'll ask the usher to throw you out."

Response C-You look the loud talkers in the eye and politely but forcibly tell them their talking is keeping you from enjoying the movie.

Example # 2

You've been standing in line for nearly an hour trying to register for a class that will reach its capacity right after you sign up. There are only three more students in front of you, when suddenly a big angry looking student jumps in front of the line.

Response A-You're pissed so you touch him on the shoulder and say, "Say buddy if you don't go to the end of the line, I'm going to kick your behind".

Response B-You shrug and throw up your hands and leave the line, thinking that's what you deserve since you don't want to make a scene.

Response C-You tap the student on the shoulder and explain how long you and the students behind you have been waiting and request that he goes to the end of the line or you will report him.

Example # 3

You have an exam first thing the next morning. You just finished studying, turned the lights out and just about the time you're ready to doze off, your neighbor starts blasting the stereo.
Response A-You pull the sheets over your head and put a finger in your ear in a vain attempt to block out the sound. You wish the noise would go away but you don't leave your bed.
Response B-You pound on the wall, yell a few obscenities and finally resort to turning up your stereo full blast to drown the other noise out.
Response C-You go next door and explain the situation and firmly request that the noise be turned down. You make it clear that you don't want to be disturbed the rest of the night.

What Are Your Political Beliefs?

Objective: This exercise is designed to help participants determine their political beliefs. Time required:30 minutes-2 hours.
Designate the four corners of your room as **Liberal, Conservative, Radical, and Moderate** (one sign per corner). Request that participants move to the corner they feel best describes their political belief. This should be an independent decision.
In each group have the participants a) choose a spokesperson, b) discuss why they chose the belief they did, c) agree on a definition of the particular belief, and d) list three things (reasons, events or activities) that clearly illustrates that they are indeed a moderate, liberal, conservative or radical.
Next have each political grouping agree on a definition of the three political beliefs they did not choose and cite one thing they feel will illustrate each of the other beliefs. Allow at least 20 minutes for this part of the exercise. After allowing for the discussion, bring the four groups together. Beginning with the "conservatives", have the spokesperson give their definition of conservative and their three illustrations. Then have the spokesperson for each of the other three groups give their definitions of conservative and cite their illustrations. Allow at least ten minutes for the whole group to discuss conservatives.
Now repeat this process with the other three political labels. Since this exercise gets heated at times, be sure to close by asking how many participants would now change their political beliefs as a result of the discussion. Discuss also the ramifications of labeling people and finally ask what was learned from this exercise.

SEATING ARRANGEMENTS PROS/CONS

Arrange the seating to produce greatest interaction. Although we strongly recommend sitting in circles for most activities there are some where this is not appropriate. Here are some other options.

Classroom style

Pros: Great for presenter and participants. Good view. Presenter can move around fairly freely. Good for visuals.

Cons: Not as good as other seating arrangements for discussions especially if you want to encourage eye contact and a sense of community. Reminds participants of school!

Horseshoe shaped

Pros: Allows for movement by the presenter and participants. Offers a good arrangement for discussions. People can see each other easily.

Cons: It's O.K. for visuals but some people may have to move in order to see.

Circle

Pros: Great for discussion. Interaction is greatly enhanced by the easy eye contact. If the speaker is sitting down during his presentation, this seating arrangement is the preferred one at the retreat. Good for role playing.

Cons: Not good for visuals nor for a speaker who likes to move around since some participants will always be behind her.

Cresent

Pros: Good for visuals. Allows movement between rows. Good for activities that are speaker focused.

Cons: Not the best for discussions among participants.

Being Affectionate

1. Have participants form a circle.
2. Select one person to stand in the middle of the circle with his/her eyes closed. (Try to select someone that appears to be left out of things).
3. Have each person in the circle go up to the person and give him/her some type of affection. (This can be a handshake, a kiss on the jaw, a pat on the back, etc.).
4. After everyone has shown this person some form of affection, continue your meeting or other activities. You don't need to discuss this activity because at times it can get emotional. When that happens have the person standing in the middle rejoin the circle and have everyone hold hands. It will be up to the facilitator to help the group talk through its feelings.
5. You can repeat this exercise whenever the need arises.

Blind Communication

1. Have the participants form two circles.
2. Have each circle count off consecutively beginning with 1, 2, 3,....
3. Next have each circle mix the numbers up so they will be out of order. (see example below)
4. Then have members of the circles (ideally circles would have between 9-15 members) close their eyes. They should also be told that they are not to speak and except for your instructions should pretend that they can't hear.
5. Next, when you say go, have the circles try to get back in numerical order without talking, speaking or looking. Laughing is permitted however.
6. Have the group clap its hands when they feel they are back in the correct order.
7. Then announce the winner.
8. Discuss the activity. Ask them what type of communication system did their group develop in order to get back into the correct order. Ask which group tried to use "memory" instead of communication to get back in order.

Black Student Union Agenda

12/4/86

Items for Decision

1. Approval of last week's minutes
2. Approval of February's social calendar (see attachment)

Items of Information

12. BSU is sponsoring a Black history quiz 2/25/87 at the student union, room 207. It starts at 7 p.m. and it is free.
13. Committee reports
14. Deadline for applying for financial aids is 3/1/87.

Black Student Union Minutes

Date: 12/4/86

Time: Meeting was called to order by Debow Washington at 6:00pm.
Present: There were 12 members present and two visitors.
Location: The meeting was held in room 221 in the memorial union.

Items for Decision

1. Minutes of 11/28/86 were approved.
2. It was decided by a 10-2 vote that the long range planning committee would prepare a report for February's calendar.

Items of Information

3. The membership committee reported that 5 new members joined.
4. Our next meeting will be 12/11/86 in room 221 of the memorial union starting at 7 p.m.
   Respectfully submitted by Al Cummings, Secretary-BSU.

ORGANIZATIONAL GOALS

Social/Cultural Goals

* Plan cultural activities for the academic year
* Identify funding sources
* Prepare year's budget
* Plan public relations campaign
* Fill out academic calendar (include room sites and alternate sites
* Complete responsibility form for each activity planned (see next page for an example of this form).

Political Goals

* Get representation on the dorm council
* Get at least one person appointed to the allocations committee
* Run at least one person for the student senate
* Meet with the campus student body president to share concerns and offer support
* Get at least one person on the student union board
* Get at least one person to write articles for the campus newspaper or other media source
* Encourage students to sign up for the various student committees on campus
* Meet with representatives from the faculty senate to share concerns

Educational Goals

* Encourage each member to create a personal time schedule that leaves ample time for study
* Create study groups and pool class notes to help members avoid academic trouble
* Establish academic incentives that reward students who make the Dean's list
* Stress class attendance and encourage students to keep absences down to an absolute minimum
* Encourage students to ask for a tutor at the beginning of the semester or as soon as they might be having difficulty

By establishing goals similar to the ones listed above your organization will be better informed, more effective and viewed as making a contribution to the entire campus.

STUDENT RESPONSIBILITY FORM

1) Name of Event_____
   Contact person_____
   Address_____
   _____
   Telephone _____
   Check payable to:_____

2) Type of event: Band___, Play___, Film___, Speaker___,
   Exhibit___, Demonstration___, Music/Lecture___,
   Slide/Lecture___, Other (specify)_____

3) Admission charge: No___, Yes___If yes how much?_____

4) Need Equipment: No___, Yes___If yes list each item needed.
   Please use the back of this form if more space is needed.

5) Where and when will event take place:
   Date _____ Time _____ Place _____

6) Date room was reserved_____Fee:_____

7) Expenses associated with the event:
   Lodging $_____ Materials (specify on back) $_____
   Meals $_____Transportation $_____Services $_____
   Equipment rental $____ Other (specify on back $_____

8) Social Security Number _____ ___ _____(required for service
                                    payment to an individual)
9) FEIN (Federal employer identification number_____

10) Hotel Reservation _____

11) Flight arrival and departure_____

12) Intra-city transportation _____

13) Person responsible for completing this form _____

Approved: _____ _____
                date   student coordinator signature

          _____ _____
                date   staff advisor

Note: Please attach a program agenda to this form and a copy of
publicity announcing the event.

QUALITY CIRCLE ASSIGNMENTS

Problems

1. What problems need to be resolved before the purpose of the organization can be accepted by all of the membership?
2. What problems need to be resolved before communication can be noticeably improved between and among members of the organization?
3. What problems need to be resolved before the organization can conduct effective meetings and establish clear priorities?

Instructions

Divide the participants into working groups comprised of 3-5 members, to address the problems listed above or ones similar.
Have each group select a spokesperson and someone to record the groups' decisions. When discussing the problems identified above each quality circle is to follow the same format:
> 1) Brainstorm answers to each of the problems by:
>> a. Not judging ideas
>> b. Requiring each person to add input
>> c. welcoming a variety in thinking/responses
>> d. energizing the group with creative thoughts

It works like this. Each person is asked to identify a problem in turn. If you don't have an answer when it's your turn to respond, say "I pass". An answer is sought from each person until everyone says I pass. During the brainstorming there are no interruptions for discussion, clarity or debate. After all the ideas have been recorded, the group spokesperson calls for a discussion of any of the problems listed. This is the time to seek clarification on any of the problems listed. Next combine into one, any ideas that are the same. (Combine only if they are the same).

Next vote on the ideas to get a rank order (priority). The highest votes get ranked first and so on. Rank only the top seven.

2) As you rank them, keep track on a separate sheet of paper the number of people who voted for a particular idea. (see example)

Problem	How many members feel this way	Total
A. Chairperson not supported	xxxxx	5
B. Poor communication among members	xxxx	4
C. Poor attendance at meeting	xxxxxx	6
D. Meetings poorly planned	xxx	3
E. Feel my input is ignored	xxxxxxx	7

3) After the top seven ideas have been identified, the next step is to determine cause and effect. For example, you will determine why members feel the chairperson is not being supported. You will need to brainstorm again and list what each person feels is the cause of the problem being discussed. This time only rank the top three causes.

(see the example).

223

<u>chairperson</u> <u>not</u> <u>supported</u>=<u>belittles</u> <u>membership</u>
      effect   cause

<u>chairperson</u> <u>not</u> <u>supported</u>=<u>committee</u> <u>roles</u> <u>unclear</u>
      effect   cause

<u>chairperson</u> <u>not</u> <u>supported</u>=<u>lazy</u> <u>members</u>
      effect   cause

4) Next your quality circle is to recommend one solution to resolve the causes identified above. Brainstorm your decisions and then vote on only one solution for each cause.

5) After you have completed the process above, bring all the groups together for their report. All group reports should follow the same format:

    a) Mention the problems your quality circle has identified in rank order. (the top seven)

    b) List and explain the causes and effects of the problems you've identified.

    c) Next list your quality circle's solutions to resolving the problems.

Someone should record all of the circle's reports. An analysis should be prepared of all the reports. What normally happens is that groups find similarities in their reports which makes the analysis easy to accomplish.

All the problems should be grouped as well as the causes and effects. The entire group should then vote on the top 3-5 problems, their related causes and effects, and finally vote on the solution for each of the 3-5 problems.

Now the organization has some specific solutions to work on for the academic year, the entire membership was involved in reaching consensus, everyone's input was solicited and members can claim ownership of the solutions. Although this tends to be a timely drawn out process, the benefits can be tremendous.

Notes

Books

Alberti, Robert E. (Ed), **Assertiveness:Innovations, Applications, Issues.** San Luis Obispo, CA:Impact Publishers, 1977.

Bradford, Leland P., **Making Meetings Work:A Guide for Leaders and Group Members.** La Jolla, CA:University Associates, 1976.

Cheek, D.K. **Assertive Black...Puzzled White.** San Luis Obispo, CA:Impact Publishers, 1976.

Taylor, Charles A., **Cultural Retreat Handbook,** Madison, WI, NMCC Inc., 1985. Includes most of the activities used in this workshop.

Annotated Books

Reference Guide to Handbooks and Annuals (1983 Edition) by J. William Pfeiffer and John E. Jones. This guide will help you find the right structured experience, instrument, lecturette, etc.,. This book describes the contents of Volumes I through IX of the **Handbooks of Structured Experiences for Human Relations Training and the 1972 through 1983 Annuals published by University Associates.** With the Reference Guide's comprehensive cross referencing system, you can look up materials by title or by author. The price is $12.50 and can be ordered from University Associates Inc., 8517 Production Ave., San Diego, CA 92121.

The Encyclopedia of Icebreakers includes structured activities that warm-up, motivate, challenge, acquaint and energize. The author is Sue Forbess-Greene. The price is $54.95 and can be ordered from University Associates Inc., 8517 Production Ave., San Diego, CA 92121, (619) 578-5900.

Playfair The author is Matt Weinstein and Joel Goodman. This book billed as everybody's guide to noncompetitive play is filled with games for people who are interested in learning about a new type of play that lets people be supportive, cooperative and open with each other. The price is $8.95 and can be ordered through:Impact Publishers, P.O.Box 1094, San Luis Obispo, CA 93406.

Lead On!, The Complete Handbook for Group Leaders. The authors are Leslie G. Lawson, Franklyn Donant and John Lawson. This book is a comprehensive guide for leaders of volunteer groups. 24 easy to follow chapters make it easy to follow. Describes essentials for novices and experienced leaders. The price is $5.95 for paper back and can be ordered from:Impact Publishers, P.O.Box 1094, San Luis Obispo, CA 93406.

Additional Resources

National Black Youth Leadership Council
Dennis Rahiim Watson, Executive Director
250 West 54 St, Suite 811
NY,NY 10019   (212) 541-7600

Race Relations:A Feature and Documentary Filmography
An annotated listing of 223 films addressing race relations.
Available from the center for the study of Human rights, 704 S.I.A.
Columbia University, NY,NY 10027. Price is $5. Make check payable to
Columbia University.

Chapter 10

A Workshop on Recruiting & Retaining Minority Students

Introduction

The following chapter represents an actual retention workshop conducted by Charles Taylor at several campuses around the country. It includes the major findings in the field as well as additional resources available to assist the campus administrator. Readers are urged to pick up a copy of Mr. Taylor's popular book, **Effective ways to Recruit and Retain Minority Students** for a complete discussion of the issues presented in this workshop.

The workshop is presented here solely to assist the campus planner structure retention problems under a holistic framework. Surveys mentioned in the workshop and related activities are included at the end of this chapter. They may be used without permission as long as proper credit is given.

EFFECTIVE WAYS TO RECRUIT AND RETAIN MINORITY STUDENTS

by Charles Taylor

I'm pleased to be invited to speak to you this evening. I hope to share with you some effective ways to recruit and retain minority students. I invite your questions and your comments throughout. If you look at the black board you'll see the agenda I'll be following:

Agenda

1. Understanding problems that Minority students face on predominantly white campuses.
2. Discussion of significant factors impacting Minority Student Retention.
3. Ten inexpensive strategies campuses can use to recruit and retain minority students.
4. Discussion of a retention model.
5. Resources that are available to assist you.

Based on my experience I would recommend that before a university begins to implement a retention plan, that it carefully address problems that I believe minority students face on predominantly white campuses. You see universities are highly complex social systems. The better students are integrated into these systems, the more likely their perseverance and graduation. A general difficulty faced by many minority students is fitting in. I mean a lot of time, energy and just plain frustration are spent by minority students trying to adjust to the environment that exists on many campuses.

1. Understanding Problems that Minority Students Face

So these problems faced by our students must be understood and addressed if any meaningful change is to occur. Problems like:

Institutional Racism

The truth is that racism exists in our society and our institutions simply mirror that society. Institutions have great power to reward and penalize. They reward by providing educational and job opportunities for some people and foreclosing them for others. No society will distribute social benefits in a perfectly equitable way, but no society need use race as a criteria to determine who will be rewarded and who will be punished. Anytime race affects those who benefit from institutional policies, you have institutional racism. The Kerner Report over two decades ago concurred that American institutions are racist. Institutional racism is perpetuated sometimes by good citizens merely carrying on business as usual. To detect it is often a very difficult task and even when it is detected it is seldom clear who is at fault? I mean who do we blame for residential segregation, for poor education in ghetto schools, for extraordinary high unemployment among blacks, for racial stereotypes in history text books, for the concentration of political power in white society.

There are many places to look for institutional practices that impact minorities in a negative fashion. Here are some indicators worth watching for.

1. All white committees
2. Absence of minorities in the campus press coverage.
3. Inflexible rules and guidelines that ignore the cultural needs of minority students.
4. Tokenism
5. High minority student attrition rates
6. Using entrance exams based solely on white middle class culture.
7. Using textbooks that don't include the Black experience.
8. Creating an all white cultural environment.

An admission office that has good intentions but uses inappropriate selection instruments to deny minority students access might be committing an act of institutional racism. Institutional racism is a factor that is almost always involved in disparities that exist on campus. Disparities in retention, hirings, promotions, etc.

It's going to take a new type of person to change institutional racism, but institutions do change under pressure. This new type person is called the new white by author Robert Terry, (**For Whites Only**). What does he mean by the new white person. He suggests a person who is intentionally political, engages in intelligent reflection, and possesses new credentials. (That is it has been his experience that only after whites have begun to work on racism can they begin to enter into significant conversations with minorities on the race question). Whites get their new credentials from their fight against racism, Minorities have their credentials by being victims of racism. When people think of racism they usually think in terms of individual behavioral racism. They think of some one burning a cross or calling someone names. The new white takes a broader perspective.

The new white asks, what do we want our campus to look like next year, five years from now? How can we increase the number of Black students and faculty? You know what the past has been like here for Blacks. You have a chance to construct a better future. The future is crucial for both the new white and minorities, for America will either be transformed or destroyed from within. So it's unwise to sit back and say we have no race problem, because we have no Blacks. The reason you have few Blacks may be because of a race problem. I mean if we don't fight passionately against racism, it's going to come back and haunt us. As Bob Terry says, racism must be the absolute enemy of the new white. Expose the contradictions, rationalizations, and disguises that are used to perpetuate racism. Face the multiple ways in which all of us are victimized by racism. Challenge verbal commitments to justice and demand just action rather than more talk.

229

Finally develop strategies and tactics appropriate to eliminating racism. Saying that you are not racist or that you don't want to be is not the same thing as doing something about it.

Bob Terry suggests that new whites raise these types of questions on campus. What percentage of workers on campus are Black? At each job level? How are employees recruited? Is promotion a possibility for all employees. Are minority suppliers and services used? Minority Bankers? Insurance Companies? Contractors?

What are the policies of the companies in which investments are made? Do we support firms that buffer the South African regime. Are Black images projected only in black media or all media? Is there a University Committee to develop and carry out a non racist policy? Are there Blacks on the Board of Regents?

I could go on and on about the questions that institutions must ask themselves internally if they are serious about addressing the problem of institutional racism. But that task must be done by caring and committed people here who are actively anti-racist. That way you'll not only be against racism but working for justice.

Mono-Cultural Curriculum

Another problem faced by minority students on predominantly white campuses is the problem of a **Mono Cultural Curriculum.**

The world is becoming increasingly non-white. By the year 2000 it is predicted that of the six billion people expected to populate the globe, five billion will be non-white. You wouldn't know that such a massive social phenomena exists by what's being presented in the classroom. The prevailing pedagogical strategy is to teach about one culture only. The Indian learns that even his existence is questioned as students are taught that Columbus discovered America. Hispanics aren't told that Spanish settlements thrived in Texas, New Mexico and California long before the English colony of Jamestown existed. Asians helped build the railroads that brought the east and west closer together, while on the back of Black slave labor, America's economy was saved. Given such a monocultural perspective it's not surprising that minorities learn their status in America is second class. It takes little imagination to figure out how people react when their existence is discussed as unimportant or completely ignored.

Even when minority groups are presented it is often pathological or in a negative context, highlighting only the oppression and powerlessness of their people. This says a lot about the educational training and ideology of the classroom professor. Professors need to take a serious look at their bibliographical and reference materials for unilateral views. They should also widen their reading list to include Black and Hispanic authors.

Educators can analyze the relationship between course content and ethnocentrism and pluralize their class presentations. If efforts such as these are not undertaken, white students (constantly bombarded with myths about white domination of each academic discipline) will continue to view themselves and their culture as superior to other groups. Such a view is extremely dangerous in a world where whites are the minority. Even if a university does not have one minority student its curriculum and staff should be multicultural. Just imagine if we could have educated Ronald Reagan in a multicultural setting. Whites growing up in all white environments become disadvantaged by their schools and may be woefully out of place in the new emerging world order where an understanding and appreciation of cultural differences are necessary for peaceful coexistence.

There are several options available to institutions of higher learning serious about correcting this inequity.

A. One can teach the values of the dominant culture forcing the minority to adapt to the dominant society.

B. One can provide token acknowledgment of minority contributions; a page here, a paragraph there, Black History Week etc., or

C. One can implement cultural pluralism in which the minority experience is an integral part of the total curriculum. This latter course of action is preferred.

Permit me to digress for a moment and give you a brief black history lesson. That way this whole issue of monoculturalism will be better explained. Blacks arrived in this country in 1619, officially, although there is substantial evidence they came earlier. Anyway in 1619, no provisions for slavery existed in English law. But the law did recognize and regulate the indenture of servants. This system was easily adopted to the new world. That's an important fact to keep in mind. You see, white servitude provided the apparatus for Black slavery. I mean they had already set up a plantation pass system. There was sexual exploitation of white indentured women, there where whipping posts, chains, branding irons, overseers and so on. All of these things were tried out and perfected on white folks before they were used on black folks.

It's critical that you understand that because if you can't understand that, then you won't grasp the true character of class/race oppression of Black people in this country. At one point early on in our history, black and white indentured servants had much in common. But at some point the commonality was removed from our history books and the true story remains untold. In order for us to understand the Black experience we need to be knowledgeable about its history.

Yesterday, black folk worked until "can't see in the morning until can't see at night" making this country strong. When Paul Revere rode through the countryside waking up people, he woke up Black minutemen as well. When George Washington crossed the Delaware, blacks were in the boat with him. We've marched in every war.

When they signed the declaration of independence, we were not included. When they wrote the constitution they said our lives were worth only 3/5 of a white person's life. Yesterday Frederick Douglass, said we have worked without wages, we have lived without hope, wept without sympathy and bled without mercy.

That is the essence of Black History yesterday. So in order for our society to produce citizens with a multicultural perspective we've got to implement cultural pluralism in which the black and minority experience is an integral part of the total curriculum. This is necessary because America is not white. She is brown, black, yellow, red and white. The contributions of all of us must be understood and taught.

Professors Expectations and Attitudes

Then there's the problem of professors expectations and attitudes. This is a social problem that requires a great deal of attention but gets the least. On nearly every campus there are likely to be some faculty members who regard the retention issue as someone else's responsibility-**"it is a great idea, but it is not my job"**.

Some of the faculty will ask if their involvement in retention efforts will be weighed as heavily as another publication, in determining tenure, promotion and salary increases. Researchers found in a study done in the 70's that 50%, half of the faculty in a national sample were opposed to actively recruiting underrepresented groups. And who's to say that attitude of (you shouldn't even be here in the first place) doesn't carry over into the classroom.

It's the instructors who ultimately make the educational system effective and relevant. Faculty can be mentors, advisors, liasons between the student and the institution, role models and friends.

If the numerous roles which faculty play were recognized it would follow that any effort to improve retention, (if it is to be successful) must be founded upon faculty support, cooperation and participation. One of the keys to creating faculty acceptance and support is to make clear to faculty early on that we are not asking them to sacrifice "standards," that what we're talking about is doing a better job for students. Our approach is to help students meet legitimate standards.

Faculty must understand that retention is not the goal but only the by-product of improved programs and services for students. Students deserve a positive environment for learning, a classroom free of negative and humiliating experiences. I have students tell me all the time that professors make them feel badly in class and often when blacks are mentioned, it's in a negative context. We need to sensitize our faculty to recognize that there is genius and creativity in our minority communities. It is time for them to expect black presidents, hispanic doctors and women professionals. It was found through interviews with graduating seniors at the University of Maryland, that the single most important thing that students felt they had gotten out of college was the relationship they formed with a faculty member,(Sedlecek, 1983). The most innovative thing an institution can do to help academically under prepared students is to make sure they have teachers who provide quality instruction and who won't view a student's economic situation, and standardized test scores as the final judgment of a student's ability. Collectively faculty have more power to improve retention on campuses than any other group.

Cultural Conflict

Next there's the problem of **cultural conflict.** When colleges fail to provide cultural support the result is usually cultural conflict. To be culturally different doesn't mean that one is culturally deprived. If I bought a sack of potatoes and asked each of you to prepare them I might get back mashed potatoes, hash browns, french fries, etc. based on your cultural norms. For me to then turn around and say a potatoe is better because it is fried instead of boiled is absurd. That's a value judgment or a nutritional judgment.

Likewise if we permit cultural ethnocentricism to cloud how we address minority student concerns, we are confusing differences with deficiencies. They are not the same. Imagine if you will, that everyday you turned on the TV there were only black faces, the newspaper you read was all about blacks and when whites were discussed either a crime had been committed or some white had broken another sports record. You came to school and you only had black teachers and you were the only white in the classroom. You wanted so badly to have your culture mentioned but it never was or only as an after thought.

How would you react? Those all "Black and Chicano" tables present in many student unions and cafeterias serve a cultural reinforcement role in many respects, although they are for the most part depicted as supporting segregation. Some students argue that it is because of minority student organizations and cultural activities that they are able to survive life on predominantly white campuses.

I think colleges need to pay closer attention to this notion of cultural conflict because college is a critical period in the development of a student's identity. It's the time when adolescence supposedly comes to an end. Students are eager to "fit in" and to be affirmed by their peers. According to researchers (Gibbs, 1974) and (Chickering, 1981) there is evidence that minority students undergo a classic identity crisis on predominantly white campuses that interferes with academic functioning.

When black students reject their culture they will have trouble with their self concepts, understanding racism and conducting realistic self-appraisals.

We can't permit our campuses to be places where the type of music, food and social outlets minority students need don't exist.

Assessment Strategies

Next let's look at the problem of **assessment strategies.** No group on earth is more tested than American children. As David Nyberg (writing in the March 26, 1986 issue of the Chronicle of Higher Education) points out, the majority test out as "lacking" in ability, aptitude or intelligence. Does that tell us something about the majority of Americans or something about the majority of tests?

The problem may not only be fraudulent test construction but fraudulent use of a valid test. Take the I.Q. test for example. As the judge found in Hobson vs Hansen, the case that abolished the tracking system in the Washington D.C. schools. When standard ability tests are given to low income black children they are less precise and less accurate so it's virtually impossible to tell whether the test score reflects the lack of ability or the lack of opportunity.

External testing for college admission is usually justified as a means for identifying the students most likely to "benefit" from a college education. Can't we come up with any better selective admission procedures, ones that are more beneficial educationally speaking. Dr. William Sedlecek thinks we can. He has developed an instrument that he claims predicts black student ability far better than the SAT or ACT. Other researchers have found that the traditional admissions' predictors are inappropriate for culturally different students. Consequently many minority students who could succeed in college are never admitted.

We need to take seriously the moral short sightedness of limiting people's life chances on the basis of "aptitude" rather than on the basis of achievement. Doesn't it make sense to make the best higher education available to as broad a range of people as possible for all of our benefits rather than restrict it to those who are able to score well on standardized tests? In order for me to drive this point home, suppose I gave you a black culture test and how you scored would determine whether you got a job or were admitted into college. Let's see how you would do. [see black culture difference test located in Chapter 7.]

Now what do these results tell me about your intelligence or your ability. It tells me you know little about black culture maybe. It would be a mistake for me to use your scores as if they alone could predict your success. When universities use test scores in this manner it's the process that becomes important. When quantification becomes the goal, social issues are out of place. Predictive artifacts are given a respectability and a validity they may not deserve.

The fallibility of test scores are no longer questioned. The practical fallout from quantification is evident in the works of researchers like Arthur Jensen. His research may have contributed to the further stratification along racial and class lines of the American classroom. I.Q. tests become a method of social control that help legitimize class distinctions in schools. So called tougher standards that result from quantification may sound like a good idea until one analyzes what grades are being asked to predict. Robert E. Lee graduated first in his class while Ulysses S. Grant stood below the middle. If we were going to make a prediction based on class rank we'd be completely right only on the one who graduated last in his class, General George Armstrong Custer.

Lack of Supportive Services

Another problem that minority students face on predominantly white campuses is the lack of **supportive services**

Yes we have students who need extra help when they come to school and there's no need to apologize for it. They need the extra help because the resources needed in their schools and communities were allocated elsewhere. Many inner city schools failed to offer calculus and chemistry. A researcher by the name of Voyich, (1974) reported that support services were crucial to student success. The absence of a support program may make even the most qualified Minority students academic casualties unnecessarily.

There is a substantial body of research that links the lack of supportive services to high attrition rates. Many schools have responded by setting up remedial programs. I know we have students who don't want to attend these classes because they feel stigmatized. Well we've got to tell them to sit through these reading and writing labs because if you can't read or write you're not going anywhere. Acknowledge the need for remediation without attaching a stigma to those participating in such programs. Using titles such a skills development provides access without labeling students.

On the other hand we have some students who try to get by speaking black english. I have no problem with black english except, you can't get through Law school with it - You can't get through Engineering school with it. There's nothing wrong with being bilingual. I want our students to be bi-cultural, multicultural and able to relate not only to their community but to the world.

Edward "Chip" Anderson in Lee Noel's book **Reducing the Dropout Rate** offers some excellent guidelines for establishing support services.

Alienation

Then there's the problem of **alienation**. Socially, predominantly white universities are structured to meet white student needs. From fraternities to polka dancing, minority students often find themselves outside the mainstream of college life. A study conducted by Centra, (1970) of 83 predominantly white institutions reveals a dual environment for black students that leads to alienation. Suen, (1983) confirmed that alienation leads to high attrition.

When you consider the low number of minority students enrolled at many predominantly white institutions a situation exists in which there is often only one Black or one Indian in the classroom. These students find themselves in an isolated position, obtaining little approval and support from their teacher or other students. They are often left out of informal study groups, and have limited access to notes from past courses. As a result many find themselves on their own. The result shows up in the high dropout rate.

From all the research that I looked at it appears that the freshman year is critical. Campuses need to do a better job of thinking through appropriate ways to bond the freshmen to their campus. Freshmen who are involved tend to stay. Promote affiliation: For example, not being involved means losing the chance to have a lead in a play or losing a part time job. Promote the feeling of belonging that campus activities offer.

Some campuses offer family memberships to the gym, others

encourage a students' spouse to come to school sponsored activities or sponsors bring a guest to class day. Some expand campus employment opportunities. When I was an administrator at UW-Oshkosh, we started a saturday children's program for minority youngsters as a way to get non-traditional students involved.

Astin, (1975) suggests that having a point of identification with the institution is important for student retention. Tell students there's the library, there's the union and there's the basketball court.

Socialization

Then there's the problem of **socialization.** Minority student adjustment at predominantly white institutions require that they adhere to white cultural norms rather quickly, ignoring their own cultural roots in the process. Since many colleges are what Orlando Taylor describes as middle class entities it's not surprising to find that students who have adopted white middle class norms are more likely to experience success in higher education. The process by which students of color are integrated into the social fabric causes many students to question the necessity of losing their ethnic identity in order to be accepted.

While I think it's important for minority students to develop their own clubs and organizations, I believe it's a mistake for them not to participate in every aspect of college life. If they are going to stay on these campuses they must have something to say about how they are going to function. The research shows that students who get involved in campus activities generally do better in classes and increase their chances for persistence.

Students who have developed interpersonal skills are usually better able to manipulate bureaucracies to their advantage. Studies also indicate that minority students who've had positive interracial contact prior to college, experience more positive interracial contacts once they get on campus.

It appears that black females face a greater sense of frustration in socializing than males. Add to that an increase in interracial dating, coupled with the depressing low number of Black males to begin with and you have a situation that's tenuous at best.

This problem of socialization has a subtle dimension that may be even more damaging. I mean we've all been socialized. Let me give you an example.

1. A group of people are gathered around a table. They are having a great time, drinking wine and laughing loudly. The music playing in the background sounds like an opera. The robust mother yells in an accented voice at her son for dropping spaghetti on the carpet. What ethnic group am I talking about?

OK let me read another one.

2. Walking down the city street, I observe some people sitting in front of a housing project listening to loud music and doing fancy dance steps ever so often. A cadilac pulls up, a good looking woman

gets out and I hear someone say, "What's happening momma"? What ethnic group do you see?

Could the first example have been an Hispanic family? Could the second example have been Italians? They were!

In order for us to confront this type of pervasive socialization-this conformity, it involves more than just putting in new information; it also requires the removal of old information. Education is as much caught as it is taught.

Just how do black students feel about the whole notion of socialization. Let me share with you a survey I conducted at UW-Oshkosh from 1977-1980. [see survey questions at end of this chapter.]

Relevance

Then there's the problem of **relevance**. American schools are more correctly described as interracial rather than integrated, cosmetic togetherness. What if every text book you were required to read presented the rainbow in all of its beauty - Black authors and Hispanic authors , Asians... What if our schools truly prepared us to respect and live in a multicultural world. It's a tragedy not only for minorities but for whites as well to go through an entire educational career and never be taught by a Black or exposed to 3/4ths of the world's population. Shakespeare is alright but what about some James Baldwin or Alex Haley.

Greater interest can be created in the subject matter if students understand its meaning to their lives. A math professor teaching migrant workers taught students how to figure out how to pay the rent by the number of bushels they picked. A typing teacher had her class type an Indian alphabet and turned the students reactions into a lesson. A chemistry teacher discussed the composition of hair products and informed students why most blacks have to oil their hair.

Our job is to help professors understand that they are working with a variety of ethnic groups and cultures and that their charge is not so much to force everyone into the same mold as it is to give everyone the relevant tools for success. We need to make it clear there is no one model American. Most Black teachers will tell you when there is genuine black interest there is seldom any complaint about Black ability.

Motivation

Finally there's the problem of **motivation**. With the previous nine social barriers facing minority students it's understandable that a lack of motivation is often present. When I work with minority students, I tell them to view these problems not as crutches but rather as challenges. Studies have found that successful minorities tended to be independent, self-assured and confident that they can change their lives by their own efforts. They expect racism and have prepared to deal with it. They have achieved some form of success outside the classroom. They tend to have a person of strong influence who provides advice in times of crisis—someone to lean on!

I believe our motivated students are going to be our future leaders. Motivated students understand there are several things they must do while in school.

1) They must study hard because **you can't teach what you don't know, nor lead where you don't go.**

2) Don't separate yourselves while you're here—get involved.

3) Achieve academically which means (a) homework done well, (b) classes attended, (c) reports finished, and (d) preparations for class accomplished.

The task for minority students on white campuses is not to retreat but to direct their anger and frustration into changing their educational environment – to make it better for those who come after.

Are there additional questions at this point?

LET'S TAKE A BREAK

Significant Factors Impacting Minority Student Retention

FACTORS ASSOCIATED WITH HIGH ATTRITION RATES

1. Inadequate Financial Aid
2. Institutional Racism
3. Low Grade Point Average
4. Undecided Major or Career Goals
5. Lack of Supportive Services
6. Alienation
7. Other

The above list (not necessarily in that order) is usually cited by the literature as the leading causes for minority student attrition. If you were to select one as being the top reason, by a show of hands, how many would select: Number 1?, 2?, 3?...

The next question you must ask is what strategies or programs presently exist to deal with the factors you've selected. What strategies or programs need to be created to address these factors?

If the #1 factor is financial aid: A new study by the American Association of Community and Junior Colleges (which by the way have a disproportionate concentration of minority students) says, money is the key problem driving low income students away. The cuts in federal aid and the new emphasis on GSL and other loans combine to close college doors to many minority students. When I was a financial aids counselor at UW-Madison over a decade ago, we had a category of students that we called a profile student—this was the student with the greatest need. We changed office policy so this student's needs could be met first. Perhaps an equally serious problem that we uncovered was that minority and low income students graduated from UW at that time with almost twice the loan debt of white students.

This is a serious problem and one that is often over looked. Financial aid counselors need to work with students to conduct budget counseling as well. Recruiters need to be honest with low income students and let them know that chances are if they graduate they can count on $6-$10,000 worth of debt long before they land that first job. If the factor is institutional racism I would recommend that a multicultural task force conduct a policy review and evaluate how institutional policies are affecting students along racial lines.

To treat everyone the same does not mean you're treating everyone fairly. If the factor is low grades, remedial services may be the answer. Reginald Wilson of the the American Council on Education and former president of Wayne Community College in Detroit recalls how his school's nursing program was 80% white even though the total enrollment of the college was 65% black until he started remedial programs. With the remedial courses, black enrollment in nursing courses shot up to more than 50%, he said. Unfortunately federal support for remedial program is fading.

With undecided majors, you might consider career counseling or get a print out of what minority students are majoring in. If the print out says most minority students are majoring in education that should flag you into taking appropriate action to ascertain that is what they want to major in as opposed to that's the only major they know about. If the factor is lack of supportive services consider establishing some, especially for that critical freshman year. If the factor is alienation, institutions must create an environment that is inviting, comfortable and makes the student feel apart of the campus.

Ten Inexpensive Ways to Recruit and Retain Minority Students

1. Personalized letter sent to parents of freshman students

Surveys conducted by myself as well as other colleagues confirm that freshmen are still greatly influenced by their parents. A personal, friendly letter of introduction allows you to establish contact with a student's parent(s), and possibly channel some of that influence to increase their son's and daughter's involvement on campus. This technique has worked quite well for a number of administrators.

2. Positive press releases mailed to hometown papers

There are few things as motivating as good publicity. One positive story in his/her hometown paper (sent out by the Public Affairs Office) has proven effective and I am aware of at least one campus that partially credits such publicity as helping to increase retention rates. Once the publicity hits home, and students have been congratulated by hometown friends, they tend to strive even harder on campus.

3. Regular articles in student newspaper

I created two stacks of student newspapers (when looking through them for information to be included in my retention book). One stack had articles (other than sports or crime) about minorities and the other stack did not. The stack that did not have any articles was about five times the size of the one that did. After looking at hundreds of such publications, you begin to wonder why minorities are missing from the press. If any publication should reflect diversity it's the campus newspaper at an institution of higher learning. When students see themselves, their friends and their culture given coverage in a variety of settings, they tend to feel apart of the campus.

4. Involving Minority Student Organizations

Student Organizations represent experience, talent and bundles of energy. When properly channeled they can help the university in recruiting and retaining students. Campuses that provide student organizations with leadership and similar developmental training find the investment pays off.

5. Create a Minority student Advisory Council

When there are few student organizations and little participation in student government, residence halls, etc., an advisory council can fill the void. A representative council can help increase student interaction and participation.

6. Encourage a Student "Replacement" campaign

Minority student organizations can be encouraged to sponsor a campaign in which (so inclined) graduating seniors and those deciding not to come back attempt to replace themselves with another student. Successful students can be honored at end of year student sponsored banquets. Student organizations have to assume the leadership role for this strategy to effectively work.

7. Have faculty create a permanent retention committee

A standing committee ensures the issues are receiving the attention they deserve while involving faculty directly in the process.

8. Sponsor get acquainted meetings by sex

Friendships contribute to a feeling of belonging. Black faculty and staff on the Newark campus-Rutgers University devised a program for black males to get together. A directory of black students by class and major was compiled and used by students to form study groups. Social activities, mentor relationships, and new friendships were the outcome. A similar group was formed for women. Now both groups are actively involved in retention efforts.

9. Create a "town-gown" committee

Students may avoid some colleges because of the reputation of the town. Institutions located in small or rural communities face even greater challenges. A town-gown committee can help smooth the transition that students must make.

10. Involve minority alumni

Create a Minority Alumni organization. Such organizations raise funds, sponsor annual workshop/conferences, and help recruit and retain faculty as well as students.

Discussion of a Retention Model

TAYLOR RETENTION MODEL

Next I want to talk about a model that can assist campuses as they begin to develop a plan of action. [A copy of the model is located at the end of this chapter.] The model is based on a holistic approach and I want to stress the relational nature of each area and urge you to avoid the tendency of reducing an analyzation of the problem to simple parts in search of the ideal solution. Every link in the model is important. Each should be carefully studied in terms of current institutional practices. If the model is applied I believe campuses will experience effective ways to recruit and retain minority students.

Pre-Collegiate

The first area in the model is **pre-collegiate:**
A pre-college program can be to campuses what HEAD START programs are to elementary schools. Both programs get students prepared for school. They assess students' academic weaknesses and strengths and provide assistance to overcome deficiencies. We must keep in mind that college has not been a "family" experience for most minority students. Therefore it often takes targeted efforts to get them thinking about college at an early age.
The most successful pre-college programs are Upward Bound type programs, in which middle and high school students actually live on campus, take college courses and interact with college faculty.
According to a report written by Delta Calvin, four years after high school graduation Upward Bound participants are four times more likely to earn a baccalaureate degree as compared to non-participants (Calvin,1984). Examples of successful pre-collegiate programs range from Upward Bound programs, to the development of feeder schools. Some colleges are maintaining correspondence with youngsters in middle school and continuing it through high school.
Another factor that can't be ignored is the high dropout rate among minority youngsters in high school. If we fail to stem that

tide, the best laid recruitment plans will fail. The data shows that in 1978 nearly a fourth of black Americans between 16 and 34 were not in school and had not graduated from high school. Although the high school graduation picture has improved somewhat, the number of minority students attending four year institutions has declined.

There are many things universities can do in this area to help black and minority kids get set, start ahead, have a better chance and bound upward.

Recruitment/Admissions

Next I'll talk about recruitment/admissions. There are many activities that colleges can implement to influence and invite minority student choice. Some universities use what they call a cultivation plan where different schools across the state are divided among admissions personnel to develop more personal relationships with students to increase enrollment. Some sponsor a minority week similar to "Discover Dartmouth" to attract minority students.

Universities must answer three distinct but interrelated questions regarding minority students recruitment and admissions, where do we find them? How do we recruit them and what things do we consider before we admit them? Let me speak briefly to each of these concerns.

Where do we find them?

While the white student population between the ages of 16-24 is projected to decrease into the 1990's, the minority student population is expected to increase. Early identification is paramount to the success of effective recruiting efforts. Some universities have created targeted admissions programs by establishing computerized applicant pools.

Data from the Census Bureau provides specific locations for concentrations of minority populations. In my retention book, I also provide tables and information on the top cities and states where Blacks and Hispanics are located.

How do we recruit them?

There's little disagreement from the research that financial aid is the most important factor to successful minority student recruitment. According to the latest census report the financial position of Hispanics and Blacks has not improved relative to whites over the past decade. Add to that the high unemployment rate in minority communities and you have a situation where students are being denied opportunity based on both class and race.

In addition to keeping many students out, limited funds also means limited choice where students can go. This choice is significant because (as I mentioned earlier) it forces a disproportionate number of minority students to enroll in two year campuses where many never make it to a four year campus.

With dwindling financial resources on the national level the issue of access threatens to widen the gulf between white and minority students. If this trend continues Dr. Manning Marable of Colgate University argues that a college education will be available only to the rich. Add to that a continuous increase in tuition and the reduction in grants and the real threat to minority educational gains becomes apparent.

What things do we consider before we admit them?

Several guidelines have emerged from the Bakke and Adams court cases that may be of help to campus planners.

A. Race and/or ethnic background can be considered as a factor for admission.

B. Minority applicants should be reviewed on an individual basis rather than on a group basis for admission purposes.

C. Although quotas are not allowed, universities can use numerical goals and timetables.

D. Separate admission programs are unacceptable to the courts.

E. Test scores should not be used exclusively to determine admission.

The Adams case seems to provide even greater flexibility for campus administrators. This case requires the desegregation of state systems of public higher education. Some significant highlights from this case are:

A. Requiring state-wide coordinated plans rather than individual institutional plans from a state.

B. Encouraging aggressive Affirmative Action which goes beyond removal of barriers to actual access.

C. Requiring states to strive for parity of enrollment.

D. Requiring universities to strive for parity of retention and progress from matriculation to graduation.

Obviously some campuses have used these guidelines more liberally than others but the prevalent trend is still to make greater use of standardized tests to determine admission. William Ihlandfeldt in his study (1984) estimates that no more than 2.8% of the total high school graduate population in 1984 of 69,149 could meet the admission criteria for Northwestern University (located in Evanston, IL) which requires a score of 1100 on the SAT and a B average in high school.

That means over 97% of America's high school graduates are automatically excluded from many of our institutions who are directly or indirectly tax supported. This selectivity based on test scores succeeds quite well in keeping students out. There are alternative admission models being proposed. The one that is generating the most interest is called NCQ - The Non Cognitive Questionnaire developed by Dr. William Sedlecek of the University of Maryland, who recently sent us an updated report. His instrument measures factors like self concept, leadership experiences, ability to set goals and he claims, predicts Black student graduation up to six years after initial matriculation while SAT scores on high school grades do not.

As staff from the Mexican American Legal Defense Fund argue there ares no statistical, constitutional, or moral reasons to limit admissions criteria strictly to standardized test scores.

Practical things that campuses can do to make the admissions process easier is to streamline and simplify the admission form itself. A university in Virginia simplified its form. The result was that many more students applied.

Orientation

The next link in my retention model is orientation. Students in general find campuses perplexing. That's why a good orientation program is critical, because it's often the first encounter a minority student has with that campus. It's important that the entire university is involved in the orientation process. This reassures students that they are a part of the total campus community. This approach also helps to reduce stigmatization by helping traditional departments recognize their responsibilities in helping minority students adjust to campus.

An effective orientation program usually has the following characteristics:

It informs students about what support services are available on campus and shows the importance of those services to their retention and graduation.

It gives them an awareness of degree requirements in their area of academic interest.

It provides academic advising to help students complete their course scheduling.

It familiarizes students with the process of registration.

It discusses educational and career options.

It provides an orientation to the non-collegiate community.

It provides students an opportunity to interact with other students, faculty and staff.

The National Orientation Directors Association has a good bibliography available to assist in creating an effective orientation program.

Many campuses are beginning to focus attention on the first year of college, when many new students, especially on large impersonal campuses are not well served; they find themselves closed out of classes, given lower priority in advising and scheduling and generally treated impersonally. According to Myers, (1981) study, it's not uncommon to find that of the students who drop out during their freshmen year, 50% drop out during the first six weeks.

If retention rates are to be improved greater care must be given to establishing a solid orientation program for Minority students.

RETENTION

Getting into college is less of an issue than it was a decade ago. The issue today is retention which has been characterized as a revolving door. Nationally only about 42% of minority students entering college go on to complete their degrees while approximately 60% of white students do so. It seems to me a minimum goal would be to have the retention rates for minority students the same as those for non-minority students. As I mentioned earlier the research clearly suggests that the freshman year is the critical place for intervention.

Indiana University at South Bend has implemented a **Beginning Student Early Warning System** where a brief student report form is sent to instructors during the 4th week of classes to identify students in need of assistance. Some campuses start even earlier by the 3rd week since that is the deadline on many campuses for students to withdraw with a full tuition refund.

Others provide faculty with a list of all freshmen and the names of their advisers to contact if the student is getting into academic difficulty. Some campuses require semester and year end reports from each college summarizing the efforts made by the college to improve retention.

If minority students make it past the freshman year the data indicates they are about as predictable as their white counterparts as far as retention goes.

Again the whole question of finances is important to retention. If students from low income backgrounds attended inferior schools and have lower academic skills they must spend more time reading, studying and preparing while at the same time more of their time and energy is required to fulfill financial, work, housing and similar responsibilities. The bottom line being those students who need the most time and energy to succeed academically have the least time and energy available to devote to their studies.

Adequate financial aid that will permit a student not to work during their freshmen year has been implemented with some success at several colleges.

To address the issue of poor prior academic preparation some universities are considering hiring elementary school teachers to teach basic skills.

Some other ideas worth exploring are roommate assignments. Some studies have found that significantly higher levels of academic achievement can be obtained by assigning middle and low achievers as roommates or assigning students by majors or upper classpersons with freshmen.

Dr. Sedlecek suggests in his research that the use of campus facilities is related to retention for students in general and black students in particular. While library use was related to retention in both blacks and whites use of nonacademic facilities was especially important for black student retention. This question of retention if it is to be properly addressed, must include a discussion of other student services such as academic advising, counseling, remedial education, faculty involvement, and student incentives. I'd like to speak briefly to each of these next.

Academic Advising

It's not unusual to find a first semester freshman's schedule that includes a calculus, chemistry, foreign language, accounting and history course. This selection is fine for some students although it may be less than ideal for others to begin their college experience with. A close look at these courses reveals one thing in common-homework almost every night and tons of reading.

The course selection also assumes a strong background and prior knowledge in rather technical areas. This is a demanding program for any student. Marginal students may find it to be the kiss of death.

Without proper advising, ill informed students often sign up for such classes based on the catalog description. They find themselves in academic difficulty before the semester barely gets underway.

Ideally any student would be able to take a demanding course load and do well. Unfortunately we live in the real world where some students' schools prepare them better than other students' schools. As a result some students need a "catching up" period before they tackle the rigors of such a demanding schedule. That's where good advising comes in. Good advising lets students know that it's not their intelligence that's being questioned, but their preparation.

The schedule that is recommended is based on the skills they brought with them. As their skills improve their course selection will tend to be more challenging. This is done so that students are given the maximum chance to succeed. In order for students to receive this type of quality advising the advisor must be extremely knowledgeable and competent. The advisor must know what prerequisites are required for certain courses. They need to know what courses can be substituted for other courses. They must possess a substantive knowledge of the curriculum. Successful advisors have more content information on courses than what's provided in the catalog. They contact professors for syllabi, reading lists and course descriptions so they can stay on top of course requirements. Knowledgeable advisors serve on advising and curriculum committees and regularly receive information from such bodies. When they sit down with a student, they have copies of the student's transcripts, test scores and other data that will help provide the best advice possible.

Good advising is usually reflected in the courses students sign up for. By obtaining copies of transcripts its fairly easy to determine whether students are using the advice they've been given. Such monitoring can be used successfully with freshman students. Coupled with a follow up procedure more serious scheduling problems can be nipped in the bud early on.

It's also helpful if the advisor establishes a personal relationship with the student. Some advisors routinely write the parents of all new freshman minority students. They explain their role on campus and try to reassure the parents in a friendly personal manner that their sibling is in good hands. Others let students know that they'll be their contact for the next two years or longer, guaranteeing students consistency in the information they receive.

Effective advising services are not performed in isolation. Advisors must meet regularly to work out problems of freshmen scheduling. They constantly strive to use scheduling and cluster techniques to improve inclass retention.

Counseling/Career Placement

Who can I turn to...doesn't have to be the theme song for minority students longing for someone to talk to about personal problems. Unfortunately on many campuses the counseling services in place go unused by minority students allowing centers by default to remain unresponsive to minority student needs. Minority students face a unique set of problems at predominantly white institutions, which I previously discussed. There are times when these problems become over bearing and students simply need someone to listen.

During this counseling moment it's important that the counseling center have trained counselors capable of providing sensitive guidance to culturally different students. This is a serious concern because it is the training that counselors receive that allows them to address students' needs. When the training permits a counselor to treat all students the same ignoring cultural signals then the counselor is not in a position to be of much assistance.

Students take their problems elsewhere and normally sensitive and caring counselors are left wondering why minority students don't come into the center more often. An effective counseling program has proven decisive in combating alienation and helping students adjust to college. Sensitive university personnel can help students feel good about being who they are.

The late Johnnie Ruth Clarke who was on the staff at Tallahassee Community College in Tallahassee, Florida felt an effectual retention plan should include the following:
- recruiting outcomes that would attract both sexes to all programs.
- better knowledge of ways to lessen cultural conflict.
- humanistic, sensitive counseling and career guidance.
- peer support within and among minority group members.
- role models on the counseling staff and faculty and in the administrative ranks.
- access to developmental studies to close educational gaps and promote positive personal growth.
- access to placement services that supports self worth and promotes personal economic sufficiency.

She implies that campus counselors may need to be retrained. They need to know how to select, administer and evaluate assessment instruments. They need an awareness of activities which promote the development of positive self concepts. Counselors should have an understanding of minority students problems from their perspective and

247

then address these problems from both a counseling and instructional perspective. In looking at black students' counselor preference, Thompson found **"the likelihood of going to the counseling center increased as counselor preference increased,"** (Thompson, 1978). He found that black students preferred black counselors for both personal and educational-vocational problems. He also found that student and counselor sex had no affect on counseling center use.

This is not to suggest that only blacks should counsel blacks but it does imply that non-blacks must be sensitive to cultural factors to be effective in counseling blacks and other minorities. Counseling involves an intimacy of sorts. It involves trust, empathy and a non-judgmental helping attitude. When a black student sits down with a white counselor to discuss perceived racism on campus, this student wants to know if the counselor can be trusted and if his/her problem will be taken seriously. If not handled properly the situation can be very intimidating and deteriorate very rapidly. When handled appropriately the counseling center will have gained a supporter and through the word of mouth grapevine would have increased its effectiveness on campus.

While the above scenario may be typical in the sense that counselors wait for students to come in with their problems, some campuses are experimenting with outreach or action counseling. This has proven to be a very good strategy in heading off more serious counseling problems, especially with new freshmen. Freshmen are asked to fill out an assessment questionnaire during the matriculation period. The questionnaire asks information about their academic backgrounds, interpersonal concerns, personal traits and similar areas. The questionnaire provides a helpful insight into the student's background. The counselor reviews this information and makes contact with the student in a non-threatening manner. Rather than limit the session to a discussion of problems, the counselor shares information about various deadlines, talks about available support services and uses the session as a get acquainted opportunity. Often this initial session is done with a group of freshmen students, helping them to understand the commonality of their concerns.

These types of activities by the counseling center tend to increase minority student use of center services and enhances rapport between students and counselors.

PLACEMENT

For many students the only contact they make with the placement office is when graduation is approaching. Placement services have expanded on most campuses during the past decade. Services now range from computerized job listings to allowing students to videotape mock job interviews. Resume writing workshops, tips in job hunting, part-time employment opportunities and self improvement seminars are all provided on many campuses.

Students undecided about career opportunities can explore with a counselor different types of careers. They can get information that tells them what type of job a particular major might lead to or what type of additional training they would need to enter the professions.

The placement office is more than just an introduction to the world of work; it's charge is to assist students in the successful culmination of an educational investment by helping them secure employment and educational opportunities commensurate with their preparation and experience. For the most part placement offices are utilized by minority students, especially seniors and graduate students. Outreach efforts need to be targeted at undergraduates to increase their participation. Universities need to do a better job of keeping statistics on the number of minority students served and placed also. There also needs to be stronger linkages between the placement office and workstudy/student employment opportunities on campus. Closer ties between these areas could result in giving students the kind of exposure to careers that is lacking at many institutions.

One of the factors Astin, (1975) identified that played a significant part in students' dropping out was indecision about major/career goals. Some universities now offer career planning courses to assist students in their decision making.

In summary, career counseling can influence student persistence in a positive manner.

Learning Resource Center

The literature is clear in identifying academic underpreparedness as a major factor explaining student dropout. Until American elementary and secondary schools no longer discriminate along class and racial lines, the poor and racial minority population will continue to enter college at a disadvantage. When underprepared students enter there have to be remedial type programs available to give them a reasonable chance of succeeding. If this is to be done their academic problems must be diagnosed early on-preferably during the matriculation period. After high risk students' needs have been diagnosed appropriate services must be prescribed.

Administrators can't rely on standardized tests alone so some campuses have installed an early warning system to monitor class performance of high risk students. A model program may be the Early Warning System in place at California State University, Northridge. Instructors are asked to fill out a form (progress report), and return it to the office of origin where appropriate follow up can begin. [An example of such a form can be found at the end of this chapter].

The real benefit of such a system is that it involves the faculty directly in retention activities. When handled appropriately the message that comes through to students is that faculty and staff care about them.

Although teaching basic skills is still a controversial issue in higher education recent successes, Noel and Levitz, (1982, p. 8), have to impress even the staunchest critics. Remedial education is working primarily because it assumes that underprepared students are not dumb, they simply lack certain academic skills. If they can be taught these skills in a non-stigmatized environment, the research indicates they can compete with their fellow classmates and go on to complete their degrees. Remedial services have been traditionally rendered either using the classroom approach or tutorial approach. The classroom approach normally involves an instructor teaching a group of under prepared students reading, writing and mathematical skills. Sometimes the course is offered for credit, sometimes not.

The tutorial approach involves a personal tutor usually skilled in a particular subject area assisting an underprepared student master that subject or skill. Both approaches can be successful. The instructional approach requires competent teachers who have high expectations. The tutorial approach requires trained tutors and adequate space. Many facilities offer a lab like setting and because of the new technology, self-tutoring is also available. Regardless of which skill building approach is used, it's evident from the literature that supportive services similar to the Learning Resource Center will help increase retention and graduation rates.

Need For Faculty Involvement in Retention

No improvement can be expected in decreasing the attrition rate without faculty leadership and involvement. Collectively and individually faculty have more power to improve retention on campuses that any other group. These are powerful statements yet the role that most faculty play in retention efforts is secondary. Beal & Noel, (1980) found that only 18% of 944 institutions they surveyed involved the faculty in any meaningful manner.

This can be explained in part by faculty resistance. Retention is often viewed, at best, as an extra curricular activity; or as someone else's responsibility. Consider the position that faculty are in. They know which students are repeatedly late for class, unprepared, take few notes, sit at the back of the class, etc. What are they to do with this information. Unfortunately too many do nothing.

Campuses face a real challenge in getting faculty to understand that assisting in retention doesn't involve a lowering of standards. The literature suggests just the opposite. When the learning environment is improved for some students, it's improved for all.

The retention issue impacts faculty directly. Half empty class rooms mean fewer dollars for instruction, research and the like. Such a situation forces faculty to either jump ship or rethink what their role should be. It's better for the health of the institution for faculty to put in place preventive measures early on than to find themselves faced with long-term declining enrollments. How important are "standards" under those circumstances?

Let's set aside the self-interest argument and concentrate on a more positive approach to justifying faculty involvement with retention. Almost every major study involving retention mentions caring and sensitive faculty as one of the key ingredients for student persistence. Astin, (1977) concluded that student-faculty interaction was the most important factor in assessing student satisfaction with their campus. Pantages and Creedon, (1978) reached similar conclusions. Beal and Noel, (1980) found the retention factor cited as most important by both two year and four year institutions was the **"caring attitude of faculty and staff".**

When faculty transmit signals that tell students they care the results are usually better motivation, class attendance and involvement in class discussions on the part of students. Faculty wield tremendous influence over students. Many a major gets chosen because a student admired faculty in a particular department. There are few residence halls or student centers one can enter and not hear discussions about professors. Students tend to hold professors in high esteem, almost in awe. As a result they have a right to expect fairness. They have a right to expect that the classroom is free of racism and sexism and that information is shared in a way that doesn't belittle them or their culture. Minority students attending predominantly white campuses especially need reassurance upfront from faculty. There is ample research to suggest that minority students educational experiences are qualitatively different than their white counterparts.

If a composite was drawn of the American professor the portrait that would emerge would be that of a middle aged white male with limited experience in interacting with minority students. This professor's life experiences and educational preparation traditionally place him at odds with students of color. When minority students enter his classroom, more than likely they are the ones who are expected to change. Nettles' (1982) research concludes that the majority of faculty members at predominantly white schools have made no special adjustments in terms of their time allocation, manner of teaching, or curriculum, and most admit that they interact less with their black students than with their white students.

Clearly a shift in faculty attitudes and practices is suggested by Nettles' findings. Without faculty change its easy to picture minority students being placed in classrooms under less than ideal circumstances. Such an environment contributes to poor class performance and the whole cycle of lower expectancy.

The picture painted above does not have to be overly pessimistic. Faculty can be trained to be effective advisors, mentors and counselors of minority students. Curriculums can be pluralized thereby enhancing the total educational surroundings for all students.

The FAMES program at Northridge college (California) has put together a booklet for faculty advisors of minority students that other campuses should find very helpful. Caring faculty recognize the new challenges that minority students represent. They also acknowledge the many positives that minority students bring to the campus as well.

They expect minority students to succeed and students respond accordingly. Caring faculty understand that their involvement with students must extend outside the classroom as well. Colleges that have been successful in cutting attrition rates find ways to involve their faculty outside the classroom. This doesn't mean that faculty are expected to attend every minority student function or spend enormous amounts of time engaged in student activities. The time faculty spend with students has to be a judgment call based on one's schedule, lifestyle and free time available. The point that needs to be made is that quality time spent does make a difference. Campuses should consider offering incentives to faculty. If the faculty role is as vital as the research indicates then institutional rewards should reflect this importance. Reduced class loads, merit pay increases and similar motivators tell faculty their participation in retention efforts is not only acknowledged but is taken seriously. This could lead to faculty giving the retention problem the priority it deserves. For example creating a permanent standing faculty committee on minority student recruitment and retention. This committee could monitor the faculty's significant advisory power over resource allocation, admission decisions, curriculum reform, graduation requirements, special services, grants solicitation, and similar areas.

Many of the programs needed by minority students require faculty support; the limited time faculty have available added to the pressures of publishing and research implies the support needed carries a high premium. Nonetheless ways must be found to generate faculty advocacy because the record is clear; students who attract faculty allies stand a much better chance of graduating.

Student Incentives

When properly motivated students make superb recruiters, peer counselors, tutors and helpers who can tremendously enhance a university's overall retention efforts. The enthusiasm and idealism they bring to projects is heartening and when this energy is channeled into a positive force the results can be astounding. When one thinks of the many fine presentations, seminars, talent shows, etc., that students have created, planned and implemented then one begins to appreciate the marvelous talent and knowledge they bring to our campuses. Too much attention is given to students' weaknesses rather than their strengths; strengths that often go unmeasured by standardized tests. These strengths need to be nurtured and supported. Many minority students have a deep social conscience and are interested in "giving back" to the community. Developmental workshops stressing leadership and organizational training can give students the type of skills that encourage their involvement in campus activities. Opportunities like these help to motivate students and allows them to feel needed on campus. When campuses create the right atmosphere it seems that minority student interaction falls in place. A supportive environment is one in which student growth is expected and fostered. Student organizations are promoted and given the resources necessary to function. When there is advocacy for Minority students on a campus the results are students helping to bring in new students and helping each other make it through.

Despite all these efforts let's face it students are still going to withdraw. It's important to structure your withdrawal policy in a way that can prevent withdrawals. It should involve the financial aids office. It should first determine the reason and secondly direct the student to an office that may be able to help solve the problem.

Graduation

With so much emphasis on recruitment and retention, it's important not to lose sight of the purpose of all these efforts-graduation. The intent must be to recruit with the goal of graduating minority students. We have a shortage of minorities in just about every field. Perhaps a goal worth pursuing on this campus and nationally is to work for parity in degree production. If this is to occur, just for black students alone, it has been estimated something like 100,000 baccalaureates would need to be produced annually. We are currently operating at about 60,000 annually. To achieve parity in the professions and for Ph.Ds would require about 3,000 degrees annually, up from the 1,000 or less currently being earned. Still another problem is the length of time it takes to graduate. Goodrich, (1977) estimated that only 5 out of 30 black students who enter a four year college graduate on schedule. Gosman, (1982) found that although the average time it takes to graduate is longer than four years for all students, minority students still take longer than white students to graduate. This tends to worsen the heavier loan debt already carried by minority students.

Campuses also should encourage students to have a degree summary made annually that lists all the courses they have taken as well as all the courses they need to take in order to graduate. When I was an academic advisor, you'd be surprised at the number of seniors I talked with who had no idea of what courses they needed to complete their degrees.

Post-Graduation

Next I'd like to talk about post-graduation issues. An increasing number of careers and job choices require preparation beyond the bachelors degree. Minority participation in graduate and professional education remains extremely low. You don't have to look very far to prove that statement. Statistics from the National Urban League and the Equal Employment Opportunity Commission find that only about 4.4% of the nation's faculty members are black. About half of these are at predominantly white institutions. According to a report by the College and University Personnel Association, white males outnumber women and minority faculty about three to one. So it's still possible for students to go through their entire educational careers and never be taught by a woman or minority professor.

Some approaches that should be considered to address this inequity is to establish affirmative action guidelines for teaching and research assistants. Provide practicum and internship opportunities for students with the goal of preparing them for teaching assistant slots. Work to increase post-doctoral opportunities for minority staff.

Alumni

The final link in the retention chain includes involving the alumni. Campuses miss a real opportunity by not involving their minority alumni on a larger scale. Alumni can serve everything from role models to recruiters, to fund raisers-you name it. Who better can "sell" the university? The extent to which black and minority groups get involved in alumni activities is often the best gauge for determining whether they feel a part of the campus or not.

If you view my model as being cyclical, then the alumni link assumes even greater importance. Some approaches which have proven successful include: The creation of a minority alumni advisory body or association; the development of alumni traditions that can be passed down from one graduating class to the next; hiring minority alumni staff and the development of a multicultural wing in the alumni house where portraits, awards, etc., can be displayed.

RESOURCES AVAILABLE TO HELP YOU GET STARTED

Now I'd like to share with you some resources that are available to help you get started. The following are books and publications I recommend you obtain for your library.
1. INCREASING STUDENT RETENTION BY LEE NOEL (available in your library).
2. NCQ (NON COGNITIVE QUESTIONNAIRE) (used by some campuses to supplement the SAT is available for $8 prepaid from:The Counseling Center, University of Maryland, College Park, MD 20742).
3. EFFECTIVE WAYS TO RECRUIT & RETAIN MINORITY STUDENTS (available through Praxis Publications Inc., P.O.Box 9869, Madison, WI 53715 for $29.95).
4. GUIDE TO MULTICULTURAL RESOURCES (available through Praxis Publications for $25.95).
5. CULTURAL RETREAT HANDBOOK (available through Praxis Publications for $19.95).
6. HANDBOOK OF MINORITY STUDENT SERVICES (available through Praxis Publications for $49.95).
7. ADDITIONAL WORKSHOPS THAT WE OFFER. (I'd be happy to send you a list of our workshop leaders). [This list is located in chapter 11 of this book].

In closing let me encourage you to begin implementing your plan of action. I hope I've given you enough suggestions to consider. I can only advise-It'll be up to you to act. One of the reasons I'm glad I came here was because of students like the ones I met today, who inspire me with their commitment and perserverance. Perhaps like you, I want to inspire hope in our young people and let them know that America can offer them more than unemployment, dope, jails or the military. I want them to know if they can believe it they can achieve it. I've enjoyed my visit here. Thank you very much for inviting me.

Activities Used in the Retention Workshop

The Black Cultural Difference test used in the workshop is located in chapter 7.

Survey of Black Students at UW-Oshkosh (1977-1979)

1. Do you feel that you put more emphasis on entertainment, education or cultural interests?

2. How would you describe success?

3. Circle the word that describes you:
   Misunderstood   Angry   Happy   Cool   Other

4. My hero is a ___Civil Rights Leader ___Religious Leader
   ___Musician ___Athlete ___Other

5. Do you think you will pursue educational goals beyond an undergraduate degree?   ___Yes ___No

6. Do you feel that black and white youth share the same interests?
   ___Yes ___No

7. What do you feel is your biggest problem in school?

8. What kind of advice would you give to whites on how to relate to black students?

9. I am influenced mostly by my:
   ___Friends___Parents___Teacher___Pastor___Other

10. The greatest social service that I feel is needed is:

    ___Health Clinics ___Day Care ___Legal Aid ___More Jobs___other

11. Circle the type of society that you want to live in:
    ___Separated ___Integrated ___Liberated ___Other

12. Circle the type of political system you want to live under:
    ___Capitalism ___Socialism ___Communism ___Other

13. Are you aware of the various organizations located on campus?

14. Have you made an effort to seek information about the organizations located on campus.

15. Do you feel you can achieve a degree of satisfaction by actively participating on campus?

16. Can you suggest reasons why some black students fail to become involved on campus?

17. Is color a factor as far as black apathy is concerned?

18. What are some reasons why blacks don't take advantage of the Multicultural Education Center?

19. What additional questions should have been asked?

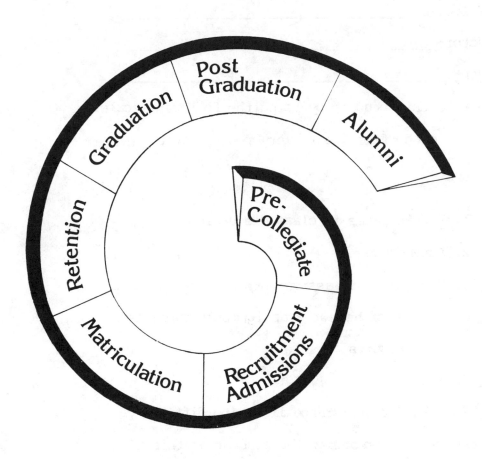

EARLY WARNING SYSTEM

STUDENT MONITORING FORM

Student Name/I.D. Number:_____

Course/Section:_____

Instructor:_____

Date Sent:_____

Please rate this student by using the following scale:

excellent good fair poor very poor unable
                                         to answer
1   2   3   4   5   6

_____ 1. Participates in class discussion

_____ 2. Attendance

_____ 3. Submits class assignments on time

_____ 4. Quality of homework assignments submitted

_____ 5. Quiz results

_____ 6. Test results

_____ 7. Asks for assistance if having difficulty

What grade would you assign the student at this time?

A A/B B B/C C D F OTHER_____

Comments: (where applicable, speak to students' interest shown in
class, and any follow up you would recommend).
* This form is to be completed by the Course Instructor/Professor
prior to the sixth week of class for those students facing academic
difficulty. This form is to be returned to the student's academic
advisor.

RETENTION NOTES

Anderson, Edward "Chip", A Retention Design Applied to an Equal Opportunity Program." In Lee Noel (Ed), **Reducing the Dropout Rate.** San Francisco:Jossey-Bass,Inc., 1978.

Astin, Alexander W., **Preventing Students from Dropping Out.** San Francisco:Jossey-Bass, Inc., 1975.

Calvin, Delta, "Reagan's FY'85 Budget to Reduce Programs for the Disadvantaged Student", **National Minority Campus Chronicle,** Vol 2, (11) April, 1984.

Centra, John A., "College Enrollment in the 1980's, Projections and Possibilities." **Journal of Higher Education,** 51 (January-February, 1980):18-39.

Chickering, A.W. and Associates, **The Modern American College: Responding to the new Reality of Diverse Students and a Changing Society.** San Francisco, Jossey-Bass, 1981.

Gibbs, J.T. "Patterns of Adaptation among Black Students at a Predominantly White University." **American Journal of Orthopsychiatry,** 1974, 44, 728-740.

Goodrich, A. **A Data Driven Model for Minorities in Predominantly White Institutions,** (Paper presented at the National Conference on Advising, Vermont, 1977).

Gosman, Erica J., and others. **Predicting Student Progression: The Influence of Race and other Students and Institutional Characteristics on College Students Performance,** Air Forum, 1982.

Ihlandfeldt, William, Admissions, (1984) in **Increasing Student Retention** by Lee Noel, et al, San Francisco:Jossey-Bass, 1985.

Myers, E. Unpublished Attrition Research Studies, St.Cloud State University, St.Cloud, MN. (1981) in **Increasing Student Retention,** Ibid, p.20.

Sedlecek, William. "Teaching Minority Students", in J.H. Cones III, J.F. Noonan, and D. Janha, **New Directions for Teaching and Learning,** no.16, San Francisco:Jossey-Bass, 1983.

Suen, Hoi K., "Alienation and Attrition of Black College Students on a Predominantly white Campus." **Journal of College Student Personnel,** v24, n2 p.117-21 (March, 1983).

Taylor, Charles A., **Effective Ways to Recruit and Retain Minority Students,** Madison: Praxis Publications Inc., 1986.

Terry, Robert W., **For Whites Only,** Grand Rapids,1970.

Voyich, D.L., **A Study of Selected Characteristics of Successful and Unsuccessful American Indian Students Enrolled at Montana State University from September 1967 to June 1972,** (Doctoral Dissertation, Montana State University, 1974).

261

Chapter 11

Resources Available to Assist You

Pre-Collegiate Resources

There are a number of model pre-college programs for campuses to emulate. Contact the National Council of Educational Opportunity Associations (NCEOA) at 1126 16th Street, N.W. Suite 200 Washington, DC 20036, (202) 775-0863.

* National Alliance of Black School Educators
  1430 K St. NW, Suite 700
  Washington, DC 20005
     Organization of Black educators, majority of which are elementary and secondary officials.

* National Chicano Council for Higher Education
  710 N. College Ave.
  Claremont, CA 91711

* National Association for Bilingual Education
  1201 16th NW
  Washington, DC 20036

* National Advisory Council on Indian Education
  Pennsylvania Building, Suite 326
  425 13th St., NW
  Washington, DC 20002

* National Association for Equal Opportunity in Higher Education
  2243 Wisconsin Ave., NW
  Washington, DC 20007

During the 70's the Alfred P. Sloan Foundation funded the establishment of a network of regional pre-college programs to increase the number of minority students in the field of engineering. These regional programs form the National Association of Pre-College Directors (NAPD). By contacting NACME (212/279-2626) you can obtain the addresses and numbers of each regional program as well as information about NAPD.

Recruitment and Admission Resources

ABAFAOILSS - The Association of Black Admissions & Financial Aid Offices of the Ivy League and Sister Schools
P.O. Box 1019, Rastor Station
Boston, MA 02123

The American Council on Education publishes an **Annual Status Report on Minorities in Higher Education,** which contains a wealth of statistics detailing minority participation at all levels of higher education.

(Contact: $5 from the Office of Minority Concerns, American Council on Education, 1 Dupont Circle, NW, Washington DC 20036. All orders must be prepaid.)

National Association for the Advancement of Black Americans in Vocational Education
3476 Renault St.
Memphis, TN 38118

New England Consortium of Black Admissions Counselors
P.O. Box 512
Hartford, CT 06112

Native American Information Center
Bacon College
Muskogee, OK 74401

National Association of College Admissions Counselors (NACAC)
9933 Lawler, Suite 500
Skokie, IL 60077   312/676-0500

American College Testing Program (ACT)
2201 North Dodge Street, P.O. Box 168
Iowa City, IA 52243

National Action Council for Minorities in Engineering (NACME)
3 West 35th Street
New York, NY 10001   212/279-2626

National Scholarship Service and Fund for Negro Students (NSSFNS)
1501 Broadway
New York, NY 10036

Who's Who Among American High School Students
Educational Communications, Inc.
721 North McKinley
Lake Forest, IL 60045

RETENTION RESOURCES

National Orientation Directors Association (NODA)
Director of Orientation
2203 Student Services Bldg
Western Michigan Univ.
Kalamazoo, MI 49008   616/383-1898

Guide to Resource Organizations for Minority Language Groups available from the National Clearinghouse for Bilingual Education InterAmerican Research Association Inc.
1555 Wilson Blvd, Suite 605
Rosslym, VA 22209

United States Student Association
200 P St. NW
Room 300
Washington,DC 20036

National Council of Educational Opportunity Associations
1126 16th St. N.W.
Washington,DC 20036   202/775-0863

National Academic Advising Association
c/o Charles W. Connell
201 Woodburn Hall
West Virginia University
Morgantown,WV 26506   304/293-4611

POST GRADUATE RESOURCES

Organization of Chinese Americans
2025 Eye St NW Suite 926
Washington, DC 20006

Association of Mexican American Educators
2600 Middlefield Rd.
Redwood, CA 94063

Organizations in American Indian Education
copies are available free from ERIC/CRESS
ERIC Clearinghouse, Box 3AP Las Cruces, NM 88003 (505) 646-4286. It
lists over 115 programs and contact personnel concerning Native
American education.
National Hispanic Center for Advanced Studies and Policy Analysis
255 E 14th St
Oakland, CA 94606

National Network of Hispanic Women
Center for Research on Women
Serra House, Stanford University
Stanford, CA 94305

Minority Graduate Locater Service
CN 6010
Princeton,NJ 08541-6010

Association of Black Psychologists
P.O. Box 2929
Washington, DC 20013

National Association of Black Social Workers
271 W 125th St
NY,NY 10027

The National Black Nurses Association
P.O. Box 18358
Boston, MA 02118

Association of Black Women in Higher Education
30 Limerick Dr.
Albany, NY 12204

American Association for Affirmative Action
119 West Hubbard 4th Floor West
Chicago, IL 60610
312/329-2512

A national professional association for equal opportunity/
affirmative action administrators and specialists, individual and
organizations sharing similar concerns; hosts an annual conference.

ALUMNI RESOURCES

The National Council of Alumni Associations
Coordinator, Steering Committee
4 Washington Square Village
NY, NY 10012

Because of space limitations we recommend one source that
literally includes educational organizations, media, civil rights
groups, and will guide you to virtually any multicultural resource:

Guide to Multicultural Resources
c/o Praxis Publications Inc
P.O. Box 9869
Madison, WI 53715 (608) 244-5633
The cost is $25.95 plus 2.50 postage & handling.

Meeting Your Entertainment Needs

There are numerous agencies, agents, organizations and services
that offer a wide variety of entertainment options. For inexpensive
programs check the listings in your yellow pages, contact local night
club owners, speakers bureaus and heads of community based
organizations. For nationally know speakers try:

American Program Bureau Inc.
850 Boylston St.
Chestnut Hills, MA 02167
1-800-225-4575
They feature everyone from Jesse Jackson, Dick Gregory, Nikki
Giovanni, Julian Bond to Kwame Toure. They are billed as the world's
largest lecture agency.

William Morris Agency
1350 Avenue of the Americas
NY,NY 10019
212/586-5100
They feature a fine tuned roster of R&B and Jazz artists
including groups like the Temptations, Chuck Berry, Smokey Robinson,
Angela Bofill, Chuck Mangione, Dionne Warwick, Aretha Franklin, Bill
Cosby and many more.

New Line Presentations
853 Broadway 16th Floor
NY,NY 10003
800/221-5150
They specialize in lectures for Minorities and Third World.
Exclusively representing Jamaica's Michael Manley, Rev. Buster Soariss
on "Motivation and Self-Respect" and many more specialized programs.

National Association for Campus Activities (NACA)
P.O.Box 6828
Columbia, SC 29260
803/782-7121
Features up and coming talent and offers showcase opportunities
for collegiate entertainers.

American Collegiate Talent Showcase (ACTS)
Box 3 ACTS
New Mexico State University
Las Cruces, NM 88003
1-800-448-ACTS
Features new talent and rising "stars" for college campuses.
ACTS encourages, develops, and helps prepare talented college students
for careers in the entertainment industry.

DIRECTORIES

In addition to the above mentioned sources, we strongly recommend the following directories for your library. These directories include thousands of entries including speakers, dancers, choirs, etc.

THE BLACK RESOURCE GUIDE
The Black Resource Guide gives you immediate access to key blacks in America. It includes celebrities, church leaders, politicians, civil rights heads and more. To order your hardbound copy send $25.00 to:Black Resource Guide Inc.
501 Oneida Place NW
Washington, D.C. 20011
202/291-4373

HISPANIC SPEAKERS NATIONAL DIRECTORY
This directory lists nearly a 100 Hispanic speakers, their addresses and phone numbers. Nearly all subject areas are covered. It can be ordered by writing or calling:
Cuaron, Silvas & Associates Inc.
1391 N. Speer St., Suite 460
Denver, CO 80204
303/892-5533

NATIVE AMERICAN DIRECTORY
This directory is perhaps the leading source of information on and about American Indians. It can be obtained from:
Fred Synder, Executive Director
National Native American CO-OP
P.O. Box 301
San Carlos, AZ 85550-0301
602/475-2229

GUIDE TO MULTICULTURAL RESOURCES
The Guide is perhaps the most comprehensive collection of programs, organizations, services, and related information available from the Black, Hispanic, Indian, and Asian communities. Anyone wishing to network with the minority community should have this book. It sells for $24.95 and is available from:
Praxis Publications INC.
P.O.Box 9869
Madison, WI 53715
608/244-5633

Workshops for your Campus to Consider

LEADERS IN THE FIELD AVAILABLE TO VISIT YOUR CAMPUS

At last there are dynamic workshops to meet all of your programming needs. NMCC Inc. is pleased to introduce its 1986 workshops series featuring eleven of the country's frontrunners in providing services that help students succeed.

Could you benefit from tested and proven ways to increase minority student involvement on campus? Would you like to know what recruitment and retention approaches work best and which to avoid? Looking for new approaches to better service minority students?

If you've answered yes to any of these questions, then we have a workshop for you. Educators who are leaders in the field are available to come to your campus and share their successful strategies and experiences.

See why our workshops come so highly recommended around the country.

Charles Taylor is currently the publisher and president of the National Minority Campus Chronicle Inc., a publishing firm that publishes a wide range of literature pertaining to Minority Student Services. He's the author and editor of four books. He serves as a consultant to college campuses throughout America in the area of Minority Student Services. He is a pioneer in developing innovative programs for college students. Mr. Taylor is a speaker much in demand and he addresses diverse groups ranging from student organizations to convocations. Although Mr. Taylor lectures on a wide variety of topics his most frequently requested workshop is Effective Ways to Recruit and Retain Minority Students based on his highly popular book.

Mary Frances Howard is Associate Dean of Students, University of North Carolina at Charlotte, North Carolina. Her work in getting students to help other students via the peer counseling approach has resulted in her being the recipient of numerous awards. She was selected woman of the year in 1986, an Outstanding Black Administrator in 1985 and 1986 and Outstanding Young Woman of America in four different years. Campuses interested in creative ways to involve minority students will want to contact Ms. Howard. She is a practitioner in the field, whose contributions have launched her into the national limelight. Her workshops inspire and motive students and faculty.

RESERVE YOUR WORKSHOP TODAY!

Workshops for Your Campus to Consider
MEET OUR WORKSHOP LEADERS

Bettye I. Latimer brings over 20 years in corporate and government work with such industry giants as Procter & Gamble, World Bank, Green Bay Packers, Hospitals, major Universities and community organizations. Today she runs her own hi-tech management consulting firm. Her insight is revealing because it's based on real experience. She has served as an Affirmative Action officer and is considered an expert in personnel related issues. She helps students prepare for the work force. If you want your students to have a headstart you'll want to consider one of Ms. Latimer's workshops. She knows the ins and outs of the Corporate Culture and is a highly sought after speaker.

Dr. K. Paul Kasambira is Director, Minority Student Services and associate professor of Teacher Education at Bradley University in Peoria, Illinois. An accomplished author, Dr. Kasambira has had numerous articles published in the United States, Canada and Africa. He is a much sought after speaker at the state, national and international level. His minority student needs assessment research has embellished him as a front runner in minority activity programming. His workshops will not only help you ascertain what student interests are but recommend results oriented solutions as well.

Dr. Herbert Exum, is Associate Dean for Research and Graduate Studies in the School of Education at North Carolina State University. He has been characterized as a sensitive and caring counselor, author and administrator who provides immediately useful ways for campuses to get minority students to utilize campus services. He has conducted leading research in effective ways to counsel Black students as well as developed new techniques for counseling Black women that promises to attract him a national following. Dr. Exum has published extensively and regularly presents papers on his research at professional meetings. A licensed pychologist, Dr. Exum can assist you in creating the type of counseling program that will appropriately address the need of minority students.

Workshops for Your Campus to Consider
MEET OUR WORKSHOP LEADERS

Sylvia Lopez-Romano is Director, Educational Equity Services at California State University-Chico California. She is well noted for her work in Cross-Cultural Communication. She has set up student affirmative action programs, directed Upward Bound projects, been honored both as a principal and a teacher and is listed in Who's Who of American Women in both 1983 and 1984. Her workshops will help you inform, attract, recruit and matriculate students to your campus.

Dr. Sandra J. Foster is an assistant professor in the School of Social Work at Grambling State University. She is the president of the Faculty Senate and was elected Teacher of the Year for 1984-85. She is known for her extensive work with Black families. Her workshops will help faculty and staff relate better to minority students as well as provide innovative ways to involve the family in the schooling process. If you are looking for a speaker to motivate Black students and help them develop coping skills, you will want to check out Dr. Foster's workshop.

Louis Sarabia is Director, Chicano Programs, New Mexico State University, Las Cruces, New Mexico. He is one of the nation's pioneers in establishing successful Chicano programs on campus. Whether you are looking for better ways to advise Chicano students or need assistance in developing a Chicano Studies curriculum, Mr. Sarabia's workshops are the place to start. Mr. Sarabia has an impressive track record of working with minority youth. Every place he has worked minority student participation has increased on campus.

Dr. Alfonzo Thurman is a tenured associate professor in the Department of Leadership and Educational Policy Studies at Northern Illinois University in DeKalb, Illinois. He is also an assistant to the Provost and Vice President for Academic Affairs. Dr. Thurman brings over a decade of experience in establishing, implementing and evaluating minority student programs. Al is recognized by his colleagues nationally as a leader in establishing programs to service minority students. If your campus is thinking about reorganizing or creating an effective program you will want to involve Dr. Thurman.

Lawrence W. Young Jr.is Director, Paul Robeson Cultural Center, the Pennslvania State University, University Park, Pennsylvania. For nearly two decades he has worked in minority student programs in higher education including federal, state, and local programs. An accomplished writer he has had articles published in many journals and newspapers and has appeared on radio and television talk shows across the country. He is both a student and teacher of Afro-American culture and its impact on the behavior of Black and White Americans. His variety of experiences as recruiter, teacher, advisor, researcher, and leader of Black students on predominantly white campuses, and his study of Afro-American culture, lend themselves to a variety of workshop and lecture possibilities.

Elba Chavez is a Financial Aid/Minority Recruitment professional at Waubonsee Community College, Sugar Grove, Illinois. She brings a fresh youthful idealism to the world of financial aids. She has done translating, interpreting, is a student recruiter and financial advisor who will help you set up the type of workshops that are effective in informing Bilingual and minority students about financial aids.

271

NMCC INC. PRESENTS WORKSHOPS FOR COLLEGE CAMPUSES
1986-87 SERIES

ELEVEN PROGRAMS.....serving the nation's campuses for:

MINORITY AWARENESS EVENTS
BLACK HISTORY MONTH
CINCO DE MAYO FESTIVITIES
NATIONAL HISPANIC WEEK
and other Minority Activities

REQUEST FORM

For more

information call

608/244-5633 or
return this form!

For information on any speakers or programs in NMCC's 1986 Workshops for Colleges series, call 608/244-5633 today or return this form with no obligation.

___Please send me complete information on these speakers and their topics: (write in speakers)

_____
_____
_____
_____

Please send the information requested to:

Name_____ Title_____

Institution/Agency_____

Address_____
　　　　　street/P.O.Box　　　　city　　　　　state　　　　　zip

Phone ( )_____　　Date _____

RESERVE YOUR WORKSHOP TODAY!!!

Chapter 12

Bibliography of Recommended Books

Asian American

Beacon Press Staff, **Who's Who Among Asian Americans, Five Thousand Brief Biographics** , Ethnic Reference Ser. No.4, Gormezano,1982.

Buaken, Manuel. **I Have Lived With the American People.** Caldwell, Idaho: Caxton Printers,1948.

Bulosan, Carlos. **America is in the Heart.** Seattle: University of Washington Press,1973.

Cheng-Tsu Wu, ed. **Chink! A Documentary History of Anti-Chinese Prejudice in America.** New York: World Publishing,1972.

Conroy, Hilary and Miyakawa, Scott, T. **East Across the Pacific.** Santa Barbara.1972.

Endo, Russell, **Asian Americans: Social and Psychological Perspectives;** Science and Behavior, 1980.

Gee, Emma. **Counter Point, Perspectives on Asian America.** University of California, Los Angeles,1976.

Hosokawa, William K. **Nisei:The Quiet American.** New York,1969.

Hsu, Francis L.K. **The Challenge of the American Dream: The Chinese in the United States.** Belmont, California: Wadsworth,1971.

Kim, Elaine, **Asian American Literature,An Introduction to the Writings and Their Social Context:**,Temple UPR,1982.

Kim, Hyeng Chan and Patterson, Wayne. **The Koreans in America. 1882-1974** Oceania Publications,1974.

Kitano, Harry I. **Asian Americans: An Annotated Bibliography.** Los Angeles: Univ. of California Asian American Studies Center,1971.

Kitano, Harry H.L. **Japanese Americans: The Evolution of a Subculture.** 2nd ed. Englewood Cliffs, New Jersey: Prentice Hall,1976.

Knoll, Tricia, **Becoming Americans:Asian Sojourners-Immigrants and Refugees in the Western United States:** Coast to Coast,1982.

Lasker, Bruno. **Filipino Immigration to the Continental United States and Hawaii.** Chicago: University of Chicago Press,1931.

Lee, Rose Hum. **The Chinese in the United States.** Hong Kong: Hong Kong University Press,1960.

Letters in Exile: An Introductory Reader on the History of Filipinos in America. Los Angeles: UCLA Asian American Studies Center,1976.

Lyman, Stanford. **The Asian in the West.** Reno and Las Vegas; University of Nevada Press,1971.

Lyman, Stanford M. **Chinese Americans.** New York: Random House,1974.

Miller, Stuart C. **The Unwelcome Immigrant: The American Image of the Chinese,1785 - 1882.** Berkeley; University of California Press,1969.

Morales, Royal F. **Makibaka: The Filipino American Struggle.** Los Angeles: Mountainview Publishers, 1974.

Monoz, Alfredo. **The Filipinos in America.** Los Angeles: Mountainview Publishers, 1971.

Nandi, Proshanta K., **The Quality of Life of Asian Americans: An Exploratory Study in a Middle Size Community** Pacific-Asian, 1980.

Nee, Victor G., and Debary, Brett. **Longtime Californian: A Documentary History of an American Chinatown.** Boston: Houghton Mifflin, 1973.

Perrin, Linda, **Coming to America: Immigrants from the Far East.** Delacorte Pub,1980.

Ogawa, Dennis. **From Japs to Japanese: The Evolution of Japanese-American Stereotypes.** Berkeley, McCutchan Publishing,1971.

Petersen, William. **Japanese Americans: Oppression and Success.** New York: Random House, 1971.

Pomeroy, William. **The Philippines: A Case History of Neo- Colonialism in Remaking Asia.** New York: Bantheon Books, 1974.

Sung, Betty L. **The Chinese in America.** New York: MacMillan,1972.

Sung, S.W. **Chinese in American Life: Some Aspects of Their History, Status, Problems, and Contributions.** Seattle: University of Washington Press,1962.

Tachiki, Amy; Wong, Eddie; and Odo, Franklin; with Wong, Buck, eds. **Roots: An Asian American Reader.** Los Angeles: UCLA Asian American Studies Center,1971.

Takashima, Shizuye. **A Child in Prison Camp.** Plattsburgh, New York: Tundra Books,1971.

Weglyn, Michi. **Years of Infamy: The Untold Story of America's Concentration Camps.** New York: William Morrow,1976.

Yep, Laurence. **Dragonwings.** New York: Harper and Row,1975.

Books About Blacks

Afro Americans

Aptheker, Herbert, ed. **A documentary history of the Negro people in the United States. Volume 1: from the colonial period to the establishment of the NAACP.** New York: Citadel,1951. Published in three parts.

Aptheker, Herbert, ed. **A documentary history of the Negro people in the United States. Volume 2: 1910-1932.** New York: Citadel, 1973.

Aptheker, Herbert, ed. **A documentary history of the Negro people in the United States. Volume 3: 1932-1945.** New York: Citadel, 1974.

Aptheker, Herbert, **American Negro Slave Revolts** New York:International Publishers,1983.

Bellegarde, Ida R., **Black Heroes and Heroines,** Bell ENT, Book 3, 1983.

Bennett, Lerone, Jr. **Before the Mayflower: A history of the Negro in America:1619-1964.** Baltimore: Penguin Books,1967.

Blackwell, James E. **The Black Community: Diversity and Unity.** New York: Dodd, Mead,1975.

Brame, Herman L., **The World Records of Black People,**Sudan Pub., 1984.

Davis, Y. Angela, ed., **If They Come in the Morning: Voices of Resistance** New York: New American Library,1971.

Davis, Y. Angela, **Women, Race and Class,** New York: Random House, 1981.

Diggs, Ellen I., **Black Chronology: From 4000 B.C. to the Abolition of the Slave Trade,** Lib. Bdg. Gk. Hall, 1983.

Douglass, Frederick, **What to the Slave is the Fourth of July?** Black Scholar Vol. 7 pp. 32-37,1976.

Drake, St. Clair and Horace Cayton, **Black Metropolis: A Study of Negro Life in a Northern City, Vol I**, New York: Harper and Row, 1962

Drimmer, Melvin, ed., **Black History: A Reappraisal** Garden City, New York: Anchor Books, 1969

Du Bois, W.E.B., **The Souls of Black Folk** Greenwich, Connecticut: Fawcett, 1961.

Fall, Thomas. **Canalboat to Freedom.** New York: Dial, 1966.

Foner, S. Philip, **Organized Labor and the Black Worker, 1619-1981** New York: International Publishers, 1981.

Franklin, John Hope. **From Slavery to Freedom: A History of Black Americans.** 4th ed. New York: Knopf, 1974.

Frazier, Thomas R., ed. **Afro American History: Primary Sources.** New York: Harcourt, 1970.

Georgakas, Dan, and Marvin Surkin, **Detroit: I Do Mind Dying, A Study in Urban Rebellion** New York: St. Martin's Press, 1975.

Genouese, E.D. **Roll Jordan Roll, The World the Slaves Made.** New York: Vintage Books, 1972.

Goldstein, Leslie Friedman, Violence as an Instrument for Social Change: The Views of Frederick Douglass, **Journal of Negro History**, Vol. 61, pp. 61-72, 1976.

Haley, Alex. **Roots.** Garden City: Doubleday, 1976.

Hamilton, Charles V., **The Black Preacher in America**, New York: William Morrow and Company, 1972.

Harding, Vincent, **There is a River: The Black Struggle for Freedom in America** New York: Harcourt, Brace, Jovanovich, 1981.

Harris, William H., **The Harder We Run: Black Workers Since the Civil War**, (New York: Oxford University Press), 1982.

Hunter, Kristin. **The Soul Brothers and Sister Lou.** New York: Scribner's, 1969.

Kaiser, Earnest, ed., **A Freedomways Reader: Afro-America in the Seventies**, New York: International Publishers, 1977.

Marable, Manning, **How Capitalism Underdeveloped Black America: Problems in Race, Political Economy and Society**, Boston: South End Press, 1983.

Marable, Manning, **"The Rainbow Coalition: Jesse Jackson and the Politics of Ethnicity"**, Cross Currents, Vol. XXXIV, no. 1 pp. 21-42, Spring 1984.

Meier, August, and Rudwick, Elliot. **From Plantation to Ghetto.** 3rd ed. New York: Hill and Wang, 1976.

Ofari, Earl, **The Myth of Black Capitalism** New York: Monthly Review Press, 1970.

Pinkney, Alphonso. **Black Americans.** 2nd ed. Englewood Cliffs, New Jersey: Prentice Hall, 1975.

Quarles, Benjamin. **The Negro in the Making of America.** New York: MacMillan, 1969.

Staples, Robert, ed., **The Black Family: Essays and Studies**, Revised Edition, Belmont, California: Wadsworth Publishing Company, 1982.

Tabb, K. William, **The Political Economy of the Black Ghetto**, New York: W.W. Norton, 1970.

Taylor, Mindred D. **Roll of Thunder Hear My cry.** New York: Dial
    Press,1976.
Thompson, Daniel C. **Sociology of the Black Experience.** Westport,
    Connecticut: Greenwood Press,1974.
Van Sertima, Ivan, **Blacks in Science Ancient and Modern,** Transaction
    Books, 1983.
Weik, Hays. **The Jazz Man.** Illustrated by Ann Grifalconi. New York:
    Atheneum,1968.

European Americans

Anderson, Charles H. **White Protestant Americans: From National Origins
    to a Religious Group.** Englewood Cliffs, New Jersey: Prentice
    Hall,1970.
Gambino, Richard. **Blood of my Blood: The Dilemma of the Italian
    Americans.** New York: Doubleday,1974.
Greeley, Andrew M. **That Most Distressful Nation: The Taming of the
    American Irish.** Chicago: Quadrangle Books,1972.
Greeley, Andrew M. **Ethnicity in the United States: A Preliminary
    Reconnaissance.** New York: Wiley,1974.
Greeley, Andrew M. **Why Can't They Be Like Us? America's White Ethnic
    Groups.** New York: Dutton,1975.
Handlin, Oscar. **Immigration as a Factor in American History.** Englewood
    Cliffs, New Jersey: Prentice Hall,1959.
Handlin, Oscar. **The Uprooted: The Epic Story of the Great Migrations
    that made the American People.** rev. ed. New York: Grosset and
    Dunlap,1973.
Hansen, Marcus Lee. **The Atlantic Migration 1607-1860.** Edited by Arthur
    M. Schlesinger, Cambridge, Massachusetts: Harvard University
    Press,1940.
Huggins, Nathan I., Martin Kilson, and Daniel M. Fox, eds., **Key Issues
    in the Afro-American Experience, Vol.II** New York: Harcourt,
    Brace, Jovanovich,1971.
Killian, Lewis M. **White Southerners.** New York: Random House,1970.
Mphahlele, Ezekiel, **Voices in the Whirlwind and other essays** New York:
    Hill and Wang,1969.
Novak, Michael. **The Rise of the Unmeltable Ethnics: Politics and
    Culture in the Seventies.** New York: MacMillan,1973.
Uya, Edet Okon, ed., **Black Brotherhood: Afro-Americans and Africa**
    Lexington, Massachusetts: D.C. Heath,1971.
Winks, Robin, ed., **Slavery: A Comparative Perspective** New York; New
    York University Press,1972.

Books About Hispanics

Cuban Americans

Lazo, Mario. **Dagger in the Heart!** New York: Twin Circle Publishing
    Company,1968.
Linehan, Edward J. Cuba's exiles bring new life to Miami". **National
    Geographic.** 144 (July 1973), pp. 68-95.

Prohias, Rafael J., and Casal, Lourdes. **The Cuban Minority in the United States.** Cuban Minority Planning Study, SRS Grant No. 08-P-55933/4-01, Florida Atlantic University, Boca Raton, Florida 1973.

Mexican Americans

Acuna, Rodolfo, **Occupied America:The Chicano's Struggle Toward Liberation.** Canfield, Harper & Row, 1980.

Acuna, Rudy. **Cultures in Conflict: Problems of the Mexican Americans.** New York: Charter School Books,1970.

Alford, Harold J. **The Proud Peoples.** New American Library, Makay 1972.

Anaya, Rodolfo A. **Bless Me Ultima.** Berkeley, California: Tonatiuh International Incorporated, 1972.

Beeson, Margaret, Majorie Adams, Rosalie King, **Memories for Tomorrow: Mexican American Recollections of Yesteryear,** Ethridge Books,1983.

Castro, Tony. **Chicano Power.** E.P. Dutton & Co. Saturday Review Press,1974.

Deblassie, Richard R. **Counseling With Mexican American Youth.** Learning Concepts, 1976.

DeGarza, Patricia. **Chicanos: The Story of Mexican Americans.** Julian Messner, 1973.

Farquhar, Margaret C. **The Indians of Mexico.** Holt, Rinehart & Winston, 1967.

Franco, John M. **Hispano American Contributors To American Life.** Benefic Press, 1973.

Galarza, Ernesto. **Barrio Boy.** South Bend, Indiana: University of Notre Dame Press, 1971.

Garcia, F. Chris **La Causa Politica: A Chicano Politics Reader.** University of Notre Dame. 1974.

Gomez, David F. **Somos Chicanos, Strangers in our own land.** Beacon , 1973.

Gonzales, Rodolfo. **I Am Joaquin.** Bantam, 1972.

Hernandez, Haug—Wagner. **Chicanos.** C.V. Mosby Co., 1976.

Hernandez, Jose Amaro, **A Mutual Aid for Survival: The Case of the Mexican American.** Krieger, June,1983.

Horowitz, Ruth, **Honor and the American Dream Culture and Identity in a Chicano Community,** Crime, law, and Deviance series, Rutgers Univ. Press,1983.

Ludwig, Ed, and Santibane, James eds. **The Chicanos Mexican American Voices.** Penguin Books Inc., 1971.

Martin, Patricia Preciado, **Images and Conversations: Mexican Americans Recall a Southwestern Past:** Univ. of Ariz. Press, 1983.

Martinez, Elizabeth S. and Enriqueta Longeaux Y Vasquez. **Viva La Raza: The Struggle of the Mexican American People.** Doubleday,1974.

McWilliams, Carey. **North From Mexico: The Spanish Speaking People of the United States.** New York: Greenwood Press,1968.

Meier, Matt S. and Rivera, Feliciano. **The Chicanos: A History of Mexican Americans.** Hill & Wang,1972.

Moore, Joan W., with Pachon, Harry. **Mexican Americans.** 2nd ed. Englewood Cliffs, New Jersey: Prentice Hall,1976.

Moquin, Wayne, with Van Doren, Charles, eds. **A Documentary History of Mexican Americans.** New York: Bantam Books,1971.

Nava, Julian. **Mexican Americans: A Brief Look at Their History.** Adl,1970.

Pinchot, Jane. **The Mexicans in America.** Lerner,1973.

Seligmann 2nd, L. Gustav, Rosaldo, Renato and Calvert, Robert, **A Chicano: The Evolution of a People.** Krieger,1982.

Servin, Manuel P. **An Awakened Minority: The Mexican American.** Bruce & Glenco Press, 1974.

Simmen, Edward, ed. **Pain and Promise: The Chicano Today.** Nal,1972

Steiner, Stan. **La Raza the Mexican Americans.** Harper Colophon,1969.

Stoddard, Ellwyn R. **Mexican Americans.** New York: Random House,1973.

Tebbel, John and Ramon E. Ruiz. **South By Southwest: The Mexican American and his Heritage.** Doubleday,1969.

Puerto Rican Americans

Cordasco, Francesco, and Bucchioni, Eugene, eds. **The Puerto Rican Experience: A Sociological Sourcebook.** Totowa, New Jersey: Littlefield Adams,1973.

Fitzpatrick, Joseph P. **Puerto Rican Americans: The meaning of immigration to the mainland.** Englewood Cliffs, New Jersey: Prentice Hall,1971.

Golding, Morton J. **A Short History of Puerto Rico.** New York: New American Library,1973.

Hauberg, Clifford. **Puerto Rico and the Puerto Ricans: A study of Puerto Rican history and immigration to the United States.** New York: Hippocrene Books,1974.

Lewis, Gordon K. **Puerto Rico: Freedom and Power in the Caribbean.** New York: Monthly Review Press,1963.

Padilla, Elena. **Up From Puerto Rico.** New York: Columbia University Press,1958.

Silen, Juan Angel. **We the Puerto Rican People.** Translated by Cedric Belfrage. New York: Monthly Review Press,1971.

Steiner, Stan. **The Islands: The World of the Puerto Ricans.** New York: Harper and Row Colophon Books,1974.

Thomas, Piri. **Down These Mean Streets.** New York: Signet,1967.

Wagenheim, Kal, with de Wagenheim, Olga Jiminez, eds. **The Puerto Ricans: A documentary history.** Garden City: Doubleday,1973.

Books About Indians

Indian Americans

Adler, Bill. **The American Indian: The First Victim.** New York: Morrow,1972

Andrist, Ralph K. **The Long Death:The Last Days of the Plains Indians** New York, MacMillan,1964.

Axtell, James, **The Indian People of Eastern American**, Oxford University Press,1981.

Baird, David W., **The Vanishing American, White Attitudes and U.S. Indian Policy**: Wesleyan University Press,1981.

Brown, Dee A. **Bury My Heart at Wounded Knee**. New York: Holt, Rinehart, and Winston, 1970 and 1971.

Clark, Ann Nolan. **In My Mother's House**. New York: Viking,1941.

Deloria, Vine **Behind the Trails of Broken Treaties: An Indian Declaration of Independence**. New York: Delacorte Press, 1974.

Deloria, Vine. **Of Utmost Good Faith**. San Francisco: Straight Arrow Books, 1971.

Deloria, Vine. **We Talk You Listen: New Tribes. New Turf**. New York: Macmillan,1970

Dippie, W. David, Barsh, Russel, Lawrence, and Henderson, **The Road: Indian Tribes and Political Liberty**, University of Calif, Berkeley,1980.

Driver, Harold E. **Indians of North America**. 2nd ed. Chicago: University of Chicago Press,1969.

Dunn, Jacob P. **Massacres of the Mountains: A History of the Indian Wars of the Far West, 1815–1875**. New York: Archer House,1958

Forbes, Jack D. **The Indian in America's Past**. Englewood Cliffs, New Jersey: Prentice-Hall, 1964.

Foreman, Grant. **Indian Removal: The Emigration of the Five Civilized Tribes of Indians**. Norman: University of Oklahoma Press, 1932.

George, Jean Craighead. **Julie of the Wolves**. New York: Harper and Row,1972.

Josephy, Alvin M. **The Indian Heritage of America**. New York: Bantam Books,1968.

Josephy, Alvin M. **Red Power: The American Indians Fight for Freedom**. New York: American Heritage Press, 1971.

LaFarge, Oliver. **A Pictorial History of the American Indian**. New York: Crown,1956.

Marriott, Alice Lee. **American Epic: The Story of the American Indian**. New York: Putnam,1969.

McLuhan, T.C., ed. **Touch the Earth: A self portrait of Indian Existence**. New York: Pocket Books,1971.

Miles, Miska. **Annie and the Old One**. Illustrated by Peter Parnall. Boston: Little Brown,1971.

Momaday, N. Scott. **House Made of Dawn**. New York: Signet,1966.

Moquin, Wayne., and Van Doren, Charles, eds. **Great Documents in American Indian History**. New York: Praeger,1973.

Oswalt, Wendell H. **This Land Was Theirs: A Study of the North American Indian**. New York: Wiley,1966 and 1973.

Paucha, Francis P. **The Indian in American History**. New York: Holt, Rinehart and Winston,1971.

Pelthmann, Irvin M. **Broken Peace Pipes: A four Hundred Year History of the American Indian**. Springfield, Illinois: Thomas,1964.

Shorris, Earl. **The Death of the Great Spirit: An Eulogy for the American Indian**. New York: Simon and Schuster,1971.

Spicer, Edward H. **A Short History of the Indians of the United States.** New York: Van Nostrand,1969.

Starkloff, Carl F. **The People of the Center: American Indian Religion and Christianity.** New York: Seabury Press, 1974

Underhill, Ruth Murry. **Red Man's America.** Chicago Press,1971.

Vogel, Virgil J. **This Country was Ours: A Documentary History of the American Indian.** New York: Harper and Row, 1972.

Jewish Americans

Blau, Joseph, and Baron, Salo, eds. **The Jews in the United States, 1790-1840: A Documentary History.** New York: Columbia University Press,1963.

Chapman, Abraham, ed. **Jewish American Literature: An Anthology.** New York: New American Library,1974.

Bellow, Saul, ed. **Great Jewish Short Stories.** New York: Dell,1963.

Frank, Anne. **The Diary of Anne Frank.** New York: Random House,1956.

Glazer, Nathan. **American Judaism.** Chicago: University of Chicago Press,1972.

Goldstein, Sidney, and Goldschieder, Calvin. **Jewish Americans: Three Generations in a Jewish Community.** Englewood Cliffs, New Jersey: Prentice Hall,1968.

Handlin, Oscar. **Adventure in Freedom: Three Hundred Years of Jewish Life in America.** New York: McGraw Hill,1954.

Howe, Irving. **World of Our Fathers: The Journey of the East European Jews to America and the Life they found and made.** New York: Simon and Schuster,1976.

Meltzer, Milton. **Never to Forget: The Jews of the Holocaust.** New York: Harper and Row,1976.

Ruderman, Jerome. **Jews in American History: A Teachers Guide.** New York: Anti-Defamation League of B'nai B'rith,1974.

Multicultural Books

Allport, Gordon W. **The Nature of Prejudice.** Garden City, New York: Doubleday,1958.

Barth, Fredrik, ed. **Ethnic Groups and Boundaries: The Social Organization of Cultural Difference.** Boston: Little Brown,1969.

Blauner, Robert. **Racial Oppression in America.** New York: Harper and Row,1972.

Colangelo, N., Foxley, C., and Dustin. **Multicultural Nonsexist Education: A human relations approach.** Dubuque, Iowa: Kendall-Hunt Publishers,1979.

Gordon, Milton M. **Assimilation in America Life.** New York: Oxford University Press,1964.

Jacobs, Paul, and Landau, Saul, with Pell, Eve. **To Serve The Devil.** 2 volumes. New York: Vintage,1971.

Rose, Peter I. **They and We: Racial and Ethnic Relations in the United States.** 2nd ed. New York: Random House,1974.

Simpson, George E., and Yinger, J. Milton. **Racial and Cultural Minorities: An analysis of prejudice and discrimination.** 4th ed. New York: Harper and Row,1972.

Books Dealing With Racism

Allen, B. "Implications of Social Reaction Research for Racism," **Psychological Reports,** Vol. 29 (1971).

Allport, Gordon. **The Nature of Prejudice.** Garden City: Doubleday & Co., Inc., Anchor Book, 1954

Baldwin, James. **The Fire Next Time.** Dell Publishers Co.,1963.

Barndt, Joseph. **Liberating our White Ghetto.** Minnesota: Ausburg Publishing, 1972.

Beck, J. **The Counselor and Black/White Relations.** Boston: Houghton Mifflin, 1973.

Billingsley, Andrew. **Black Families in White America.** Englewood Cliffs: Prentice Hall, 1968.

Boggs, James. **Racism and the Class Struggle.** New York Monthly Review Press. 1970.

Brown, Claude. **Manchild in The Promised Land.** New American Library, Inc. 1937.

Campbell, Anguss. **White Attitudes Toward Black People.** Ann Arbor: Institute on Social Research Press, 1971.

Citron, A. **The Rightness of Whiteness: World of the White Child in a Segregated Society** (pamphlet). Detroit: Ohio Regional Educational Lab, 1969

Cleaver, Eldridge. **Soul on Ice.** New York: Dell Publishing Co. 1968.

Davis, Angela. **If They Come in the Morning.** New York; Third World Press, 1971.

Fanon, Frantz. **Wretched of the Earth.** Grove Press.

Freire, Paulo. **Pedagogy of the Oppressed.** Merder & Merder, New York,1969.

Grier, William H. & Cobbs, Price H. **Black Rage.** Bantam Books Inc.1968.

Haley, A., ed. **Autobiography of Malcolm X.** New York; Grove, 1967.

Hernton, Calvin. **Sex and Racism in America.** New York Bantam,1970.

Johnson, J.W. **Autobiography of an Ex Colored Man.** New York; Hill & Wang, 1960.

Jones, J. **Prejudice and Racism.** Reading,Mass; Addison & Wesley, 1972.

Joyce, Frank. **An Analysis of American Racism.** (pamphlet), Boston: N.E. Free Press, N.D.

Kerner Commission. **National Advisory Commission on Civil Rights.** New York: Bantam, 1968.

King, Larry. **Confessions of a White Racist.** New York: Viking Press, 1971.

Knowles, Louis and Prewitt, Kenneth. **Institutional Racism in America.** Englewood Cliffs: Prentice Hall,1969.

Kovel, J. **White Racism: A Psychohistory.** New York: Pantheon, 1970.

Niel, Alice. **The Shortchanged Children of Suburbia.** New York: Institute of Human Relations Press, 1967.

Ryan, William. **Blaming the Victim.** New York: Pantheon Books, 1971.
Terry,R. **For Whites Only.** Grand Rapids, Mich.: Eerdmans, Puritan
   1970.
Welsing, F.C. **Cress Theory of Color Confrontation.** Washington, D.C.
   Howard University, 1972.
Yette, Samuel F. **The Choice.** New York: Putnam. 1971.

Related Books of Interest

1. EFFECTIVE WAYS TO RECRUIT AND RETAIN MINORITY STUDENTS

This publication is a must for universities and colleges. It provides a coordinated approach to recruiting and retaining minority students, speaks to factors that create retention problems, features successful programs from around the country and lists dozens of ideas you can implement on your campus immediately. ($29.95)

2. CULTURAL RETREAT HANDBOOK

Looking for ways to break down racial barriers, and ways to get minority and white students to interact, then this book is for you. This handbook shows you step by step how to conduct a retreat and is filled with activities to ensure your retreat's success. ($19.95)

3. GUIDE TO MULTICULTURAL RESOURCES

The guide is a comprehensive collection of programs, organizations, businesses, services and related information from the Black, Hispanic, Indian, and Asian communities. Anyone wishing to network with the minority community should have this book. Includes names, addresses and phone numbers of hundreds of entries. ($24.95)

4. THE HANDBOOK OF MINORITY STUDENT SERVICES

Everything students, faculty, and administrators need to establish successful minority programs on campus. A necessary book for student services staff and campus planners. ($49.95)

To order any of the above books add $2.50 shipping & handling and mail check or money order to:

Praxis Publications Inc.
P.O. Box 9869
Madison, WI 53715
For add'l info call 608/244-5633

Appendices

284

INFORMATION ON A SELF-EVALUATION INSTRUMENT

How does your campus decide if its student support services are actually benefiting minority students, especially if there are problems with lower than desired retention rates? What type of characteristics should an effective minority services delivery system possess? We would like to share with you information about a new instrument that will help you answer these questions. The **Minority Student Services Delivery System** self-evaluation instrument is both research based and field tested. It provides a much needed framework for assessing institutional commitment to minority programs. It is especially designed to help colleges answer questions like: **How do we determine priorities in our delivery system? Where in the student support services areas are we the strongest? the weakest?**

The instrument permits seventeen critical departmental and program components to be evaluated such as pre-collegiate activities, recruitment efforts, financial aid, social factors, faculty involvement, etc. It is structured in such a way that the data generated from the instrument will tell you specifically which programs are viewed as effective. Through survey items and discussion questions, users are led through an engaging self-evaluation process. Comparisons are not made with other campuses; nor does the instrument attempt to establish one set of standards all institutions should follow. Rather it provides guidelines and programmatic suggestions that can assist you in defining what is adequate and proper for your campus. Many of the instrument's programmatic suggestions don't require new monies and can be implemented with existing staff.

Whether your school is contemplating reorganizing, eliminating or creating a minority student program, this instrument should prove useful by raising the types of questions that will assist individuals in reaching fair decisions. It is available from the Praxis Publications Inc. for only $13.95. Kindly fill out the attached form and we'll promptly send you your instrument.

SELF-EVALUATION INSTRUMENT
ORDER NOW-HERE'S HOW

Please send me____copy(s) of **Minority Student Services Delivery System Self-Evaluation Instrument** at $13.50 each plus $1.50 postage/shipping.

Name_____Title_____

_____   _____
Institution/Agency   Street/P.O.Box

_____   _____   _____
City   State   Zip
(___)_____   _____   _____
Telephone   Date   Signature

Make check payable to PP Inc. and mail to: PP Inc. P.O.Box 9869, Madison, WI 53715 (608)244-5633. **Money back guarantee.** If you're not completely satisfied with your purchase return it undamaged within 30 days for a full refund.

Bradley University Minority Student Services Program Needs Assessment Survey

The Office of Minority Student Services is interested in improving the quality of services delivered to minority students. As a student your response to this survey will assist our office in supporting programs with the highest interests and needs.

Programming is "the creating, planning and implementation of activities for students and staff that builds a sense of community, responsibility and enthusiasm on campus," i.e. intramural sports participation, parties, speakers, live entertainment.

Please mark all appropriate responses with a check(✓). Your personal written comments will especially be helpful and receive particular attention.

PART I PERSONAL DATA

(1)
___Female ___Male Year in School ___FR ___SO ___JR ___SR ___GRAD
Transfer student ___Yes ___No Major_____
Hometown_____ State/Republic_____
Where do you live?

(2)
___Off campus dwelling   ___Bradley Apartment Complex
___Residence Halls   ___Greek
___At home with family   ___Other (please specify)_____

PART II DECISION FACTORS-Check as many as appropriate in all categories.
What is the best day(s) and time(s) for your attendance at campus Programs?

(3)

SUN	MON	TUES	WED
___Before noon	___Before noon	___Before noon	___Before noon
___Noon to 1pm	___Noon to 1pm	___Noon to 1pm	___Noon to 1pm
___1pm to 3pm	___1pm to 3pm	___1pm to 3pm	___1pm to 3pm
___3pm to 5pm	___3pm to 5pm	___3pm to 5pm	___3pm to 5pm
___5pm to 7pm	___5pm to 7pm	___5pm to 7pm	___5pm to 7pm
___7pm to 11pm	___7pm to 11pm	___7pm to 11pm	___7pm to 11pm

THUR	FRI	SAT
___Before noon	___Before noon	___Before noon
___Noon to 1pm	___Noon to 1pm	___Noon to 1pm
___1pm to 3pm	___1pm to 3pm	___1pm to 3pm
___3pm to 5pm	___3pm to 5pm	___3pm to 5pm
___5pm to 7pm	___5pm to 7pm	___5pm to 7pm
___7pm to 11pm	___7pm to 11pm	___7pm to 11pm
	___11pm to 2am	___11pm to 2am
	___After 2am	___After 2am

What is the best way to inform you of campus activities?

(4)
___Bradley Scout   ___Monthly flyer   ___Word of mouth
___Bulletin Boards   ___Blackboards   ___Mailbox flyer
___Radio/TV   ___Posters   ___Your organization reps.
___Other_____

I would prefer to attend the following types of programs: (check as many as appropriate)

(5)
___Art exhibits   ___Dances   ___Plays
___Nightclub events   ___Lectures/Speakers   ___Pop music concerts
___Movies   ___Sports events   (i.e. Lionel Richie,
___Other_____   Tina Turner)

What types of music do you prefer? (check as many as appropriate)

(6)
___Soul   ___Country Rock   ___Gospel/Religious   ___Punk
___Rock 'n' Roll   ___Folk   ___Disco   ___Country/Western
___Hard Rock   ___Pop   ___New Wave   ___Swing
___Jazz   ___Reggae   ___Rhythm and Blues   ___Classical
___Other_____

What type of movies do you prefer? (check as many as appropriate)

(7)
___Comedy   ___Mystery   ___Foreign
___Western   ___Horror   ___Classic
___Science Fiction   ___X-rated   ___Black starring films
___Musical
Specific Suggestions_____

What type of speaker/lecture presentations do you prefer?

(8)
___Current events   ___Religious   ___International issues
___Political   ___Minority issues   ___Scientific
___Comedy   ___Academic   ___Self-help
Specific Suggestions_____

PART III ACTIVITY/INTEREST PROFILE-Membership in campus organizations

(9)
___Greek-please specify_____   ___Scout
___Intramural Sports   ___Student Senate
___Activities Council (ACBU)   ___Black Student Alliance
___Professional or Honorary fraternity   ___Special Interest groups
   please specify_____   (i.e. Dorm Council, Little
___Varsity Athletics   Sister, Sweetheart, Psychology
   please specify_____   Club)
    specify_____

Does the admission price determine your participation in campus activities?

(10)
___Yes   ___No   Specify the prices you are willing to pay.
___$1-$2   ___$2.50-$4   ___$4-$6   ___$7-$8   ___$9 and up

What locations are most conducive to your participation in campus programs?

(11)
___Residence Halls   ___Garrett Center   ___Quad/Outside
___Fieldhouse   ___Student Center   ___Civic Center
___Hartmann Center   ___Academic Auditoriums   ___Other (please specify)
   _____

In which academic <u>areas</u> would you like to have review or tutor sessions? (check as many as appropriate)

(12)

___Accounting	___Speech	___Mathematics
___Business Management	___Education	___Computer Science
___Economics	___Engineering (specify)	___History/Religion
___Marketing	_____	___Sciences (specify)
		_____

What new or additional types of programming would you like to see provided by
• Minority Student Services?

1. _____

2. _____

3. _____

Additional Comments/Suggestions (Attach an additional page if necessary)

Thank you for cooperating on this survey. Your responses will be heavily weighed in pursuing expanded programming for minority students at Bradley.

Dr. K. Paul Kasambira   Joyce Means
Acting Director of Minority Student Services   Graduate Assistant

Please return to your R.A. or to the Garrett Center, Room 211 by May 10, 1985.

© 1985 K. Paul Kasambira